I0062705

"*The Home Depot revolutionized so many areas of the retail business, and for the first time one of the people who was there gives you an inside look at how it was done. This is a book that everyone in the retail business should read, and people in other industries will also gather some great advice on how to run their businesses.*"

— Chris Roush, Dean and Professor, School of Communications, Quinnipiac University, author of *Inside Home Depot.*

"*In **Breakthrough Retailing**, both a compelling and entertaining story of the building of Home Depot's incredible culture as well as a textbook on the principles of developing a successful retail enterprise, home-improvement industry legend Jim Inglis shares his wide-ranging experiences of an amazing career.*"

— Paul Hylbert, Chairman, Kodiak Building Partners

"**Breakthrough Retailing** *chronicles Jim's journey and the changes and evolution of Home Depot in a well-paced manner, and is almost hypnotic in the way it draws you into the tale of this amazing business. It was also interesting to think of many of the changes and evolutions that The Home Depot has made that have flowed into Bunnings' DNA as well.*"

— Michael Schneider, Managing Director, Bunnings Ltd. Australia and New Zealand

"**Breakthrough Retailing** *provides the present and future fundamentals on which to build a successful home-improvement business. The principles that Jim exhibits, plus his tireless support, allowed the formation of the largest and most successful home-improvement chain in Latin America.*"

— Enrique Gundermann, Chairman, IKEA, Chile, Peru, & Colombia

"*I am sure this book will become a classic of retail training. **Breakthrough Retailing** covers all the important subjects we have needed to face in order to set up the operation here. The logistics part is of enormous importance these days, which is explained in a very clear way.*"

— Patricio Silva, President, Sodimac Mexico

"*From my point of view, **Breakthrough Retailing** is a successful compilation of essential words of wisdom of the retail trade, topped with interesting and profound stories from the extensive personal background of Jim Inglis in the home-improvement industry.*"

— Erich Harsch, CEO, Hornbach Baumarkt AG, Germany

"*I very much enjoyed reviewing **Breakthrough Retailing**. It provides an excellent blend of business information and practical lessons in an easy-to-read style. I look forward to using several of Jim's illustrations in my MBA operations classes, particularly regarding his insights into inventory management and GMROI.*"

— Lane Cohee, Professor, Palm Beach Atlantic University, Rinker School of Business

BREAK-THROUGH

RETAILING

HOW A
BLEEDING ORANGE CULTURE
CAN CHANGE EVERYTHING!

JIM INGLIS

Breakthrough Retailing: How a Bleeding Orange Culture Can Change Everything

Copyright © 2021 Inglis Retailing, LTD

Published by IR Publishing

Hardcover ISBN: 978-1-7375841-0-0

Paperback ISBN: 978-1-7375841-1-7

eISBN: 978-1-7375841-2-4

Cover and Interior Design: Design9Studios

This book is dedicated with admiration to all the "orange-blooded" associates who have worn the Orange Apron.

This is your story.

CONTENTS

ACKNOWLEDGMENTS

This book has been in the back of my mind for a number of years. Suggestions of business associates, family, and friends encouraged me to finally put these thoughts into writing.

I am grateful to my business clients who have allowed me to both teach and also learn as we developed strategic plans for growth. I have received words of encouragement from Enrique Gundermann, former CEO of Sodimac in Chile, and Michael Schneider, CEO of Bunnings in Australia. Thanks to Patricio Silva of Sodimac Mexico for his numerous suggestions and also to Erich Harsch of Hornbach in Germany for reviewing my manuscript.

People I admire in the business and educational community have provided great insight and advice. Paul Hylbert, chairman of Kodiak Building Partners, provided some keen insight and corrections that I greatly appreciate. Chris Roush, from Quinnipiac University, provided inspiration by writing his book, *Inside Home Depot,* and encouraging me to write this one. Thanks also to Sam Voorhies at Palm Beach Atlantic University, who critiqued my manuscript and also provided contacts that helped transform the manuscript into a book.

Friends and associates like Eduardo Isaacson and Bonnie Fitch read an early draft and provided suggestions and encouragement.

I am particularly excited by the suggestion of Palm Coast Atlantic University's Professor Lane Cohee that Breakthrough Retailing could be considered as a potential resource for students of business.

I would like to especially recognize John Herbert, executive director of the Global Home Improvement Network in Germany for his overall support and for preparing the Foreword for this book. John has been quick to remind me that there is benefit to staying active and involved in the retail home-improvement industry.

Thanks so much to Anita Palmer, who took the first pass at editing my manuscript and provided so many improvements to make the book more interesting and readable. She also took the time to point me in the right direction for the next steps, including introducing me to others who would prove to be helpful. This included editing by Jeanette Littleton, and Kate Hoyman, who was so helpful with the layout and book cover. I am also grateful to Amanda Bird for her final review and editing.

I must thank my wife, Sue, for putting up with my hours and hours of working on my computer while the various drafts of the book were developed in virtual isolation. Then, her help in proofing the finished document, with her incredible talent for finding the smallest error was very helpful. Thanks, Sue, for being in my corner for the past fifty-seven years.

I must also salute an anonymous friend who provided great assistance. Thanks – you know who you are!

FOREWORD

In my more than fifty years of retail experience, I have read many books on retailing, but never one as inspiring as Jim Inglis's *Breakthrough Retailing.*

In *Part I, Building The Home Depot: A Winning Culture*, Jim recounts the three founders of The Home Depot—Bernie Marcus, Arthur Blank, and Pat Farrah—each with different talents, formed a truly magical team that resulted in the almost unequalled phenomenal success of The Home Depot.

He tells how the founders understood their role in this retail business to be that of servant leaders to those on the shop floor. He explains the inverted pyramid-shaped organigram, in which the associates in the stores were at the top of the organizational chart because they were the ones who had direct contact with the customers.

In all my many years in retailing, I have never experienced a working environment where the associates on the shop floor received so much respect and attention from all members of management. It is so appropriate that The Home Depot does not have a head office; it has a Store Support Center.

The other incredible strength of the founders described by Jim was their focus on The Home Depot's excellent customer service and its "religion" offering the best possible products at the lowest price, all to "delight the customer."

In *Part II, Foundation Cracks: Structure Fatigue*, you'll learn of the many problems that developed at The Home Depot in the era of Bob Nardelli. Nardelli, whom Conde Nast Portfolio later named one of the worst American CEOs of all time, joined as chair and CEO in December 2000 and was out in January 2007.

During the six years Nardelli was at the helm, his relentless cost-cutting strategies and the loss of long-time Home Depot executives severely damaged morale and almost drained The Home Depot of its "orange blood."

During the time Nardelli was at The Home Depot, sales and profits did increase, but the stock price declined by 5 percent, while the stock price of Lowe's, the main competitor, increased by 180 percent. What was worse was that the mythic magic of The Home Depot's reputation was gone forever.

In *Part III, Reconstruction: Rebuilding Dominance*, Jim gives a superbly balanced assessment of The Home Depot as it is today, and how it has regained some of its dominance under the excellent leadership of Frank Blake and now Craig Menear. The Home Depot no longer enjoys the same cult following by homeowners as before the Nardelli era, when The Home Depot was everybody's favorite store. But it is back to enjoying excellent growth and record profits.

In *Part IV, Blueprints for Success: Principles for Any Retail Operation*, Jim perfectly highlights the core principles of a successful retail company. With many years of retail experience behind me, I consider his views to be spot on. It is not surprising that Jim has become one of the most recognized and respected global experts in the home-improvement retailing industry today.

Breakthrough Retailing: How a Bleeding Orange Culture Can Change Everything is a joy to read. Never ever have I been so engaged and motivated to read a book. I raced through its twenty-one chapters with much delight. Not only does it provide expert lessons for the management of retail companies, it also is an excellent handbook for all retail merchants.

And it will bring back happy memories for the tens of thousands of past and present associates of The Home Depot who, like me, still "bleed orange."

—John W. Herbert

John W. Herbert has spent more than fifty years in international retailing senior management positions in the UK, Germany, and the US. In January 2001, he was appointed president of The Home Depot EXPO Design Center for the West Coast. Since 2004 he has been the general secretary of the European DIY Retail Association, and he later founded the Global Home Improvement Network, which now has 216 of the leading global home-improvement companies operating in seventy-four countries.

PREFACE

I am perhaps best known in the retail world for my past position of Executive Vice President of Merchandising at The Home Depot. However, the thirteen years spent growing The Home Depot was just one stop in a sixty-year retail journey. This was a journey that was to take me around the world on an adventure that would have made Marco Polo envious!

It all started when, as a seventeen-year-old high school graduate, I entered my first retail job in 1961 at Sackett & Peters, a store in Whittier, California. This was one of the early innovators in the burgeoning do-it-yourself trend of the 1960s. I started out as a sales clerk in the electrical department and was soon noticed by Bob Sackett, one of the owners. He rapidly promoted me to manager of the department, and over the next ten years, I became general merchandise manager of the company. Bob customized my work schedule so I could attend church on Sunday mornings. He adjusted my hours during the week so I could work toward a marketing degree and, later, MBA in marketing at California State University in Fullerton, while managing the merchandising and marketing responsibilities at the store.

My journey then took me to Dallas, Texas, to help launch the Texas stores for the San Diego-based Handyman chain, which had become a leading home center on the West Coast. I was soon transferred back to the Handyman corporate office in San Diego as a division merchandise manager. There I learned a great deal about retailing from mentor Rene Samuel. Rene taught me, "The world needs not to be taught nearly as much as to be reminded." While working at Handyman, I had the pleasure to teach marketing at California State University in San Diego. This experience has given me a lasting love of teaching.

The journey continued in 1978, when I became vice president of merchandising for the Dixieline Lumber Company, the dominant wholesale lumber and building material company in San Diego County. There I worked for Bill Cowling, who was a lumberman's lumberman. My job was to create a do-it-yourself retail arm to complement this strong wholesale lumber business. I saw the pride with which Cowling built the Dixieline business to always be the best alternative for his customers. There were no shortcuts in the pursuit of excellence.

Pat Farrah contacted me in the spring of 1983 and flew to meet with me in San Diego. This is when my retail journey began to take on warp speed. Pat had previously managed a home center chain in Southern California but had gone to Atlanta a few years earlier to open a new retail concept in the home-improvement industry called The Home Depot. Pat asked me to fly to Orlando to attend the grand opening of The Home Depot's newest stores. I took the trip and, upon arriving in Orlando, was met by Bernie Marcus, The Home Depot's CEO, who gave me a tour of the new stores. Subsequently I was offered a position as the merchant in charge of paint and furniture.

This was not an easy decision, but I took a leap of faith, moving my family to Atlanta, believing The Home Depot represented the future of the home-improvement industry. Very quickly I was made responsible for half of the company's merchandising departments while reporting to Pat. Two years later, I returned to the West Coast as vice president of West Coast merchandising and spent the next five years opening stores in the western states. My journey then brought me back to Atlanta as executive vice president of merchandising, and I was ultimately elected to the corporate board of directors. During this time, I was also on the board of the National Kitchen and Bath Association. I learned so much from Pat Farrah, Arthur Blank, and Bernie Marcus, founders of The Home Depot. My entire understanding of retailing principles changed as I came to understand The Home Depot retail paradigms.

However, this was not the end of my journey. In many ways it was really just an exciting new start. I resigned from The Home Depot in 1996. I subsequently joined the Dixieline board of directors and renewed my involvement with the company. I also served on the boards of Atlanta-based K&G Men's Wear and Chamberlain Manufacturing.

Simultaneously, I was serving as COO of The Maxim Group, a national franchise operator of flooring stores. Here, I went through a learning experience in another aspect of the home-improvement business.

The journey next took me to South America in 1998 to work with Sodimac, which operated home centers and building material stores in the Chilean market. This proved to be a twenty-year relationship, as we redefined the Sodimac business model to incorporate a big-box format and then expanded from Chile into Argentina, Peru, Columbia, Brazil, Uruguay, and Mexico. I was privileged to work with Guillermo Aguero and then his successor, Sandro Solari, and later Enrique Gundermann. These were all great merchants. I learned many lessons from the Sodimac experience. Opening stores in developing countries teaches a person the need for flexibility and quick responses to changing circumstances. This environment encouraged and rewarded creativity.

My journey was about to cross the ocean to Europe. My relationship with Sodimac resulted in an invitation from Otmar Hornbach, the CEO of Hornbach Baumarkt, to work with his stores in Germany, Luxembourg, and Austria. This began a twenty-year relationship as more stores were opened in Switzerland, Czech Republic, Slovenia, The Netherlands, Sweden, and Romania. I admired Otmar Hornbach, who was a master at retail strategy. I worked closely with his son, Steffen Hornbach, who ultimately took over the reins as CEO. Steffen kept his hand on the pulse of the company and was an incredible example of driving the business with hands-on management. At Hornbach I learned the importance of due diligence to ensure the greatest likelihood that any program implemented would succeed.

While working with Sodimac and Hornbach, I embarked on opening a series of high-tech interior design stores in the U.S. I was honored to have both Sodimac and Hornbach as investors, along with the department store Sears and the leading European home improvement retailer, Kingfisher, which operated the B&Q stores in the U.K. and the Castorama stores in France. Kingfisher's CEO, Sir Geoff Mulcahy, was a great partner in helping start and later wind down this business. Being an innovator includes successes and failures, which can be painful learning experiences.

The journey next took me to Asia, where I joined the board of The Home World Group. This company operated numerous shopping centers in Northern China, twelve of which contained HomeWay Home Centers, which were eventually sold to The Home Depot. There, I had the privilege of working with Mr. Du Sha, who is an incredible entrepreneur. He was very instrumental in bringing modern big-box chain store retailing to China. I learned many things in China. The main takeaway was that there are three ways to do anything: the right way, the wrong way, and the Chinese way. Western companies that fail to understand this enter China at their peril.

The next stop on my Asian journey was Niigata, Japan, to meet Mr. Kenichi Sasage, who had created an incredible chain of 1,000 small hardware & agricultural supply stores across Japan. He was embarking on opening big-box home centers and introduced to me by the people at American-based Masco Corporation. This was the start of another twenty-year relationship, advising both Mr. Sasage and COO, Mr. Yuichiro Sasage, who subsequently assumed the CEO responsibilities and continued Komeri's incredible growth. Japan is the second-largest international market for home-improvement, and Komeri developed multiple store formats in order to serve the entire market, from very small stores to some of the largest in Japan.

The journey continued "down under" to Australia and New Zealand, where I was invited by Peter (PJ) Davis, COO of the Bunnings home-improvement stores, to help strategize their preparation for the American based Lowe's home-improvement stores' invasion of Australia. The next few years were a time of dynamic growth as Bunnings met the competitive challenge, so that Lowe's ultimately exited the Australian market. The Bunnings stores, under the leadership of CEO Michael Schneider, certainly represent "best of breed" in the home center industry. The Bunnings brand is always top rated with Australian customers, and their financial numbers are the envy of the industry.

In 2015 I received the Global Lifetime Achievement Award in London from the European Do-It-Yourself Retailers Association (EDRA). This high honor recognized and rewarded my many travels and journeys advising many of the best retailers in the home-improvement industry. What a pleasure to know that great merchandising can motivate customers to invest in their homes and enjoy an improved life style, while low pricing can improve their standard of living.

How was I able to travel the world and be so involved in the international world of home center retailing and still have a home life? My wife, Sue, has been an incredible gift. She was a cashier in that first store where I worked sixty years ago. My success has been our success. We have two daughters and eight grandchildren.

This has been an incredible career journey that I did not plan. So how did it come about? I believe my path was directed. The scriptures say if we acknowledge God in all our ways, He will direct our path. I do acknowledge Him and will be eternally grateful for His mercy and providence.

This book will zero in on the portion of my journey that tells the incredible story of The Home Depot's success through the lens of its *Bleeding Orange* culture. It will then explain the winning principles needed to be a high-productivity retailer.

I have had a wonderful career advising my clients and teaching merchandising principles to their staffs. Friends and colleagues have often told me I should share my retailing insights with a larger audience. "Write a book!" they said. So I am taking their advice by telling my story and sharing my perspectives on retailing.

Here it is!

Jim Inglis
Atlanta, Georgia

PART I

BUILDING THE HOME DEPOT:
A WINNING CULTURE

THE HOME DEPOT:
THE EARLY DAYS

Orange blood? Absolutely. *"Bleeding Orange"* was the battle cry of the believers who pioneered The Home Depot. "Cut me anywhere and I'll bleed orange!" Any one jumping on board The Home Depot bandwagon at the very beginning was taking a leap of faith. You had to believe.

The Home Depot's first full year of business was 1980. Its big-box home center concept was, to put it mildly, unorthodox. All the powers in the home-improvement industry were lined up against it. If you were to ask any of the leading tool manufacturers, or the major hardware wholesalers, or the competing traditional home centers—or even impartial trade journalists—about the prospects for the newly opened stores called The Home Depot in Atlanta, Georgia, their responses would be resoundingly negative.

The common line went something like this: "The stores are too big, the prices are too low, the inventories are too large. It's all being done with smoke and mirrors. Frankly, I wouldn't trust those guys. They all come from California."

Nevertheless, I too, came from California and made my own leap of faith by joining The Home Depot's team in Atlanta during the early Spring of 1983. The company was in its fourth year of business and I spent the next thirteen years spreading *the orange gospel* across America. Ultimately, I became the executive vice president of merchandising and served on the corporate board of directors while we revolutionized the way home-improvement products were sold.

Innovation hardly ever comes from the industry leaders. In fact, they will fight with all their power to maintain the status quo.

THE WORLD BEFORE THE HOME DEPOT

The twenty-year period between 1960 and 1980, prior to the start of The Home Depot, was the golden era for traditional home centers. Multiple stores were rapidly opening across the country, especially in the growing suburbs. The concept was to offer a one-stop store that catered to homeowners who, in the past, had to shop at specialty paint stores, plumbing stores, lumber yards, and garden centers aimed primarily at the professional customer. These DIYers (do-it-yourselfers) now could feel comfortable in a store that welcomed the non-professional customer.

This DIY format was first seen in the early 1960s at both ends of the country. On the East Coast, the early entries were Grossmans in Boston, followed by Rickel Home Centers in New Jersey. On the West Coast, the first big success story was Builders Emporium in Southern California.

Over the next two decades, the home center format spread to every metropolitan area in the U.S. It was emulated in Europe with home centers like B&Q in England, Castorama in France, Bricocenter in Belgium, and Obi in Germany. Ultimately, this traditional home center format would even be duplicated in South America, Australia, and Japan.

THE GROWTH AND DEATH OF TRADITIONAL HOME CENTERS

In 1980 the industry was operated somewhat like a club of friendly competitors running homogeneous stores. The U.S. market was divided into geographical fiefdoms, with regional groups operating chains in each region.

People in the Boston area may remember Somerville Lumber, in addition to Grossman's. The New Jersey market was dominated by Rickle Home Centers and neighboring New York by Pergament. Washington, D.C., was Hechinger's territory. Atlanta had Handy City. The Florida market was controlled by Scotty's in the north and Lindsley Lumber in the south. Chicago had home centers like Courtesy Lumber and Handy Andy. Handy Dan dominated Texas. The largest chains in California included Handyman and Orchard Supply, as well as Builders Emporium. Ernst and Pay 'n Pak in the Northwest round out this partial list of regional home center chains that all disappeared. They were run over by an orange freight train called The Home Depot. (See page 34 for a more complete list of these chains)

These traditional home center stores looked pretty much the same, sourced their merchandise from the same type of regional wholesalers, and priced their products with the same high markups. (And they all died pretty much the same way, too, after The Home Depot entered their marketplace.)

The Hechinger stores in the Washington, D.C., area epitomized the ideal home center that most of the other home-improvement stores wished to emulate. Retailers from the U.S. and around the world made pilgrimages to Hechinger stores, seeking merchandising ideas, which they would duplicate in their own markets.

Ironically, Hechinger ultimately proved to be one of the easiest competitors for The Home Depot to crush. The Hechinger stores *looked good* to the industry watchers but did not *work good [sic]* for their customers.

The traditional home center model called for a store of 20,000-30,000 square feet. (For comparison, the first Home Depot warehouses were 60,000; today the typical square footage averages 105,000.) The purchasing process had two steps: large regional wholesalers fed products into these stores on a weekly basis, using a cost-plus arrangement that netted the wholesalers a margin of sixteen to twenty percent. The home centers added another gross profit averaging around thirty-eight percent. This inefficient channel of distribution, with margins piling on top of margins, was an open door for The Home Depot to ultimately destroy their price image and take their customers.

There were usually multiple home center companies operating in the same geographical market, often across the street from each other, in a competitive relationship that pretty much assured each company would get its fair share of the homeowner's business. The structure of the home center industry assured the existence of many stores with relatively low sales volume and high margins. The customers got convenience on a limited assortment of DIY home-improvement products but not low prices or great service.

Then came the Big Orange Box that changed the home-improvement business forever.

THE NEW HOME CENTER PARADIGM

The Home Depot's concept was to operate huge warehouse-type stores that could take direct shipments from vendors, thereby cutting out dependence on the large regional wholesalers that had previously controlled the major markets. In doing so, we eliminated the middleman margins that were built into the traditional supply chain. The first step was purchasing better.

The Home Depot's big-box type facilities were twice the size of existing home centers and used high cube pallet racking to maximize holding power, thereby allowing volume purchases and wide assortments. The DNA of the company was to drive down costs and pass much of the savings on to our customers, which could amount to 20 percent or more on a DIY home-improvement project. This clear focus on giving the customers a better deal empowered us to be a market disrupter based on price and value.

To be the Everyday Low Price Leader, you must also have the Everyday Low Cost Supply Chain.

Customers immediately noticed The Home Depot was different—and better. People could see and feel the difference the moment they entered the store. To begin with, we ripped out the floor tiles and ceiling tiles of the second-use buildings we leased for those early Atlanta stores. That created a low-overhead ambience and kept operating costs at a minimum. In addition, the product assortment was overpowering, and our salespeople were actually knowledgeable and helpful.

The message was, The Home Depot is not like those other stores selling home-improvement products. The impact was Wow! It was not long before neighbor told neighbor about the big orange boxes, and the revolution in home-improvement was under way.

PERFECTING THE STORE MODEL

Soon after the first four stores were established in Atlanta, we added four more in Miami. Just as in Atlanta, these stores were located in 60,000-square-foot facilities that were subdivided from larger JC Penney discount stores called Treasure Island. They were much smaller than The Home Depot's stores of today but double the physical size of the traditional home centers in the market at that time.

In the fourth year of business, The Home Depot's store prototype increased to 80,000 square feet when the first two Orlando, Florida, stores opened in 1983. The store size increased again in 1985 to 100,000 square feet when the West Coast stores made their debut. Each time the size of the stores increased, the total sales of these larger stores also increased, and the sales per square foot increased as well. This meant that productivity was improving. Purchasing power increased, store efficiency improved, and all of that led to even better pricing and services for the customer.

The Home Depot *Bleeding Orange* culture always demanded that we push the envelope to the extreme. Later the company experimented with larger, 135,000-square-foot stores, in order to answer the question, "How high is up?"

While sales did increase in these larger stores, the sales per square foot in these super-stores declined. That indicated a reduction in productivity. After that - the prototype reverted to the 100,000-square-foot prototype, which proved to be the most productive footprint, and remains the format of most of The Home Depot stores today.

STORE PLACEMENT AND PRODUCTIVITY

A predictive sales model was developed, based on statistical analysis of customer buying habits, using actual cash register history, combined with demographic government data. Using this approach, the model could accurately project the annual purchases of any proposed store site, by analyzing postal zip codes in each store's catchment area. The model could specify the most likely annual home-improvement purchases of the average home in any specified zip code.

This provided a new-store site model using a location matrix that could specify the placement of multiple stores in an urban market grid to maximize the synergistic productivity of the 100,000-square-foot store format in any metroplex.

The idea was not to have high-volume stores in key locations and lower-volume stores in marginal locations. Instead, the model helped develop a market matrix that would assure store size could be standardized which is the key to productivity.

AGGRESSIVE GROWTH PLANS

An extrapolation of this data, combined with results of the first three years of operations and applied to the entire country, indicated it would be possible to grow The Home Depot's store count to 1,000 stores in the United States without serious cannibalization of sales in existing stores. We knew that by growing our store base by 25 percent per year, we would hit this goal by the year 2000.

Constant growth to open those 1000 stores became our goal. We continued to aggressively open new stores and spread the *Bleeding Orange* culture from border to border and coast to coast. As the base of stores increased, the number of stores opened each year to maintain the 25 percent growth goal also grew. Soon we would be opening more than one hundred big-box stores per year.

WAREHOUSE PRICING WINS

The Home Depot philosophy was to achieve economies of scale in purchasing and store operations, which could then allow more aggressive low pricing. That, in turn, helped grow our market share, gaining even more economies.

While the average gross margin in these early days ran about 28 percent, pricing cannot be reduced to a simple formula or some preset margin objective. Volume buying allowed higher margins on some unique products; but there were some products sold at lower margins - or even negative margin, if necessary, in order to offer the lowest prices in the market. The objective was to make sure the customer was purchasing at our store and nowhere else. The actual cost of a particular product was essentially irrelevant to the retail price.

This was a new supply-chain paradigm and pricing attitude that put the existing traditional home centers at an existential disadvantage. These traditional home centers priced their products with fixed gross-margin requirements and simply did not have the cost efficiencies to compete with The Home Depot prices. The homeowners quickly recognized the value of buying at "warehouse prices."

The Home Depot brand represented saving money. Our not-too-subtle promotional message was that the homeowner no longer had to shop at the expensive retail stores that had been ripping them off. Our grand opening advertising stated, *"Sale Starts Today and Last Forever!"*

Most retailers price defensively and consider pricing a threat. Winning retailers price offensively and consider pricing a tool.

HOW THE COMPETITION TRIED TO COMPETE

When The Home Depot entered a new metropolitan market, the reaction was almost always the same. First, the locally based home centers would invariably issue a press release outlining the long history of their company in the marketplace and bragging about the incredible loyalty of their customers, which allowed them to have the most stores and a dominant position in the local market, *et cetera, et cetera.*

However, the retailers quickly discovered that their customers were not all that loyal. In fact, to their dismay, they learned that customers are fickle and in charge. Our market surveys showed that most customers disliked their traditional home centers and were frustrated with poor service. When these customers experienced The Home Depot's difference in assortment, value, and service, they never went back to their old stores.

It was rewarding to see how fast customers changed their buying habits. It was even more fun to watch the existing market leaders struggle to respond to the new reality. These fat cats had taken their customers for granted and now were found wanting.

When the reality of the impact of The Home Depot's grand opening on their market share would finally hit them, the traditional home center operators would take a hard look at their stores and not like the lackluster appearance of their stores. While they had no idea of the dynamics The Home Depot would bring to their market, they knew they had to do something. So, they would begin to remodel their stores to make them more attractive.

We were delighted to see them tear up their stores and create confusion and dissonance for their customers right when we were entering their market with a better mousetrap that would offer a far better value proposition. It created chaos for their "loyal" customers, and it required new capital investment at a time when they had no real chance of recouping the expenditure. It made no economic sense.

Their remodeling efforts were akin to rearranging the deck chairs on the Titanic. In truth, it was too late; their ship was already sinking.

Yet, every competitor started putting lipstick on their pigs to "modernize" their stores. This was totally counterproductive. Their stores were enhanced to look more *retail*, while we worked hard to make our stores look more *wholesale*. Our stores were not neat and pretty. The early ones were second-use buildings with used store fixtures, concrete floors, and hand-written signage. We were the antithesis of a modern retail store. We offered a bare-bones format that was designed to be fully functional.

We may have not have always *looked* good, but we *worked good [sic]*— and that was all that mattered.

WINNING THE PRICE WAR

Then, in desperation, the traditional stores would try to fight fire with fire by lowering prices on a specific list of the most price-sensitive items. The problem was that their two-step supply chain was inefficient and costly, and it put them at a cost disadvantage.

This was complicated by the fact that their stores were small and, as a result, had limited ability to stock inventory in depth. While their strategy was to lower prices, they did not have the inventory depth to allow them to sell more quantity. As a result, when prices were lowered, they essentially sold the same quantity of these products but at a lower price and with less gross margin.

The Home Depot, on the other hand, had large stores with the capability to hold huge quantities of product. Therefore, while our gross margin might be low, we could sell huge quantities of the price-sensitive products, thereby creating a significant flow of gross profit dollars, resulting in a very favorable return on investment. The gross margin dollars that a company takes to the bank proves success, and we were taking wheelbarrows of money to our bank, as the traditional home centers watched their profits evaporate.

The lower pricing backfired for these competitors. The result was lower gross sales and less gross profit dollars in their recently remodeled stores, resulting in mounting financial losses. These traditional home centers would soon capitulate on price. They would come to the desperate conclusion that they could maintain their higher prices by emphasizing the convenience of their multiple locations, which made their stores relatively closer to their customers. Their last competitive advantage was convenience. But convenience alone will always prove to be a weak competitive posture.

Our advertising constantly conveyed the motto, *Worth the Trip from Anywhere.* It recognized our need to be able to justify the extra time and effort it often took for customers to get to our stores. The metrics of our big-box stores demanded that we have high per-store sales volume. That required us to pull traffic past the more convenient stores.

Aggressive pricing was an important magnet. The positioning line that was always married to The Home Depot's logo was *Low Prices Are Just the Beginning.* Our policy was to set a permanent gap between our price and the competition's prices and to maintain this gap whether our competitor's price went up or down.

THE LOGIC TO AGGRESSIVE PRICING

We knew what the competitors did not know. We understood the benefit of generating real gross profit dollars. We were looking for tangible dollars, not some abstract gross margin percentage goal. Our first job was always to generate high sales, which created high inventory turnover and was best accomplished by having the lowest prices. We embraced the low margin commodity items as a critical part of our product mix, while our competitors deemphasized these important project categories. Our competitors were fixated on maintaining high gross margin percentages, while we were fixated on generating a high count of customer feet in our stores.

Our pricing instincts were diametrically opposed to the rest of the industry. When we would prepare our budgets, it was not unusual to project lower margins on future business. This would be forbidden in most retailers. However, at The Home Depot the only questions were how much more could we sell and what would be the impact on inventory turnover and GMROI (Gross Margin Return on Inventory Investment)?

The traditional retailers did not even understand the question, let alone have an answer. GMROI is a measure of the gross margin dollars the company takes to the bank in any given time period, divided by the inventory investment at cost during that period. Understanding the importance of constantly working to increase GMROI provided us with a tool to measure productivity, which proved to be an invaluable, competitive advantage in the marketplace.

Ultimately, the traditional home centers would decide that they also wanted (and needed) this price gap so they could somehow regain their profitability. We would watch them back off their new low-pricing initiative and set their prices above ours. That's when we knew we had won the war! They were now dead men walking and simply didn't know it.

Increasing GMROI is always a winning strategy, while increasing gross margin percentage can be a dangerous losing strategy.

These guys were in a hole, and they just kept digging deeper and deeper. That hole was, in fact, their grave.

People are not blind or stupid, and they are always looking for value. It was amazing to see how some of the larger traditional home centers with huge resources were checkmated as our relatively smaller team of *Bleeding Orange* zealots entered their market.

Customers tend to love grand openings and going-out-of-business sales. The Home Depot offered the grand openings, which were followed by our competitor's going-out-of-business sale.

THE DRIVE FOR MARKET DOMINANCE

More than thirty-two strong, regional, traditional home center companies simply ceased to exist as The Home Depot rolled into their market and sucked out the oxygen by out-assorting, out-servicing, and out-pricing them. One by one they fell, just like a row of dominos—inundated by a tsunami of orange blood.

Check out the chart that shows the major home center chains, grouped by geographical area, at the time of The Home Depot's first grand opening. You can see that there were multiple home centers overlapping in the same space. None of them had the vision, drive, or culture to consider taking their competitors out. Price wars were to be avoided. They were willing to accept their "fair market share" and offer a somewhat mediocre shopping experience to their customers. They were not prepared to compete with a company like The Home Depot that would not play by their safe rules.

Traditional U.S. Home Centers Pre-Home Depot - 1980

NORTHEAST
Rickel Home Centers
Channel Lumber
Pergament
Hechinger
Somerville Lumber
Grossman's

SOUTHEAST
Scotty's
Handy City
Lindsley Lumber

MIDWEST
Courtesy Lumber
Republic Lumber
Handy Andy
Central Hardware
Forest City
Knox Lumber

SOUTHWEST
Handy Dan
Payless Cashway
Cashway El Paso

WEST COAST
Builders Emporium
Handyman
Angels
Bonanza
Ole's
Lin-Brook Hardware
Pay 'N Pak
Homeowner's Emporium
Orchard Supply
Ernst
Cooper Lumber
Sacket & Peters
All American Home Center
Lumberjack

When most of these competitors closed their doors, their real estate was redeveloped into other business applications. We often said that our goal was to create new bowling centers across the country! Some of these home centers temporarily merged. But when you combine three or four sick horses to pull a wagon, you still have three or four sick horses.

However, a few retailers tried to reformat their businesses and protect their market share by opening their own version of the big-box home center. For a period of time, twelve such home center chains competed with The Home Depot for the U.S. market share. All appeared to be weak clones of The Home Depot. Most of these efforts ended in failure, primarily because they could see the big-box part of the strategy and could duplicate size, but they did not understand the business philosophy behind our warehouse format nor the dynamics of the *Bleeding Orange* culture, which was the key to The Home Depot's strength.

Only two of these big-box knock-offs survived: Lowe's operates nationwide, while Menards is located primarily in the Midwest. Lowe's essentially had been a lumberyard operator focused on the professional customer. Headquartered in the hills of North Carolina, the stores were mostly in rural markets. Lowe's didn't wake up to the new DIY big-box home center reality until about eight years after The Home Depot started the big-box revolution. It has never achieved the productivity of The Home Depot.

Menards began as a rural supplier of pole barns for the farming community and evolved into a big-box home center but is only located in the Midwest. This growth limitation was a result of their private capital structure and their highly centralized supply chain.

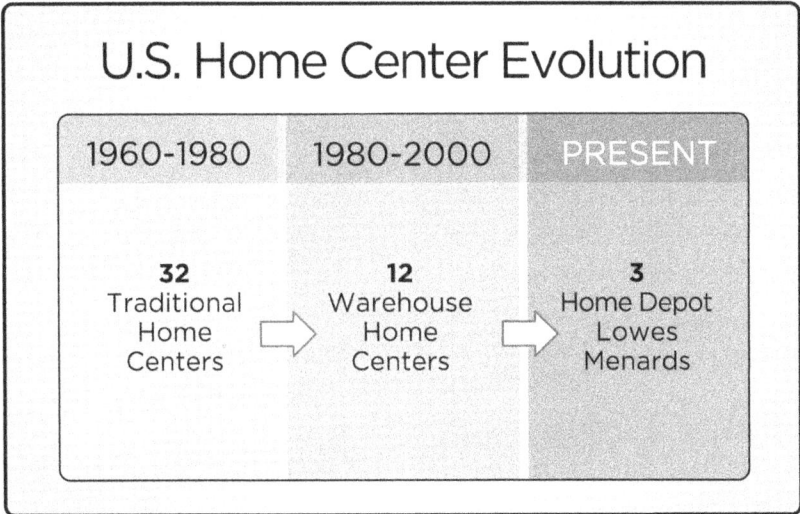

U.S. Home Center Evolution

1960-1980	1980-2000	PRESENT
32 Traditional Home Centers	**12** Warehouse Home Centers	**3** Home Depot Lowes Menards

THE BUILDERS SQUARE CHALLENGE

Builders Square is a good illustration of a doomed big-box copy. An industry veteran named Frank Denny started it. Denny had been the CEO of the Handy Dan home-improvement chain of traditional home centers. Handy Dan was cobbled together by the W.R. Grace shipping company as they purchased many of the traditional regional home center retailers across the county. It had become the largest retail group in the home center business and the only company with a national footprint. However, the acquired regional chains retained their local brand identification and remained relatively independent.

One by one, The Home Depot entered each of Handy Dan's local markets and put these traditional stores out of business, starting with their Handy City stores in Atlanta. Denny realized that he was riding a bunch of sick horses and decided to copy the enemy.

He raised some private capital and went to San Antonio, Texas, where he opened Builders Square, modeled after The Home Depot. He opened a few more stores and then quickly sold the company to Kmart, which at that time was a powerful company with deep pockets.

The strategy of Builders Square, at that point, was to open in every major metropolitan market before The Home Depot could get there. So, with Kmart's money, the Builders Square brand spread rapidly across the U.S.

The fast entry into so many diverse markets spread the company's assets and management's attention thin. In addition, the geographical dispersion of the stores created logistical problems that put Builders Square at a cost disadvantage. But the biggest problem was that the focus on rapid growth did not allow time for a cohesive culture to develop. The company's colors were blue and orange, but the culture was colorless. The strategy that did develop was based on rapid growth at any price, without a true focus on the customer or the financial disciplines needed for long-term viability.

That is the curse of having too much money and growing too fast. Builders Square was missing that *Bleeding Orange* magic. The Builders Square brand did not become dominant in any of the new markets after San Antonio.

The Builders Square strategy was to enter the most markets as quickly as possible. The Home Depot strategy was to pace our growth in order to perform well and maintain our dynamic culture. As we entered new markets, we also backfilled into existing markets to achieve a dominant position. Therefore, we grew more slowly into new cities than Builders Square.

However, when The Home Depot finally arrived in a Builders Square market with a cluster of stores, it was bye-bye Builders Square. The customers could feel the difference that the *Bleeding Orange* culture made in their shopping experience.

It was just a matter of time before Kmart pulled the plug on their unprofitable experiment, and we created a few more bowling alleys.

THE FAILURE OF SEARS

The poster child for inefficient competitors was certainly Sears.

Founded in 1893 and known worldwide for its iconic catalogue, Sears, Roebuck and Co. had developed by the 1980s into the country's largest chain of department stores. In the post-World War II era, Sears also became the dominant supplier of home-improvement products for the American home, whether it was paint, tools, appliances, lighting fixtures, or about any category you could name! Nearly every homeowner in American had a Sears credit card.

This company was truly an American institution. It was Sears' game to lose—and they did

The best loyalty program is simply to be the best store. Give the customer no reason to shop elsewhere.

One of the first threats came from the traditional home centers that began to chip away at the Sears formula. It was far easier to shop for a home-improvement project at a freestanding home center with shopping carts and central check-outs than in an inconvenient mall with its department store environment. However, Sears had become a real estate owner of malls, so the company needed to protect the mall traffic with their own stores. Home-improvement customers were moving away from malls, but Sears was chained to their mall investments.

The Sears credit business was very profitable. This caused Sears to think of itself as a financial company rather than aspiring to being the greatest retailer in the country. Ultimately financial people ran the company instead of merchants, which resulted in numerous financial services, but no real innovation in the retail business. With all the focus on real estate and financial products the merchandising group lost its preeminence. It was locked in a time warp that was no longer relevant, especially now that the customer had new and better choices.

Delighting the customer with great merchandising, superior products, and great value had been the hallmark of Sears retail innovation and success. However, the real merchants were put in financial handcuffs and ultimately eliminated. They no longer ran the business; only the numbers mattered. In the Sears deck of cards, gross margin percentage was king, and the customer was the joker. The customer was taken for granted as Sears' management set rigid gross margin percentage goals based on outdated market conditions. They simply ignored new competition and changing customer expectations. Sears was living in past glory.

While the traditional home centers chipped away at Sears' market share, the *coup de grâce* was the opening of The Home Depot. We challenged Sears for category dominance. Sears' response was to simply drop product category after product category and accept less and less market share to protect its high gross margins and antiquated way of selling home-improvement products. High gross margins were Sears's security blanket, and they were not about to change. Sears committed suicide, and we loved it!

Here's an illustration. In the mid-1990s Sears announced that they had seen the light and were implementing EDLP (Everyday Low Pricing). On the specified first day that this new merchandising policy was to start, we had an army of The Home Depot people at the doors of Sears stores. We wanted to see what new price points they would set so we could quickly discount our prices and discredit this new initiative.

We quickly realized that Sears had not seen the light. All the sale pricing had been removed from the stores, but it was plain to see that Sears had not truly embraced lower margins and had no intention of driving down their regular high prices. They were telling the customers that they were instituting everyday low prices, while in reality they were even more firmly protecting their everyday high prices. It was an ill-advised marketing strategy by a financial company that had forgotten how to be merchandising-driven.

Sears focused on protecting gross margin percentage and lost their customers' loyalty in the process, leading to its ultimate bankruptcy.

Sears Flirts with The Home Depot

As a sidelight, Sears contacted us in 1995 with the suggestion that we begin selling Kenmore Appliances at our Home Depot Expo stores. Kenmore, at that time, was the number-one brand of appliances in the United States, and it was the exclusive private label of Sears. The proposal was very tempting, as it would give us an immediate advantage in the major appliance industry, where we were not strong.

The decision was taken to Bernie Marcus and Arthur Blank, our top management. This decision was a big deal.

The argument in favor of the deal was that, in addition to gaining a great appliance program, a successful Kenmore program could create a relationship with Sears that might open the door to obtain their other private label programs. This would allow us to achieve quantum jumps in dominating certain categories. In addition to Kenmore, Sears had extraordinarily strong private label programs in the categories of paint (Easy Living and Weatherbeater), tools (Craftsman), and automotive (DieHard).

The negative argument was that Sears was still a competitor, and all competitors were, by definition, the enemy. The final decision was to pass on the Sears offer. Our senior management reasoned that while the addition of Kenmore would be a coup for The Home Depot establishing a strong presence in the major appliance industry, the negative impact on the orange blood culture would simply be wrong. How could we tell our employees that our goal was to take market share from Sears and dominate the market while throwing Sears a lifeline by selling their appliances in The Home Depot stores?

This shows the importance that The Home Depot management placed on keeping the culture on track. Our associates were taught to attack the competition and take no prisoners.

"Attack, Attack, Attack!"

The *Bleeding Orange* culture won the argument and forced the decision.

Sears was ultimately run by bankers, where The Home Depot was run by merchants. This impacts the company's mission and how success is measured.

SUPPLY CHAIN RESISTANCE

Most of the major manufacturers with the top brands originally resisted selling direct to The Home Depot. They were determined to protect their market share by supporting the two-step wholesale distribution system that was firmly established in the marketplace.

Market share is the Holy Grail to manufacturers. Their initial reaction to The Home Depot—this aggressive, disrespectful disrupter with its new format upsetting the comfortable status quo of the industry—was to boycott us.

Why should they bet on this upstart with only a few stores and a bizarre desire to buy directly from the manufacturer? Why should they threaten their entire national distribution system to cross the line and offer direct factory pricing to this newcomer? Wouldn't direct selling to The Home Depot result in lower prices to the public? Clearly this would then prevent their existing two-step wholesaler/retailer supply chain from maintaining their traditional margins.

These fearful vendors could not envision that the market for their products would actually *expand* by selling through The Home Depot. They tended to see the market as a zero sum game. Therefore, their first response to becoming supplier to The Home Depot was an emphatic, "No!"

When you focus on the customer, the right numbers are likely to follow. The opposite is not true when you start with the numbers.

DEALING WITH MYOPIC VENDOR MANAGEMENT

I remember a meeting with the CEO of Halo Lighting and our merchants in Chicago. Halo was the largest producer of recessed and commercial lighting fixtures in the country. Their product was generally the brand specified by architects on most construction projects. My team and I met the CEO and his people in the Halo corporate boardroom. The CEO entered the room, and his first words were, "I know why you are here, and you will be successful over my dead body." Nice way to start a negotiation!

Halo was not an outlier. Vendor after vendor made it clear that they would not support The Home Depot, only to later capitulate as we took market share. Today, Halo is a major product line in The Home Depot.

In a free market the customer will ultimately win, and any market void will ultimately be filled. Many of these major brands were choosing to protect their existing distribution while ignoring the wishes of their ultimate homeowner customer. They were ignoring the changing market and refused to recognize that the customers had chosen a new and better solution to their home-improvement needs.

We were able to fulfill our customers' needs, often by going around the barrier of the dominant brands and finding vendors who were willing to break ranks with the industry. We had developed a voracious appetite for merchandise, and it was difficult to obtain all the products and brands we wanted. Sometimes we had to take the number two or three brand in order to compete against the number one market leader. We might have to go offshore to secure the needed products. One way or another, we would fill the market void and prevail.

Fortunately, DIY customers are rarely brand insistent, so our low prices and great service gave them confidence to buy the products available in our stores. Customers vote with their dollars, and they were voting for The Home Depot. We could now rapidly grow our sales and negatively impact the market share of the dominant industry brands. We were closer to the customer, as they were shopping in our stores. Clearly, the customers were willing to change their buying habits if given better value.

Our increased buying power eventually caused vendors to sit up and take notice. The battle was won slowly but surely, over time. Those manufacturers who were slow learners lost considerable market share before recognizing the new reality of The Home Depot's market influence.

The Home Depot's philosophy was simply, "Don't give the customer any reason to ever shop anywhere else for home-improvement products."

"You either make dust or eat dust."

— *H. Jackson Brown, Jr.*

Brands can be particularly important to the professional customers, and even the homeowners who may not have brand insistence certainly do have brand awareness. Therefore, we continually knocked on the door of the key vendors to obtain their branded products.

Our task was to paint a picture to the vendors of how the structure of the home-improvement industry was going to change dramatically and convince these suppliers they needed to get on board The Home Depot's express train. More than once I explained to an intransigent supplier that only a limited number of seats were available, and they needed to get on board soon or risk missing the train completely.

Old rules had to be broken. We were upsetting the norms and would not politely take only our "fair share" of the market. We were going to consolidate the fragmented home-improvement retail business. It took time - a lot of time - but most vendors eventually asked for a seat on The Home Depot's train to protect and grow their market share.

THE PEOPLE IMPERATIVE FOR SUCCESS

At the beginning we had only limited capital and few systems. We were a band of zealots on a mission. This was the orange-blooded brotherhood. We were not the elite of the industry. Our leadership staff team resumes included few college degrees. We had no consultants, key performance indicators, 360-degree reviews, Lean management, or Six Sigma black belts. We were street fighters. Our team was composed of ordinary people achieving extraordinary results.

We valued street smarts over the management method *du jour* so often loved by university professors and business consulting firms. While they had a pecuniary interest in presenting the newest management fad, our approach was to listen to the customer, apply common sense, and overreact with urgency.

Sure, the stores were huge, the prices were incredible, and the assortments wide and deep. But the secret weapon was always our Bleeding Orange customer-centric culture. This was driven by a staff of hungry people who knew that they could be more successful and richer than their parents if they gave one hundred percent of their effort to please all our customers all of the time. Since we were a small start-up, we had to keep it simple. The main criteria to be a successful employee at the Home Depot was to: 1) Have a strong work ethic; 2) Be honest; 3) Be drug free. That's it!

RETAIL DETAIL #1

"I began a revolution with eighty-two men. If I had it to do over again, I would do it with fifteen and absolute faith. It does not matter how small you are if you have faith and a plan of action."

— Fidel Castro

STORE LEVEL EXPERTISE

To seal the deal with new customers, we hired real product experts as sales associates to provide friendly, helpful advice. It seems unbelievable now, but that was rarely available in the traditional home center stores. Our recruitment efforts focused on hiring retired tradesmen who really knew their stuff. We also looked for sales experts who knew how to design and sell projects.

Some of these people were full time, but many were part-timers, which was just fine. We were willing to pay top wages for people who had expertise and did not want full-time work but who could help our customers and train other employees. Flexible hours also appealed to many of our sales associates and helped us provide the right expertise at the right time for our customers. We paid higher wages than our competitors. Our guideline was simply to pay people what they were worth. There were no union agreements that preset the pay scales or limited our ability to reward competence and positive sales results.

Our competitors might pay lip service to having good employees, but they didn't put their money where their mouth was. The result was that The Home Depot's investment in great people proved to be a *unique, sustainable, compelling, competitive advantage.*

This focus on quality went a long way toward creating the employees' pride in the job, which was a hallmark of the *Bleeding Orange* culture. This pride encouraged an attitude of ownership which, in turn, motivated our people to go above and beyond the call of duty. The overriding guideline was always to do the right thing and to empower the front-line associates to always take the positive initiative in serving their customers.

GOING THE EXTRA MILE

The Home Depot people would go the extra mile to satisfy the customer. If an item was out of stock, it was not unusual for employees to go to a nearby competitor and buy the product to get it back in stock quickly. A store employee would secure the missing item and then deliver it to the customer's home.

An elderly lady visited one of our stores in a wheelchair. She wanted to buy a wheelchair ramp for her front porch. Her budget was $25. Obviously, not only did she not have enough money for the project, she also didn't have the ability to build the needed ramp. So, the store manager authorized the needed supplies at no charge and arranged for a group of employees to volunteer their time and services for this customer. The woman got access to her home and The Home Depot exhibited its *Bleeding Orange* culture at its best.

Our return policy was to take back anything that the customer wished to return for any reason. The idea was to save the customer, not to win the return argument. Our objective was always to preserve the customer's lifetime purchase potential in any decision that could impact loyalty. Our most important asset was clearly our customer's trust in The Home Depot, and we could not afford to tarnish that.

This formula of wide assortment, low prices, and great service was an unstoppable market force against the traditional retailers. In market after market, traditional home centers closed as The Home Depot offered customers a better option for their home-improvement needs. This also led to the demise of the large, independent, regional wholesalers that fed products to these stores, which was a sea change in the logistics of the home-improvement industry.

MILLIONAIRE REBELS

The company went public on the New York Stock Exchange in 1983. Generous stock options to every management-level job in the company resulted in a team dedicated to success and growth. We knew our growth depended on being the best alternative for our customers to purchase home-improvement products. Customer service was always job number one, and we needed a highly motivated team that was customer focused and willing to base their future on The Home Depot's success.

The Home Depot's stock price skyrocketed as our success became known. According to The Motley Fool, if you had invested a thousand dollars in The Home Depot's initial stock offering, today it would be worth over $11 million![1]

Before long we had store managers and merchandising staff who had become millionaires. Expensive sport cars were now parked in our parking lots and gold Rolex watches were beginning to show up more frequently along with the orange aprons. This ostentatious show of pride and accomplishment by The Home Depot zealots provided proof positive to any doubters that *Bleeding Orange* paid off big time.

I remember when our CFO purchased a new Rolex watch. Shortly after, we were in a monthly stat meeting to review our financial results with all the senior management. Pat Farrah, our VP of merchandising, had just returned from Taiwan with a pocket full of fake Rolex watches. At the start of our meeting, Pat, a jokester, asked if he could see the new genuine Rolex watch, and it was handed to him. While the meeting went on, Pat put the genuine watch in his pocket and retrieved one of the fake watches.

As the meeting progressed Pat began to pretend that he was upset and began waving the "Rolex" watch in the air. Finally in pretense of anger, Pat stood up and threw the watch onto our cement floor, where it broke into a thousand pieces. The room went silent as everyone stared in shock at the pieces of what they assumed to be the real Rolex watch. After a couple of seconds Pat broke into laughter, returned the original watch to its owner, and everyone breathed a sigh of relief.

Welcome to the world of The Home Depot! We had a well-deserved reputation for being unorthodox and perhaps a little crazy. We approached the marketplace with a certain irreverence for the status quo. Our success was based on the simple idea that we had to give customers no reason to shop elsewhere for their home-improvement needs. Our *modus operandi* was to find a need and urgently fill it. This did not have to be complicated. We just had to be action oriented and keep moving forward. Damn the torpedoes–full speed ahead!

INTIMIDATING THE COMPETITION

Our band of zealots had transformed into a fearsome *orange machine* as we entered each new market. After Atlanta we swept into Miami, Orlando, and Tampa, before heading west into Louisiana, then out to Arizona and California. Ultimately, we would paint the whole country orange.

A good example of the *Bleeding Orange* zeal could be seen when we opened our first store in the Tampa market. Our grand opening team donned The Home Depot orange aprons and held a cheering session in the parking lot of Lindsley Lumber, the closest competitor. When the Lindsley management team came out of the store to see what the commotion was about, the store manager was presented with a bouquet of black roses, signifying the coming demise of his store. It was prophetic, and within a brief time, the Lindsley store was closed.

The in-your-face culture could be criticized as rude and crude, but it was effective at paralyzing the competition.

When we opened our West Coast merchandising office in Southern California, about eight traditional home center competitors were established in that marketplace. A photograph of each company's CEO was posted in our conference room. A red X was then marked through the photo as each competitor was put out of business. This was a way of encouraging our staff in the early days of the West Coast market, that although we were starting small, we were nevertheless in Bleeding Orange "Attack, Attack, Attack" mode.

Our public statements were also bold, but they focused more on the idea of driving down high prices. We often used a kind of black humor in our advertising, conveying The Home Depot as the *grim reaper* who was killing high prices—which also implied a certain existential threat to our competitors. Or we would show our mascot, *Homer*, walking his pet piranha on a leash. The piranha represented our voracious appetite to consume more market share by driving down prices.

EMBRACING CHANGE

In retrospect, it might seem that the magic of The Home Depot's strategy was the result of some grand master scheme mapped out ahead of time. The truth of the matter is that much of The Home Depot's success was developed by experimenting and taking risks on the run. We were a dynamic, changing company and we learned how to learn.

"Culture eats strategy for breakfast."
— Peter Drucker

This learning process started with not being defensive and being willing to take criticism. Self-criticism, for us, was a virtue and our way of life. Passionate arguments and candid observations led us to always increase our internal thermostat in order to perform at a higher level for our customers. As a result, our competitors were constantly surprised, as we never stood still. We were unpredictable.

The art of the ambush is to do what your competitors least expect.

Certainly, delighting our customers was the compass needle that kept us moving the right direction. We were learning on the job as we forged ahead with vigor. Our *modus operandi* was to stay in the lead while running scared, constantly looking over our shoulders.

[1]Bowman, Jeremy, "If You Had Invested $1,000 in Home Depot's IPO, This Is How Much You'd Have Now," Dec 13, 2019, The Motley Fool (www.fool.com).

HOME DEPOT:
THE PEOPLE, THE CULTURE

First, let's define the term *merchant*. In most retail companies a group of people is responsible for the merchandising function of the business; they are most often called b*uyers* or *category managers*. I prefer to use the term *merchant* or *merchandiser,* because it better describes their primary responsibility, which is to create sales.

The way I look at it, the merchants define both the online and offline product mix, negotiate merchandise cost with the vendors, set the retail pricing and promotion plans, and specify the store layout and point-of-sale merchandising. The merchant role requires an eclectic job description. Many pieces of the retailing puzzle need to be brought together in a coordinated strategy and plan.

Most retailers, though, see the main work of the merchant as the buying function. This implies that the main skills, and most of the time and effort, should focus on negotiating with the vendors to lower costs. When the job is so narrowly restricted, many of the merchandising activities and decisions are either overlooked or delegated to others in the bureaucracy. The narrow definition of the merchant's job is an innovation killer. Off-loading the merchant's decision-making authority to various support groups often creates a company in which forces are pushing in opposite directions instead of being focused on the customer by a competent merchant.

At The Home Depot, we understood that the main job of the merchants was not to purchase but to sell. Everyone in the organization had to be focused on delighting the customer, which meant focusing on sales. The key concept was to first delight the customer, with the result that the customers would vote for our stores by purchasing products with their dollars. The resulting sales volume would provide the buying power we would need to further drive down costs.

It's a chicken-and-egg situation. The chicken is getting increased sales; the egg is the reward of lower product costs. The merchant at The Home Depot was, in effect, a lawyer for the customer, responsible for driving sales by creating the right merchandising mix to delight and create regular shoppers. Generating sales through customer service must always be job number one.

Increasing sales covers a multitude of sins.

MERCHANDISING MAGIC

Every merchandising-oriented company needs a "merchant prince" to lead the charge. At The Home Depot this initially was Pat Farrah, one of the founding partners of the company. Pat was a larger-than-life, charismatic Irishman who had the drive and chutzpah to attract a loyal group of merchandising zealots to join the march across the U.S., opening The Home Depot stores with incredible vigor. (I was one of those zealots.)

A typical week for our merchandising group would entail spending the first part of Monday in our Atlanta office. Then we would be on an airplane that afternoon to visit The Home Depot stores spreading across the country. We worked at the stores until returning to Atlanta on Friday and used the weekend to clean up the paperwork. Our management style was to be *ground-engaged,* which meant we had firsthand experience and knowledge of what was going on in our stores in every market. We were actively giving orange-blooded culture transfusions to our people by teaching our associates The Home Depot philosophy:

• For the customers: Give them no reason to buy elsewhere.

• For the competition: Kick ass and take no prisoners.

• For the employees: Take ownership and do the right thing.

The *Bleeding Orange* culture was transferred to the troops by the role model we set as we worked in the stores. It was understood that the corporate team of merchants should be store-engaged in mind, spirit, and body. The really great merchandising ideas are best formulated in the stores. Very few light bulbs of creativity fire up while people are sitting at a desk in the corporate office.

The vendors soon discovered that the best way to have a meeting with The Home Depot was to find out which stores the merchants would be visiting that week and plan to rendezvous in that market. There were even cases where manufacturer representatives booked flights on the same airplane in order to have an opportunity to interact with one of our merchants. Our merchandising team was on the move!

There are two types of people: those who see an opportunity and say, Why?, and those who see the same opportunity and say, Why not? The latter group are the merchants.

The merchants never had enough time to exploit all the possibilities created by our growth; they had to keep running like the Energizer Bunny™. There could always be a good excuse to stay in the corporate office. However, being plugged into a store was their ultimate power source. The longer the merchants lingered in the corporate office, the less energy they had to be creative problem solvers. In the stores, the merchants got their batteries charged with innovative ideas, motivation, and confidence to climb the next mountain.

Good decisions and productive plans require empathy with the stores, which comes through interaction. We were running a race with no finish line and energized as each store achieved new successes.

HUNGRY MERCHANTS

The *Bleeding Orange* culture was very much like a religious movement in that it required belief and total commitment to the cause, as we were constantly recruiting new people to fuel the growth. To find and recruit the right new merchants, we tended not to use headhunters. Rather, we would contact the industry vendors who knew which buyers were the good guys and which were not. We would then reach out to the most highly recommended candidates to tell them The Home Depot story and paint the vision of our mission and future growth. We would challenge them to step up and be a part of our orange-blooded team.

Our offer to them did not typically increase their salary but did include a large number of stock options. The candidates who took our offer were the kind of people who were willing to take the leap of faith and bet on their ability to help us grow the company. These were people who were committed to the long march, with confidence in the reward that would come via The Home Depot's success.

These new recruits typically took a step back in their career to get on the bandwagon. A former district manager might first be assigned to train for a store manager position. A former store manager might first serve as a department manager. A former division merchandise manager might find himself in a merchant position. In this way, the team relearned the business by embracing The Home Depot's new business paradigms. The resulting team had no illusions that they had landed a soft job. Rather, they were people hungry for success.

Our search for the best lumber expert in the country provides a good example of the cultural change required to join The Home Depot. I had received the name of a top candidate from our lumber vendors and, after contacting him, I brought him to Atlanta to tell him our story and have him experience the store environment and the company culture.

The meeting went well, and he was agreeable to the salary and stock option proposal. Then, at the end of our discussion, he said there was just one more issue. His current company provided membership in his local country club, and he wanted us to pay his country club membership in Atlanta. I told him we did not have corporate memberships in country clubs, and besides, he wouldn't have time to enjoy it if we did.

That was the end of our negotiation. He returned home while we renewed our search. A month later he called me and said, "Hi Jim, I just called to tell you that I don't care about country clubs anymore."

I replied, "Great! Welcome to The Home Depot team."

FOCUSING ON THE STORES

Another characteristic of The Home Depot management team was servant leadership, which was an unknown concept to most retail veterans back then. We had to hunt far and wide to find servant leaders. Traditionally, retailers concentrated the power and decision-making at the corporate level and expected the troops to simply follow the standard operating procedures manual. We had no such manual. Our merchants needed to listen to our store associates and respond with urgency to provide them with the products and services they needed to delight our customers.

It was important for people coming on board to understand that they were not hired hands bringing their old, proven methods and culture with them. They needed to leave that baggage behind. In most cases, these people came from larger, hierarchical organizations. They were trained to manage from the corporate office down to the stores. They had to quickly realize that we empowered the stores to delight our customers. This company was driven from the stores up. Our job was to serve the stores.

Did that mean that all strategic and tactical decisions were made at store level? No. It did mean that every member of the management understood that our priorities were set by solving the store's problems with respect and providing store personnel the tools they needed to win. By solving the store problems and empowering our store associates we could establish the *best practices* and maintain a winning culture.

Our management team members in each store knew they were expected to take ownership in the decisions that impacted their customers. They also knew they would not be criticized for exercising good judgment in taking care of the customer. The whole concept of ownership, responsibility, and empowerment at the local level was an incredible tool for developing customer satisfaction and loyalty. The uncommonly positive morale of our store management and sales associates evolved from this concept of individual ownership.

MERCHANDISING TO A DIFFERENT DRUM BEAT

Pat Farrah knew there was a mystique to The Home Depot's culture, and he worked to create an environment that would encourage staff to think outside the box. His leadership was unorthodox by design.

It was not unusual for our group to work all day in our stores and then meet at a restaurant or bar in the evening to start working on the next month's advertising campaign and catalog into the late hours of the night. After dinner and a significant amount of Bacardi rum we would have the next month's catalogue outlined with felt pen on the restaurant's tablecloths. Then we would purchase the tablecloths and mail them to Atlanta for the next month's promotional effort. This led to some interesting and novel promotions.

We developed our 1985 Christmas catalogue while sitting on the top of a houseboat in the middle of Lake Lanier, Georgia, during the hottest part of August. It is hard to think of Christmas trees covered with snow when the temperature is 95 degrees Fahrenheit and the humidity percentage is about the same. Most retailers advertise gifts and Christmas decorations in December; we were probably the first to run a full catalogue at Christmastime on commodity building materials and tools. Surprisingly, it worked. We never did the obvious and predictable.

Pat encouraged us to walk proudly and represent a winning persona. We were the believers who had embraced the vision and we were now the role models of success and winning. This was how leadership was defined at The Home Depot: It was *walking the talk*. Heaven help the merchant who sat down during a store walk. Role models don't sit down. We were on the march and had no time to rest on past success. There were always new opportunities to exploit and challenges to overcome.

We knew The Home Depot could become the dominant home center in any market we entered, as long as we maintained our momentum and never blinked. Pat led the charge by example, and the company moved forward with *Bleeding Orange* enthusiasm.

THE THREE FOUNDERS' UNIQUE ROLES

Pat Farrah was the merchandising guru who created the *Bleeding Orange* culture. Arthur Blank was the financial genius who created the budgets and discipline to keep the company on track. Bernie Marcus was the ombudsman who was the spokesman for the stakeholders. The combination was truly magic.

PAT FARRAH: INNOVATIVE VISIONARY

The initial concept of a warehouse home center sprang from Pat Farrah's vision. Pat had been the general manager of National Lumber, a traditional home center in the Los Angeles market. Pat left National Lumber and, with the financial help of some friends and business associates in 1977, opened Homeco in Long Beach, California, which truly was the first big-box home-improvement store.

Pat had seen the success of the San Diego-based Price Club (which eventually evolved into Costco). He saw the efficiency of the warehouse concept and was able to relate it to the home-improvement industry. However, he believed that the DIY home-improvement market could not operate like the self-service, limited-assortment Price Club format. Pat believed that if you did it right, you could combine low warehouse prices with a broad product assortment and helpful service.

At that time, most manufacturers produced a catalog of their products with a printed recommended retail price for the retail customer and a different list of wholesale prices at which retailers purchased. There were, in some cases, fair trade laws in place to reinforce the manufacturers' control over retail pricing. Pat determined to purchase products direct from the manufacturer and offer the wholesale price directly to the customer. This was unorthodox and disruptive, but that was Pat's style and his strategy at Homeco.

Homeco was an incredible success in bringing high customer traffic from all over Southern California to its Long Beach location. Why not? The customers were able to purchase at wholesale prices and get products and services beyond what was available in the smaller traditional DIY stores.

Meanwhile, across town, Bernie Marcus was the CEO of Handy Dan, the largest traditional home center chain. Handy Dan operated under many different local brands throughout the country. The Los Angeles stores were called Angel's. Handy Dan, in turn, was owned, at that time, by Daylin, a large publicly held retail conglomerate.

In 1978 there was a labor dispute in the Northern California division of Handy Dan known as Bonanza. The CEO of Daylin used this situation to remove both Bernie Marcus and his finance vice president, Arthur Blank, from Handy Dan. This proved to be fortuitous, as Bernie was subsequently contacted by Ken Langone, a New York investment banker who encouraged him to consider opening a new chain of home centers.

Bernie and Arthur were headquartered in the Los Angeles area and were very much aware of Pat Farrah's Homeco phenomenon in nearby Long Beach. Bernie certainly knew the weaknesses of the traditional home center model. He could see that the Homeco model approximated many of his ideas for creating a better home center standard. Bernie and Arthur decided to approach Pat about bringing new capital into Homeco and expanding the concept into a nationwide chain.

Pat was open to the idea. But an audit of Homeco's financial condition soon revealed that, while the store was achieving incredible sales, it had serious financial problems. Wholesale pricing was brilliant. However, that idea needed to be married to a low-cost supply chain with proper financial systems and discipline.

Pat's warehouse concept had clearly created excitement in the retail home-improvement business. Now the challenge was to repackage the concept into a viable and scalable business. The new strategy would be to relaunch this big-box home center concept in a smaller market than the Long Beach/Los Angeles marketplace, which had many competitors and was an expensive media market for advertising and promotion. The ideal location would be somewhere in a smaller Sunbelt city where the Homeco merchandising concept could quickly dominate the market. That was the plan. The decision was to close Homeco and start with a clean slate.

Bernie Marcus, Arthur Blank, and Pat Farrah established a new team. They searched the Southern U.S. for the best location, finally settling on Atlanta, Georgia. The Home Depot launched four stores in Atlanta with the financing package arranged by Ken Langone.

ARTHUR BLANK: DRIVER OF EXCELLENCE

Arthur Blank's background was financial, so his primary role was to bring the financial discipline to our dynamic merchandising strategies. In many retail companies, the top management tends to put the merchandising group into a budgetary straitjacket by micromanaging the gross margin number to supposedly protect the bottom line.

Arthur didn't do that. He understood the magic happening in our stores and embraced the resourcefulness of the *Bleeding Orange* culture that created excitement for the customers. He encouraged our merchants to use pricing to aggressively attack the market.

At the same time, he knew the numbers better than anyone and made sure The Home Depot team clearly understood the financial principles required to ensure that the company was fiscally sound. He insisted we evaluate the performance of our merchandising group based on GMROI (gross margin return on inventory investment) and our store operating group based on ROI (return on investment in the stores). This provided the right metrics to measure our performance and freed us from the tyranny of establishing inflexible gross margin percentage criteria that tripped up so many of our competitors.

This also meant Arthur had to expect and demand increasing sales and robust inventory turns. He could accept lower margins, but only in return for greater market share and higher inventory turns. This is what drove the productivity engine at The Home Depot.

Arthur kept close tabs on every budget and every headcount in every department. He acknowledged that expenses would increase in a growing business but was adamant that every expense—whether payroll, corporate overhead, utilities, advertising, or any other expenditure—needed to decrease as a percentage of sales every year. He was right. Only with this philosophy could we keep one step ahead of our competition by having the complete assurance that we would always remain the low-cost channel of distribution.

We had to know that if we were in a price war with one of our competitors, we would always win due to our low-cost advantage. Our goal was to drive down the homeowner's cost for home improvement, which had to start with driving down our own costs. Sometimes this led to heated exchanges in budget meetings, but the principle was maintained.

This focus on cost control extended to capital investments as well. The eventual creation of covered loading zones at the exits where customers loaded building materials into their vehicles represented a hard-won battle. The original stores had no clear area for loading as customers exited the store. In fact, the driveway often directed the traffic entering or exiting the parking lot to travel right in front of the exit door.

We determined that it would be better to route this traffic in a pattern away from the building material exit door and to put a canopy over the area to allow a safe, all-weather, loading zone. Then the issue arose of justifying the cost of the covered roof. How to you quantify safety or put a price on customer convenience? How can you ask the customers about a service or convenience that doesn't exist? This is where common sense and gut-level experience runs into the financial wall. We found ourselves in a fight between the *why not?* people and the *why?* people.

Fortunately, the decision was made to invest in the loading zone and its canopy. Almost all The Home Depot stores have this loading zone today, and nobody in his or her right mind would suggest removing it. The concern about justifying all costs was right and had to be a key part of every spending decision. These fights over expenses were often emotional and hard-fought. They were not always pleasant, but the exercise always helped define the *best practice.* This is defined as a solution that drives down costs while simultaneously increasing customer service and satisfaction.

Another tough decision regarding operating costs involved the issue of lighting levels in the stores. An energy expert was hired to help drive down utility costs, which then provoked an argument over just how much illumination the stores required. Our energy expert, affectionately known as The Prince of Darkness, espoused a standard for store lighting approximating the brightness of twilight at the winter solstice.

As merchants, we constantly fought for more light to best display the products and to make the shopping experience more pleasant. Depending on the placement of the light fixtures on the ceiling and the height of the counters, we often found areas of the store that needed much more light. Our lighting expert would take out his lumens meter and show us that we were mistaken. We had a clear and specific idea of what he should do with his lumens meter!

The Prince of Darkness had his facts right, but his criteria for brightness was not truly customer focused. Fortunately for today's retailers, the LED light bulb has brought bright lighting at much lower costs. However, there will always be energy experts running around with their light meters. This struggle of cost versus benefit required hard thinking and prevented spending capital or taking on expenses without justification. It is a healthy exercise to have legitimate arguments over the budget numbers, as long as the customer ultimately wins.

It was, of course, critical to come to a consensus on budgets so the numbers became a common goal. Budgets were not created at the top and pushed down. Rather, every manager had to know the numbers and be able to present a rational budget to senior management.

Arthur expected and demanded that we know our numbers and commit to stretch goals when we presented our budgets. This was particularly true when it came to sales and inventory turnover. He would allow, and often encourage, lower gross margin percentages, knowing we could hit our gross margin dollar goals with the right combination of sales and inventory turn.

This focus on gross margin dollars allowed us to drive prices down to a point where our competitors dared not to tread. Arthur's metrics allowed our merchants to make promotional and pricing decisions that essentially broke the rules that our competition continued to use to set prices and operate their businesses. Our competitors didn't understand our pricing philosophy but concluded that The Home Depot merchants were just a little crazy, and it was just best not to mess with us when it came to pricing.

Arthur supplied the hammer we needed to drive the nails into the coffin of our competition. There was simply no question that the customers would return to our stores once they experienced the benefits of low prices, right products, and great service. It was our job to make sure the customer was standing in our store instead of a competitor's.

Every quarter Arthur would conduct financial review meetings to dive deeply into the financial results for the quarter. These meetings were not held in the corporate office but out in the regions. This kept the management group intimately in touch with the stores and enabled members of the field management to visit and observe stores outside of their geographical area. Arthur kept us all focused on the stores.

BERNIE MARCUS: ENTREPRENEUR EXTRAORDINAIRE

Bernie Marcus was our CEO and Chairman. He was an incredible manager and charismatic leader, who made it his business to interact with all stakeholders. He listened to their praises and, more importantly, their complaints. He was considered the friend of the investor, the vendors, the customers, and the store employees. Bernie's management style was MBWA (Management by Wandering Around), which gave him keen insight into what was going on in the business.

Bernie rarely had to sign off on specific merchandising programs, so he was free to criticize any corporate program getting bad reviews. His way of relating to people tended to open candid discussions to probe the views of numerous stakeholders into the brand image of our company. He knew the corporate bureaucracy in a successful, growing company would tend to become hierarchical and arrogant. He saw his job as keeping the corporate group ground engaged and humble. He was highly effective at achieving this.

At our annual store managers' meeting, the corporate officers would sit on the front row of the auditorium. Bernie would walk into the audience and begin asking store managers about their challenges and problems. Soon the store managers were pointing out their various frustrations with corporate issues and decisions. (Bernie knew whom to ask!) Once an issue was on the table, Bernie would turn to the appropriate vice president or director and ask what could be done to fix this store's problem. Pity the officer who made any attempt to justify a problem or to defend the indefensible! Bernie wanted a pro-active answer for the store, and he wanted it now.

With the growing success of The Home Depot, it would have been easy for the management team to believe their own press reports about how awesome we were. Bernie would not let this happen. He always made sure we focused on our stores, admitted our errors, and responded with positive solutions.

Bernie had a chart framed and hung in the office of every officer in the company to make sure we kept focused on the right priorities. It showed, in seven steps, how easy and predictable it was to evolve from a successful, innovative business to an arrogant, bureaucratic establishment that has lost its customer-centric culture. Bernie was a warrior when it came to fighting the bureaucracy. He knew the greatest danger to The Home Depot success story was internal, not external.

The day you start to believe your own glowing news reports is when innovation and progress stop.

If you knew nothing about The Home Depot and were in an early staff meeting, listening to the sometimes heated discussions, you might assume that our company was in serious trouble and on the verge of collapse. We never patted ourselves on the back for past accomplishments; we criticized ourselves for missed opportunities and set new standards for performance. The constant theme was that we must keep listening to our customers and responding with positive urgency to our stores. We understood that the biggest danger to our success was self-satisfaction. We could not stand still and allow our competition to catch up with us. We could not become fat, happy, and lazy. Bernie would keep asking the right questions of the right people in order to keep this from happening.

Listening was one of Bernie's greatest talents. Most of us listen while thinking about a defensive response, but not Bernie. He knew how to probe for the truth. People felt comfortable sharing their true thoughts and feelings because he was never defensive and always appreciative. Bernie's reports on the stakeholder's attitudes were always enlightening and valuable, although sometimes painful.

The combined talents of the company founders created an unusual company with a unique culture. Pat Farrah left the company in year five to concentrate on his love of competitive sailing. However, the *Bleeding Orange* culture he helped create was firmly rooted and continued to be the magic elixir that would define The Home Depot for years. It was my privilege to ultimately assume the merchandising mantle and take responsibility for driving the merchandising, marketing, and logistic departments. Although Pat had left the company, his shadow pointed the way throughout the following years.

THE BOWATER ACQUISITION

The Home Depot's growth was both dynamic and fluid. We were discovering our own merchandising strength and reacting to opportunities as we grew. In 1984 we almost grew too fast when we acquired the Bowater Home Center chain based in Dallas, Texas.

Bowater was a British lumber trading company that had considered being an early investor in The Home Depot but decided instead to imitate The Home Depot format with their own warehouse-type home center stores. At that time, The Home Depot had twenty-two stores in Georgia, Florida, Louisiana, and Arizona. Bowater had opened eight stores, located in Texas and Louisiana.

While this acquisition of the Bowater stores instantly gave us new markets, we underestimated the impact of this kind of rapid growth. The effort required us to merge two different IT systems and to instantly infuse the *Bleeding Orange* culture into an entirely new group of employees. This proved to be more difficult than expected.

The IT fix proved to be expensive and time consuming. The unpleasant result was a dire bottom line, significantly below our projections. The major cause was inventory shrinkage during the transition period.

Transfusing our *Bleeding Orange* culture overnight into the existing Bowater employee base proved to be impossible. Bowater's passive culture – not a winning attribute – was inbred into its people. The stores didn't even approach The Home Depot's level of sales and productivity because their culture was not customer-centric. Their management team had no sense of urgency to address these shortcomings and resisted change. We quickly learned how difficult it was to erase a bad culture and impart a whole new vision to a defensive group of people.

It is human nature to resist change, especially when it demands a new commitment of time, effort, enthusiasm, and urgency. The Home Depot culture demanded a *leap of faith* based on the idea that hard work has its own rewards. We simply could not force the orange blood transfusion fast enough to prevent employee push back. A few caught the vision, but most of the Bowater people did not last through the first year. In reality, we did not buy an organization; we simply purchased real estate.

MANAGING GROWTH

This was a huge wake-up call to us. We realized for the first time we were not invincible, despite our public image to that effect. This merger threatened the viability of The Home Depot, as we were still in start-up mode and had much to prove. We had to postpone entry into some new markets to slow our growth and get the company back on track. We needed to rethink how to grow and inculcate the *Bleeding Orange* culture.

This was when we established the policy of growing our store count at a maximum of twenty-five percent per year. While that may seem like a speed limit, it is nevertheless an aggressive growth pattern and was very demanding, requiring compounded annual growth on a constantly increasing store base. This perpetual compounded growth of stores required more and more people.

We became more aware that our main job was training the troops and spreading our unique culture. We had to keep the herd moving toward true north. This required dedicated leadership and hands-on involvement in developing the people in our stores. We all wore our orange aprons with pride. Every person in management had to understand that his or her main job was not the title on a business card but, rather, teaching, teaching, and teaching. If you were to walk into one of The Home Depot's stores early in morning, before opening, you would see product knowledge meetings going on in various departments. We all had to take an active part in leading a competent army of orange-blooded zealots, dedicated to revolutionizing the home center business.

CANADIAN EXPANSION

Ten years after the Bowater acquisition, we entered the Canadian market, with the purchase of the seven-store big-box Aikenhead's Home Improvement Warehouse. We had just opened our first Canadian stores in Vancouver, British Columbia, but we saw this acquisition as a way to rapidly expand and to eliminate the only other big-box home center competitor in Canada.

Aikenhead's was originally the name of a famous hardware store in Canada. A traditional home center chain in Canada known as Busy Beaver, owned by Molson Companies (famous for its breweries), transformed the brand into Aikenhead's Home Improvement Warehouse. The move was Molson's effort to keep The Home Depot south of the Canadian border. It didn't work.

Aikenhead's was headed by an ex-Home Depot VP so it was no surprise that these Canadian stores looked like a clone of The Home Depot, in green instead of orange. This initially seemed like it would be a smoother transition than the Bowater experience, since the stores were similar to our own. We were now a much larger and financially stronger company than at the time of the Bowater acquisition. So what could go wrong?

As in the earlier merger, system integration proved troublesome – a problem that seems inherent to merging retail companies. We also encountered even stronger resistance to The Home Depot's *Bleeding Orange* culture due to Canadian distrust of the U.S. management team. We initially put some of our veteran U.S. managers into the key management positions, including the role of "country president". The negative response of the Canadian staff soon alerted us to the need to recall these veteran managers.

Once again, we found how difficult it is to transplant our culture into another company and, in this case, another country. Canada was about the same population as California, but we quickly discovered that we could not treat Canada as just another state. We had to put Canadians in charge of running this division and allow interaction over time to infuse the *Bleeding Orange* culture. A great deal of time and employee turnover transpired before this was ultimately accomplished.

The Bowater and Aikenhead's acquisitions were learning experiences. We saw just how unique our culture was, and how foreign it was to other retailers—even to those attempting to duplicate our big-box format.

DEVELOPING SPECIAL PEOPLE

The Home Depot's *Bleeding Orange* culture drove us to win—always. Once you bought into The Home Depot vision, the commitment became an all-encompassing force in your life. This resulted in a team of people who were never satisfied to give less than 100 percent. The first part of the word culture is *cult*. In many ways The Home Depot culture operated as a cult that demanded much, with a promise of future greatness.

A phrase from the Bible could apply to the process of inculcating the orange-blooded culture: *Many are called, but few are chosen.* Many people wished to join The Home Depot parade once they saw our success, but not all would wholeheartedly commit to becoming a true believer and finish the march. Movers and shakers tend to be people who are willing to break the norms and overreact with urgency. These were the people that succeeded at The Home Depot. This resulted in an interesting group of characters with unique idiosyncrasies.

I remember traveling in a car driven by the merchandising vice president for our new Northeast market. He was preparing to show us the East Plainfield, New Jersey, store building which had recently been turned over to us by the building contractor. It was a big-box structure that would soon be full of home-improvement products, but at that time was totally empty.

As we drove up to the store in our VP's custom Lincoln convertible, he did not slow down. Instead, he accelerated as we streaked through the door that would become the lumber entrance, hit the brakes, and spun the car in a 360-degree circle in the middle of the store. Wow! That was one crazy merchant—which was okay with us.

In many ways, we were looking for mavericks. A likely question a new recruit might be asked was, "Have you ever had a speeding ticket?" An affirmative answer was a plus; we were looking for self-starters with a sense of urgency.

> *"Success or failure in business is caused more by the mental attitude even than by mental capacities."*
>
> — Walter Scott

While many converts did ultimately catch the vision and become orange-blooded zealots, others could not make the transition from their old, orthodox retail maxims to embrace the more aggressive attack mode of The Home Depot.

It is interesting to look back on the early times when we were working against all odds with limited resources, and realize that those were the good old days. The task was huge, the hours long, and the work hard, but the attitude was positive, and we were having fun! The Home Depot's crew worked hard and played hard. People will work at an exceptional level once they buy into a cause that is bigger than themselves. That was the essence of the *Bleeding Orange* magic.

Wild and Crazy

Here are six true-life stories that might give you a sense of The Home Depot's culture at work:

The Welcome Party

Our new marketing vice president had just been hired from Circuit City, a major chain of electronic stores. No one told him The Home Depot was a no-tie, no-jacket kind of workplace. So naturally, on his first day at work, he showed up in suit and tie ready to impress the troops.

He was invited to attend an introduction meeting with the merchandisers that afternoon. When he walked through the doorway of the conference room, he was greeted by the entire staff sitting around the conference table nude from the waist up. (The crew at that time was all men, by the way!) After his initial shock, his tie was ceremoniously cut off so he could join the *Bleeding Orange* club.

Nothing to Hide

One lumber department merchant had a reputation for being a sandbagger who would always present low goals to assure a full bonus each year. He would suggest pessimistic market conditions to justify conservative budget projections in order to assure receiving a large bonus at year end. These dire situations might include statements such as: Perhaps the weather was bad, and the trees could not be cut. Maybe the woodpeckers had made nests in the trees, and the environmentalists would not allow logging. Or demand had collapsed, and prices were depressed. It was always a sad story!

The budgeting process was designed so each merchant would present his or her department's budget to the entire senior management team at an annual meeting chaired by Arthur Blank, who knew the numbers frontwards and backwards. These were tough meetings.

Our sandbagger knew his reputation was becoming a problem. As he began his presentation, he unbuttoned his shirt, which he then removed. Then, he unbuckled his belt. People started to glance around. Yes, next the pants came off. He went on with his presentation like a strip poker player, until he finally stripped down buck-naked. Not a pretty sight! He finished with the statement that he was being totally honest and had nothing to hide. (The management team at that time was, again, all males.)

Exotic Meetings

Pat Farrah, our merchandising guru, would schedule our quarterly merchandising strategy sessions at glamorous venues like Key West, Florida, Acapulco, Mexico, or Santa Catalina Island, California. This might seem extravagant, but Pat knew the importance of building an aura around the *Bleeding Orange* culture. He wanted to exemplify the truth that The Home Depot merchants didn't just think outside the box, they lived outside the box! The purpose of the meetings was to encourage creativity and innovation, and the venue was part of the equation.

The Home Depot Mystique

Pat would also plan an annual all-night poker game at his waterfront home in Fort Lauderdale, Florida. Vendors were invited to attend and put up a stake in the game. That money was then used to purchase a sports car, which became the prize for the winner. These poker parties were legendary in our industry. People flew in from all over the country to attend. It was truly the lifestyle of the rich and famous. You can probably imagine the scene. Well, maybe you can't! It was all part of The Home Depot's mystique and Pat's persona.

Challenging Job Interview

One evening Pat and I took a job candidate and his wife to dinner. Pat immediately went for the escargot appetizer. He turned to our candidate, and said, "Steve, would you like some escargot?"

Steve declined.

"Have you ever tasted escargot, Steve?" Pat asked.

Steve admitted he hadn't.

Pat said, "Steve, at The Home Depot we are never afraid to try new things."

Steve decided to order escargot.

As dinner progressed, Pat continued to challenge Steve on numerous issues. I could see that Steve and his wife were becoming increasingly uncomfortable.

Finally, Steve looked at Pat and said, "Pat, you have to think of me as an escargot and try me!"

Pat smiled and said, "Steve, you're hired!"

Winter Bonding

Arthur Blank would host an annual outing for all the corporate officers as a bonding exercise. Each of these adventures involved some sort of challenge. In fact, Bernie joked that Arthur was trying to kill us all.

One year we all flew in our corporate jets to Grand Junction, Colorado, at the start of winter. We then transferred to a group of single-engine small planes and, after scraping ice off the wings, took off for the high desert area of southeastern Utah. We had been told we were going to spend a week riding horses and chasing cattle.

We landed in a forsaken cow pasture as snow was falling. We were escorted into a horse trailer, our transportation to the ranch. We then discovered that not only were there no private rooms, but there were also no sleeping facilities. This was not the renowned and luxurious Canyon Ranch! It was a dilapidated cow ranch, miles from civilization. Some of the team slept in an old school bus. Others bedded down in the barn, which had no roof but a clear view of the stars. It was, without doubt, the coldest week of my life. So much for becoming cowboys in the West! We bonded in misery, but that is about all I can say for it.

The following year our marketing VP convinced Arthur to rent a fleet of sailboats in the Caribbean, and we sailed the British Virgin Islands. Much better!

Being a wild and crazy group fixated on pushing the envelope was a huge part of the *Bleeding Orange* culture. Everything about The Home Depot had to be written large. This was an important part of The Home Depot magic.

CREATING BELIEVERS

Every person in The Home Depot management, from store managers to senior executives, spent a week participating in Outward Bound. This survival school, started in England, challenges individuals with seemingly impossible tasks that can be accomplished with the right skills and attitude. The founder of the organization had observed that in accidents at sea, the older crewmembers seemed to survive, while the younger ones perished.

The Home Depot people would be placed in teams of five or six associates. Our provisions constituted little more than a bag of beans, a small tin cup, a sleeping bag, and a tent. Each day the Outward Bound guides would put us through skill practice, such as negotiating a rope course. We might have to climb a granite cliff using only our hands and feet or jump backwards off a precipice to rappel down the cliff face.

Teams that went through Outward Bound formed a special bond. We had faced the test and survived together. The message: The seemingly impossible was, in fact, possible—and expected. Each person learned to be responsible for results. Not only that, but the person must take ownership of his or her part of the business, with no excuses for failure. The *Bleeding Orange* culture of The Home Depot expected people to take on any challenge, with the expectation of winning.

TAKING OWNERSHIP

The consistent management direction of The Home Depot was to push decisions down and out. This meant we had to empower people at all levels to accept responsibility and then give them the authority to take ownership of their jobs. This led to *"orange blood pride"*—a pride of ownership that could be sensed from the division manager to the district manager to the store manager to the department manager to the sales associate.

75

Of course, this also created a certain amount of chaos. But it was a positive, creative chaos. Great results came from ordinary people performing at extraordinary levels. Customer satisfaction was the goal, and everyone was empowered to make it happen.

PERFORMANCE-BASED BONUSES

In a sales-driven company the best measurement of customer satisfaction is the votes people make with their purchasing dollars. Hitting and exceeding sales goals was expected and required—and rewarded.

Every merchant in the buying office and every member of store management had the potential to receive a bonus of 50 percent of their base pay. To qualify for this bonus, each employee had to meet the sales plan for his or her department or store. Keep in mind that the sales numbers were always a stretch number. This kept a keen focus on creating sales and finding new ways to grow comparable store sales, which meant beating last year's numbers. Meeting the sales plan was the price of admission to the bonus race. Once the sales number was achieved, the associate was assured a bonus of ten percent of the base annual salary. The other forty points of potential bonus was based on a return-on-investment formula.

The biggest factor in computing return on investment is inventory. Inventory turnover, therefore, became of utmost importance to both merchandising and store management. What is the best way to increase inventory turnover? The answer is to increase sales volume. What is the best way to increase sales? The obvious answer is low prices. That was the logic that resulted in establishing the right pricing for the customers, which in turn drove the sales and profits required to generate bonuses for The Home Depot's motivated team.

WALKING THE TALK

No aisle numbers were posted at the front of our counters during the first twenty years of The Home Depot's history. Most retail stores, including The

Home Depot today, number their aisles to help point the customer in the right direction. But early in our history, we emphasized to our store sales associates that they should never point the customer in a direction; they should always escort the individual to the appropriate counter or introduce them to the person who could provide the assistance they required. Hence, there was simply no need for aisle numbers that could tempt salespeople to underperform by just directing the customer to an aisle.

This was not open to debate. Management was not willing to make it easy to give the customer less than great service. Once again, the orange-blooded culture was reinforced. It certainly wasn't the easiest solution, but for The Home Depot, at that time, it was the right approach.

Every employee was indoctrinated with the understanding that he or she must make eye contact with every customer he or she passed. They were instructed to never ask, "Can I help you?" That phrase almost always solicits an automatic answer of, "No." Rather, we encouraged our associates to ask open-ended questions to start dialogue, such as, "What project are you working on today?"

Good customer service requires an intimacy with the customer and cannot be a vague, feel-good cliché. It must be demonstrated over and over by walking the talk. Great customer service stories always needed to be told and be retold, reinforced, and celebrated.

REVVING UP THE TROOPS

The Home Depot morning pep rally was standard procedure in every store. These meetings set the agenda for the day and always included employee recognition and celebration of customer service. The ethos of these morning sessions approximated the atmosphere you might expect at a religious revival meeting: *Hallelujah!*

The daily pep rally always ended by calling out the letters H-O-M-E-D-E-P-O-T, and then yelling the question "What does that stand for?" The answer was, "Customer Service! The question would be asked again, and the answer again was, "Customer service!" The question was asked a third time, and the answer was always, "KICK ASS!"

The yardstick of success was winning the customer's loyalty, even if it meant walking through walls.

Following the morning rally, one store manager in Greta, Louisiana, would hand a dollar bill to every sales associate. Then, during the day, he would walk the store and watch to see if each customer was being greeted in the proper manner. If anyone failed to make eye contact and start a conversation, the manager would ask for his dollar back. Every sales associate knew what he expected and inspected.

SPREADING THE CULTURE

When we opened stores in New York and New Jersey, we were told not to employ the Southern friendliness and rah-rah pep rallies we had practiced in Atlanta, because the more stoic Northeast persona would not respond. This assumption proved false.

Our New York and New Jersey stores quickly posted the highest sales-volume stores. Our Northeastern employees embraced the *Bleeding Orange* culture and made friendly customer service their job number one. Customers loved the new shopping experience at The Home Depot. Bottom line: A smile and warm greeting is appreciated by everyone. It was all right to smile and say, "Hi, y'all!" to folks in New York, although, "Hi, you guys!" was probably even better.

TOTAL CUSTOMER SATISFACTION

In every store we posted a big sign that read, "*Thank you for shopping at The Home Depot. If you have a complaint or compliment, please call Ben Hill at this number.*" We had a small staff of Ben Hills at our call center! They listened to every comment from our customers and were empowered to make sure that the customer was always satisfied.

Where did Ben Hill come from? All I know is that a sign near the Atlanta airport directed travelers to the small town of Ben Hill, somewhere on the outskirts of Atlanta. Somehow, Ben Hill became our customer ombudsman. (Our cartoon of Ben Hill had a remarkable resemblance to Pat Farrah, our merchandising guru, though.) It required no customer research or focus group sessions to take a name off a street sign and turn it into a symbol of great service. Bright ideas stem from a creative environment.

The customer was always right, even if he or she was wrong. Although this was ingrained into the culture, there could always be the outlier employee who mistakenly believed the store's resources and assets must be protected, not realizing that the trust of the customer is, in fact, the most valuable asset. It was much smarter, and usually cheaper, to solve any problem immediately at the lowest level of the company than to have the problem rise to the Ben Hill level.

The store management teams knew they were empowered to satisfy the customers. No manager wanted to be advised that one of his customers was a Ben Hill caller. If a problem did get to Ben Hill, the customer would quickly have their problem solved to their satisfaction. The flip side was that customers often called not to complain, but to compliment employees and thank The Home Depot for such great service.

PAYING FOR PERFORMANCE

Every store manager knew that one of the mandatory requirements was to establish a team of competent sales associates who could assist customers with their projects. The store manager had great authority in regard to managing the store.

Our staff was expected do whatever was required to get the job done— and the job was to satisfy our customers. Our associates were always authorized to do the right thing and were trusted to make that judgment. We did not hire any minimum wage people at The Home Depot. Our goal was to hire experts who could immediately help our customers or to bring on board people with the drive and ambition to become experts.

The operating philosophy was that people who had knowledge and experience and who bled orange should be rewarded more than those who lacked those qualities. The goal was to encourage excellence rather than be fair to all and accept mediocrity.

How did we control costs? We didn't control hourly rates of pay with rigid pay scales, but we did control payroll hours based on a matrix that compared the sales volume of the store and the average ticket of the store. In other words, the store managers had a specified and limited number of hours to spend to operate the store, so it was to their advantage to hire the most productive employees.

A positive relationship was established between pay and productivity. Of course, more sales could result in more budgeted hours. Once again, the main issue is the importance of focusing on sales. Many retailers confuse the importance of having quality sales associates as opposed to simply having a quantity of salespeople on the shop floor. Quality always trumps quantity in achieving sales goals and customer loyalty.

SHARED VISION, UNIFIED GOALS

In many companies the line between the merchandising group and store operations can be a hostile zone. Their objectives are not always in sync. We worked hard at The Home Depot to make sure that line was not a wall but a very fuzzy, overlapping relationship between these two key groups.

The common goal was to delight our customers. The common enemy was the competition. The proper success measurement was, first, exceeding previous sales and then maximizing GMROI for the merchants and ROI for the stores. In both of these return-on-investment formulas, a favorable bonus payoff was heavily influenced by increasing inventory turnover. The best way to accomplish this goal was to increase sales. The merchandising and store operations groups could agree together and focus on the one overriding goal of driving sales by gaining the customer's dollar votes.

Communication between these two groups became more and more critical as the store count of the company increased. While the number of stores grew in a linear fashion, the resulting communication complexity tended to grow geometrically. This ultimately led to the merchants' establishing a weekly store visit, where they could perform detailed store walks with a district manager and the store management team.

Each merchant was on a prescribed schedule that assured interaction with every district manager on at least a quarterly basis. These store visits were considered to be *holy* times, which means set apart. This meant that these dates were not changeable or negotiable but treated as vital to maintaining our customer focus.

This was a time for the merchants to evaluate every eight-foot linear section of their department and listen to the store associates, in order to understand what was working and what was not. It was critical for the merchants to gain insight from the store associates—the troops on the frontline—and have empathy for their issues and problems. Likewise, it was important to foster enthusiasm and support amongst the store associates by helping them understand the innovations and initiatives they could expect to see in the future.

These two groups, merchandising and store operations, were the heart and soul of our dynamic retail organization. They had to get everything right for the company to earn the customers' dollar votes and loyalty. It was understood at every echelon that the job was to provide these groups with the infrastructure and tools needed to succeed. At the end of the day, the corporate hierarchy had to have a servant attitude toward the stores, which were, in turn, servants to our customers.

MANAGING THE BUREAUCRACY

It can be easy for the many departments within the corporate infrastructure to lose track of this servant attitude maxim and to begin issuing policies and procedures that are often a burden to the stores and, therefore, not helpful to the customers. We often called these corporate units the Alphabet Departments, since they were usually referred to by initials such as IT (information technology), LPS (loss prevention systems), AP (accounts payable), NCD (new concept development), HR (human resources), and so on.

The people in these types of corporate departments want to do a good job and, in the process, they call meetings, issue directives, and send memos, creating work for everyone down the line in the process. All this seems to show that the corporate infrastructure is, in fact, working hard and doing their part. Unfortunately, these folks do not always understand the harm they do by overloading the stores with paperwork, meetings, and regulations that ultimately prevent the store associates from focusing on job number one, which is always customer service.

The bureaucracy must often be pushed back. Too often, these corporate departments become self-sufficient silos that forget that their main job—and the very existence of their department—is to help the stores delight their customers. These isolated silos can become very defensive of their own internal bureaucracy, which can lead to serious communication problems and turf wars. The important rule for these support teams to know is that their first job must be *customer retention*. The second is their alphabet title.

PREVENTING CORPORATE OVERREACH

For example, it sometimes seems that the loss prevention team would be happy if we simply kept the customers out of the stores. They typically work to prevent theft or assure safety without considering the real impact on the shopability of the store or the efficiency of the salespeople. This excessive focus on their objectives creates conflict, as we strive to delight the customer and enhance the shopping experience.

Self-serving, make-work activity must be pushed back when it becomes counterproductive. Good merchants must serve as ersatz advocates for the customers and defend their rights to a great shopping experience. To ensure they are smart and effective, corporate policies and procedures must be bounced off the front-line store associates.

On more than one occasion, our store management work force would collect the memos and directives flowing down to their stores and present these burdens to the offending corporate group. This invariably resulted in steps being taken to lighten the load being pushed down to the stores. The oft-repeated adage at The Home Depot was, "Crap flows downhill." This acknowledgement prevented a lot of store abuse.

Fortunately, the strong Bleeding Orange culture at The Home Depot helped keep our priorities focused on the stores and our customers. We had a senior management that knew how to keep the bureaucracy humble and focused on having a servant attitude. Everyone at the corporate office quickly learned that they did not work at the company *head-quarters*. Rather, they worked at the *Store Support Center*. This was not a cliché—it was a core philosophy of the company.

MULTIPLE LEVELS OF TEACHING, TRAINING

Knowledge is power. In a growing company, everyone must be actively involved in empowering through education and training. *Decentralization* and empowerment can only be effective when knowledge is prevalent.

Every new employee participated in a series of monthly, scheduled training sessions that provided the employee with knowledge of company culture, systems, procedures, selling skills, and product knowledge (PK). Additionally, every week in every store and in every department, it was mandatory to hold PK classes prior to store opening.

The human resources department set the curriculum for the training programs and kept track of each employee's progress. They were responsible for training the trainers—the store management teams that took ownership in training their people.

Every person promoted to a management position anywhere in the company would spend a week in Atlanta, in educational classes with the officers of the company. CEO Bernie Marcus, Arthur Blank, our president, and every corporate vice president knew that one day of each month would be devoted to conducting training classes for these new managers. Each officer would be scheduled to explain not just the company policies but the logic and philosophy behind these policies.

On Bernie Marcus's monthly "road show" visits to stores, he always brought along key officers and directors. As he engaged store personnel and listened to their concerns, he had at his elbow the resources to solve issues critical to the store—on the spot. The key word was urgency.

Arthur Blank always conducted quarterly financial reviews in the field. In addition to reviewing numbers, the management team could spend quality time in the stores, getting an improved understanding of the holistic operation of the stores in that market. This was a teaching and learning experience.

Our merchandising department would set up traveling road shows with the vendors, visiting each metropolitan market to introduce new programs and to get the stores ready for coming seasons. They might conduct a workshop in which the store employees participated in a floor tile installation project. They might meet at a resort and use the lawn and garden tools we would be selling the next spring to trim the resort's lawns and plants. We wanted our salespeople to be experienced doers.

We also contracted with the National Kitchen and Bath Association to provide training on kitchen and bath design. This included design workshops for our kitchen and bath department sales associates. They would learn how to interact with the customers to help them envision their dream and then create kitchen and bath designs using CAD software.

Customers discern very quickly whether a sales associate has the knowledge and competence to be trusted with their project. They appreciate interacting with knowledgeable staff who can make suggestions to take their project to the next level of delight.

Most states in the U.S. have programs to certify nursery experts. We enrolled our garden department associates in these government agricultural and horticultural training programs. There is no better way to keep dedicated people and show your interest in their career success and growth than to invest in their education.

USING TECHNOLOGY TO EDUCATE, COMMUNICATE

As the store count grew to hundreds and then over a thousand locations, we needed a way to keep the intimate relationship between the Store Support Center and store personnel. To reach out to our expanding number of associates and inculcate the Bleeding Orange culture, we set up a full-scale video production and satellite transmission studio at the store support center.

This provided the tools to initiate our HDTV broadcast system, which could produce and then stream live broadcast into each store. It also included a call center so the store personnel could participate in a two-way dialogue during the broadcast. All of this happened long before the Internet made this type of communication easy. The Home Depot was an innovator in using technology for intracompany communications.

Allowing the employees at our expanding number of stores to interact with the founders and senior management of the company exposed a broad base of new employees to the *Bleeding Orange* culture directly from the people who created it. We learned quickly that this new tool could be overused in a way that took productivity away from the store. It was important to set priorities and tailor each broadcast to a specific, *need-to-know audience.*

For example, if the subject matter of the broadcast was kitchen design, we would want the audience to consist primarily of associates in the kitchen and bath department. The subject matter would probably not be relevant to the people in the garden department. Each of our store's departments needed to be staffed by people with specific knowledge in their particular product categories. We did not move people from one department to another simply to provide sales floor coverage on a specific day. Many stores do shift people around as if they were homogenous pawns, but our people were experts in their own area of specialization. Our objective was to *hire the right people, train the right people, and keep the right people.*

CELEBRATING GOOD WORK

Once a quarter, when the financial results were made public, there would be a live *"Breakfast with Bernie and Arthur"* broadcast in all stores. All the employees and their families were invited to visit the store and share in the celebration.

The Home Depot demanded much time and effort from its employees, so it was important for employees and their families to feel they were part of something successful and good. The company culture needed to be shared and the *orange gospel* spread to the troops throughout the company. Communication, education, and training were all part of building a sense of respect and camaraderie.

People do not work for money alone. Productive people are self-motivated. But they also need recognition beyond money that acknowledges they are important and are exceeding expectations. Good sales people have strong egos that need to be stroked.

Every manager carried a pocket full of service badges. These badges could be displayed on the orange work aprons that all The Home Depot people wore. Whenever a manager noticed a store associate providing excellent customer service, he or she rewarded the associate with a badge. When customers gave a helpful employee a compliment, this was cause for celebration and bestowal of another service badge.

The associates proudly wore these badges on their aprons. Upon receiving ten badges, they could turn the badges in for a master service badge and one hundred dollars. This showed that management observed the associates' behavior and cared about their attitude toward the customers. Associates quickly learned that their first job was to interact with customers, not just stock the shelves.

TAKING CUSTOMER SERVICE TO THE NEXT LEVEL

In most of our competitors' stores, the employees occupied themselves with tasks like rearranging the merchandise, in order to look busy to the boss, instead of approaching customers with a smile and conversation. The favorite way to waste time in so many retail stores is to spend hours facing the merchandise. This means pulling product forward on the shelf, which gives the impression that this stuff never sells. Such stores have the sterile look of a museum, instead of a vibrant store that is alive. It seems like a customer could break into flames without an associate's lifting a hand to put out the fire, as long as those cartons are properly aligned. At The Home Depot, the main job wasn't facing products, it was approaching each customer as if he or she were on fire. Customers entering The Home Depot immediately felt the cultural difference. As they entered a department, they were personally greeted. This created a dialogue that pleasantly surprised customers and led to increased sales. In addition, recognizing each customer and making eye contact is one of the most effective deterrents to shoplifting. It is more effective to have associates who are aware of each customer and motivated to make contact with them than to have a platoon of security officers wandering through the store looking for thieves.

We had to teach many of our store managers to respect salespeople who could design and sell projects. This seems obvious, but it was often more difficult than one would think. Good store managers were multitasking experts, and their natural tendency was to look for new employees like themselves. These managers were often retail veterans who had, themselves, started their retail careers stocking counters and unloading trucks.

We had to sensitize store management to the importance of having the proper balance of associates who could physically stock and maintain the store, as well as experts who could generate project sales. Productivity needed to be properly defined.

For example, making sales of products like millwork (doors and windows) or kitchen and bath cabinets requires people with design and project-selling talents. The best salespeople with such expertise are often mature people who may not be good at driving forklifts and climbing ladders. These are the experts customers can trust with their projects

SELLING WITH PRIDE

It was important to make selling *cool* so that every associate would strive to become a sales expert. Selling can have a negative connotation when it is focused on paying commissions, using high-pressure tactics, and selling products that customers do not want or need. That is bad selling. Good selling is truly helping the customer make the right decision. This includes first qualifying the customer to understand his or her dream and then defining the project parameters.

The next steps are designing the project to, ideally, exceed the original vision and, finally, asking for the order. This is the essence of good selling, which is also excellent customer service. Bad selling hurts a company's image; good selling creates appreciation, loyalty, and big-ticket sales. Our sales associates never worked on a commission basis. Bonuses were paid to entire departments. All the associates worked as a team to provide great service to every customer, whether the project was big or small. All the associates needed to understand that every customer was important, whether he or she came into the store to buy a cabinet hinge or a complete kitchen. We wanted a healthy selling attitude that put the customer's need first, not a sales commission. The customer who receives great service on a widget today is the customer who does not hesitate to return with a twenty-thousand-dollar project tomorrow.

A COMPANY WITH A HEART

The Home Depot associates knew they were part of something big. They were part of a movement that would carry them to new levels of team accomplishment, career recognition, and personal rewards. They also felt pride in the fact that The Home Depot's community involvement went beyond operating stores, driving down prices, and exceeding financial goals.

Local community involvement and outreach to people in need was expected and celebrated. Each store received funding to support local charities, and employees were given opportunities—sometimes paid and sometimes voluntary—to help others. This involvement included building Habitat houses, making playgrounds for poor, urban areas, responding to local weather disasters, and rebuilding homes for elderly people or others in need.

At a corporate merchandising level, The Home Depot played a key role in sponsoring a dinner each year at the National Hardware Show that raised millions of dollars annually for the City of Hope hospital.

This outreach to people in need was a part of a culture of *tikkun olam*, a Jewish term signifying acts of kindness to perfect or repair the world. *Tikkun olam* was ingrained into the *Bleeding Orange* culture by Bernie Marcus and Arthur Blank.

The charity side of The Home Depot was not simply a matter of proper public relations. It represented a belief in *tzedakah*, a Hebrew word that describes the ethical obligation to give back to the community, not just financially, but also with time and effort. It's about improving our world and always doing the right thing.

INVESTING IN PEOPLE—BONDING WITH CUSTOMERS

The Home Depot spent millions of dollars and hours of training on projects to improve the competence and morale of employees. Make no mistake, The Home Depot was a profit-driven company, and management understood that these efforts were costly. However, we also knew that investing in our people and the community maximized long-term profits.

The company clearly had financial goals, and every employee knew and understood their role in achieving these objectives. They further understood the personal rewards for attaining these financial goals.

But the *Bleeding Orange* culture also promoted a feeling of pride and accomplishment in being part of something big that really mattered. While not everyone was wired to embrace this dynamic culture, those who did became orange-blooded zealots.

RETAIL DETAIL #17

If you think good employees are expensive, try bad employees.

The customer's appreciation of The Home Depot associate's product knowledge, competence, and service was the most important key to building loyalty and a winning brand. No matter what a company's marketing and advertising programs communicate in the print or electronic media, the moment of truth is when the customer enters the store and encounters the first associate. The timing of that first encounter and the quality of the interaction determines the customer's lasting attitude toward the store and the company brand.

It was not the size of the store, the broad assortment of products, or even the low prices that created the bonding relationship with our customers. It was the winning culture that made The Home Depot unique and separated us from all the other competitors. Price will bring customers in, but great service that creates a unique shopping experience brings them back.

The Home Depot was the homeowners' toy store, where they could find new ideas, products, and tools to improve their standard of living by improving their homes. We had ladies throwing birthday parties for their husbands in the store after operating hours. We actually had a wedding in the lumber department! This is what happens when customers say, "That's my store."

The *Bleeding Orange* culture was always expressed in the attitude of our people, which the customers could recognize and feel. We keep coming back to the importance of *hiring the right person, training the right person, and keeping the right person.*

PRICING:
OUR OFFENSIVE WEAPON

We were a learning organization. We embraced outside-the-box thinking and celebrated trial and error. Some of our guiding principles were cast in cement. But one area that evolved significantly during the company's first five years was The Home Depot's pricing strategy.

Pricing is one of the most difficult areas of retail to execute consistently. Disrupting an entire industry and constructing a new business model from scratch is a dynamic, rapidly evolving process. The Home Depot believed pricing should be an offensive tool to grow our market share and increase the size of the home-improvement market. It was one of the company's true north pillars.

We were always an aggressive price leader; it was core to our pricing philosophy and strategy. Taking price leadership in the market without blinking and going eye-to-eye with competition can be painful in the short run and will be met with competitive challenges. This is particularly true when setting advertising and promotional policies. Thus, our pricing tactics significantly changed over time, as we responded to an evolving marketplace and changed the market paradigms.

PRICING FOR TRAFFIC

Our competitors engaged in what is known as high/low pricing. This practice involves establishing regular pricing that is at or above the market price and then offering limited-time specials on select items. These companies wanted to protect their gross margin percentage with high prices, but they wanted to look competitive and generate store traffic.

They made the mistake of believing that special promotions would create a good price image for their brand. They failed to recognize that the very essence of limited-time advertising communicated to the customer that their everyday prices were high.

High/low pricing can indeed generate foot traffic. But it does not build a trust relationship with the customer that establishes a strong brand loyalty. Advertising for these events reduces credibility, requiring more advertising and more promotional expense to achieve the same or, more likely, declining results.

At the beginning, The Home Depot did use limited-time, special pricing in our promotions. What made our initial pricing policy offensive (in both senses of the term!) to the competitors was that our regular prices were truly discounted, in contrast to our home center competitors. In addition, we would buy truckload quantities from our vendors at significant discounts and pass the savings on to the customers in special buys that were often below our normal acquisition costs.

Our ability to purchase huge quantities gave us a price advantage over our competition and allowed promotional prices that left our competition scratching their heads. We also instituted a price guarantee that offered an additional ten percent price reduction off our competitors' advertised prices. This was a revolutionary concept when we introduced it decades ago and worked well to get the attention of our target market—the DIY homeowner.

NEW COMPETITION, NEW PRICING STRATEGY

At the beginning, The Home Depot exclusively focused on the DIY homeowner customer. In fact, we were not comfortable doing business with professional tradesmen. They would come to our stores and take advantage of the promotional pricing, often purchasing our entire inventory of incredibly low-priced specials. Then they'd leave without purchasing any related products.

Our limited-time pricing and promotional policies were not developing loyalty when it came to the pros. Not only that, but the practice played havoc with our inventory levels, often causing us to be sold out of our advertised specials and thereby disappointing our target market of homeowners.

When we entered the California market in 1985, we learned there was a better strategy that would change our entire pricing philosophy.

EMBRACING EVERYDAY LOW PRICING

While we were growing our business in the Southeast (Atlanta, Miami, Orlando, Tampa, and New Orleans), an emerging big-box home center chain was already opening stores in California. These stores, called HomeClub, were based on the Price Club/Costco warehouse model of charging a membership fee. HomeClub did not have the wide assortment and helpful service that The Home Depot made part of its brand, but it did take a no-frills approach to selling home-improvement products at true wholesale prices. For a while it worked.

The Home Depot was eyeing California. We realized we could not enter the market duplicating the pricing and promotional programs of our eastern stores because of the far more competitive pricing structure at HomeClub. California was a completely different market reality from the eastern markets. New market dynamics required a new pricing strategy.

We needed to reduce our initial margins to acknowledge West Coast reality. This new, reduced-margin pricing structure made limited-time advertised specials uneconomical. It also made them unnecessary. Instead, we embraced *everyday low pricing* (EDLP) and created a higher-revenue model in the process.

The Home Depot now became the undisputed low-price leader in the home-improvement business. We promoted our new pricing policy with the rallying cry *Day-in/Day-out Prices*. We entered the California market in attack mode.

LOW PRICES JUST THE BEGINNING

All items identical to HomeClub's product mix were priced at the exact HomeClub price. That meant shoppers at The Home Depot could get the item more cheaply because we had no membership fee. This, along with our wide assortments and great customer service, offered more. We met customers' price expectations while offering benefits beyond price. This was a big step forward that would only work if we could achieve a dramatically higher level of sales in our West Coast stores. Fortunately, we did.

This was a valuable lesson. The California strategy taught us to first level the playing field in pricing and then win the war on great services. It was a winning formula for both the homeowner and the professional customer.

We opened our first two California stores in the Orange County cities of Fullerton and Huntington Beach. The new strategy meant these stores had much lower initial margins than our East Coast stores. I was responsible for West Coast merchandising at that time. I still recall the phone call I received from Atlanta after our initial low margins had been established and incorporated into our opening store budgets. I was told there was concern that our California margins would destroy the company.

However, in keeping with our aggressive *Bleeding Orange* culture, this risky experiment was allowed to continue. The end result was not the destruction of The Home Depot—quite the opposite.

MARKET CONSOLIDATION

Our first two California stores were soon exceeding a million dollars a week in sales—a new record for The Home Depot stores. We were able to take market share from HomeClub, which ultimately led to its demise. We were relentless. Our grand opening advertising in California announced that The Home Depot would buy back HomeClub membership cards since members would not need them anymore!

This was when HomeClub blinked. They realized price alone would not create loyalty. The company changed ownership, dropped their membership, and changed their name to HomeBase. It was too late. Now they were playing our game, which we had already won in the customer's mind.

Our HomeClub/HomeBase attack had other outcomes. Traditional home centers were caught in the competitive crossfire and did not survive. This included Builders Emporium, Home Owners Emporium, Angels, Ole's Home Centers, National Lumber, Cooper Lumber, Sackett & Peters, Angels, and Handyman.

The death of these traditional home centers also killed the major hardware wholesalers, like California Hardware and American Wholesale, as well as a number of specialty importers and wholesalers. As we gobbled up market share in California, we were changing the home-improvement business forever.

The rewarding surprise was that at the end of the year, the maintained margin for the West Coast stores was actually higher than the maintained margin of the East Coast stores. While the East Coast started out with higher initial margins when the products arrived at the stores, the deep promotional discounts created markdowns that eroded the margins to a level below the West Coast numbers.

The verdict was in. The West Coast stores demonstrated higher average sales per store, higher rate of inventory turn, and higher maintained margins. All of this equated to higher GMROI. We had evolved a category-killer concept that would revolutionize how The Home Depot would go to market.

AGGREGATING A NEW CUSTOMER BASE

Our new *day-in/day-out pricing* brought a huge benefit. With consistently lower pricing, we became a trusted supplier to the professional customers, who were now purchasing a wide range of products for their customers' repair, remodeling, and maintenance projects. They could now trust our EDLP pricing to be right all the time. We could greet the professional customers with open arms since they were buying their total project needs from us and proving to be loyal and consistent customers. This pro-business stance allowed us to hit the million-dollar sales number weekly, as our professional sales grew from nothing to 30 percent of our total volume in a relatively short time.

We had created a strong market for our stock on Wall Street, partially on the premise that we were focused on the DIY customer. That allowed us to be seen as a somewhat counter cyclical business. We were, as a result, careful about publicly acknowledging our new professional customer initiative. The general market consensus was that the pro-business segment of the building material business was highly cyclical and, therefore, risky.

We were actually focused on very specific segments of the professional business market that were not so cyclical. Our professional customer was defined as the *repair, remodel, and maintenance contractor,* as opposed to the *new construction builders.* This repair, remodel, and maintenance segment of the pro market has the potential to grow continually, since the country's housing stock continues to age year after year and requires work. The number of older homes needing repair vastly outnumbers the quantity of new homes built each year.

SYNERGISTIC MARKET SEGMENTS

A demographic trend was also changing how the homeowner actually accomplished home-improvement projects. Because homeowners get older every year, over time they become less likely to undertake home-improvement projects. Meanwhile the homes are also growing older and requiring more attention. This leads to a demand for more and more professional home-improvement services.

Baby Boomers were initially our primary target customer group. Every year they continued to age, which tended to change their attitude toward home-improvement projects. This created a growth opportunity for the professional side of the business. Serving the DIY homeowner would continue to be our core business, but this would be a maturing business, while the professional customer would be our growth opportunity going forward.

We found great synergies in regard to products, assortments, and pricing between our DIY and our targeted pro customers. This selected, professional clientele tended to focus on doing relatively small projects, so they found The Home Depot's multiple locations to be convenient and trusted supply depots for their daily and weekly job requirements. Our large stores created a convenient building material warehouse close to their jobsite, which was typically the customer's home.

Focus on this professional customer actually allowed us to better serve the homeowner by establishing the right pro-quality products, the right pro services, and the right pro prices. We could extend these benefits to all our customers and honestly promote the message that homeowners could *Buy Like the Pros!*

DEFINING THE RIGHT PRO MARKET

We did not solicit business from the new-construction professional. This, indeed, is a highly cyclical market segment that is not compatible with the big-box home center business. New construction requires business locations that can rapidly expand in good times and contract when the cycle slows. Our stores did not meet this profile. The new construction business requires commissioned salespeople who can assist in resolving technical issues for their clients and lock in advanced bids for products with prices guaranteed to a future date. This type of bid pricing is not compatible with the EDLP strategy.

Also, many products required in new construction are of a size and weight not practical for home center stores to inventory. These construction projects are often tied to a credit commitment that could be very risky during business downturns. The new construction business was simply not in our wheelhouse.

SAVING TIME IS SAVING MONEY

The fact that homeowners now shopped side-by-side with the professionals and bought at the same prices changed how these professional contractors conducted their business. In the past, tradesmen would charge a fee for their labor and also make a profit on the product they were installing. This changed when the customer could buy at the wholesale price in our stores. Most professionals realized they needed to price their labor appropriately and no longer expect to make an additional profit on selling products to their customers.

Why were the professional customers willing to make this change? Primarily because The Home Depot freed up time— and time is money. They no longer had to go to separate, specialized wholesale supply houses across town for different products. Putting all the products required for a project under one roof saved them shopping time, which they could now devote to being on the job, making money with their valuable labor.

The fact that we were open early morning to late night and operated seven days a week was also a huge convenience, since traditional wholesalers had restricted hours of business. This made it easy for the professional customers to obtain quality products on their own schedules.

ADDING SERVICE TO THE PRICE EQUATION

Combining these services with a flexible credit program and dependable jobsite delivery made our stores even more attractive to professional customers. We established a Pro-Desk in each store to expedite the professionals' shopping experience and to help create a personal relationship. We leveled the playing field on price and provided the bonus of newfound time.

The smarter professionals also realized that it was often to their advantage to let the customer purchase the materials for the job to save them time, thus freeing up working capital they previously had tied up in purchasing products for their customers. We were saving the professional tradesmen time and money.

The result of The Home Depot's increasing share of the professional building material market created a sea change in the business model of the specialty wholesaler. While in the past they sold to the repair, remodel, and maintenance contractor as well as the new construction professional, our appeal to the former group shifted the wholesalers into a much more cyclical new-construction market with much lower margins. We took the portion of the market that would be most compatible with the big-box home center format and left the less stable segment to the wholesalers.

We had now revolutionized both the DIY home center market and the pro-oriented wholesaler business. The Home Depot was enlarging the home-improvement market and then taking a bigger share of it.

Lowe's and The Home Depot Trade Target Markets

Here is an interesting sidelight. During the period when we rapidly embraced the professional customer, Lowe's Companies began to run away from the professional customer.

Lowe's was the largest volume building material company in the country during the first eight years of The Home Depot's existence. They were primarily focused on the professional customer. We passed Lowe's in total sales volume in 1988, and their board decided to devote all their energy to being a big-box retailer focused on the DIY customer.

It is truly amazing that a huge, successful company like Lowe's could decide to completely redefine their business in terms of target markets, store concept, and locations. This 180-degree turn in their business strategy changed everything in their market and impacted The Home Depot's competitive strategies as well.

Lowe's became hyper-focused on being the best DIY store for the homeowner, while The Home Depot's strategy changed to aiming product, service, and pricing at the professional and then passing those advantages on as a bonus to the DIY customer. This difference in vision and strategy put Lowe's at a competitive disadvantage that they have yet to overcome.

ROLLING OUT EDLP NATIONWIDE

When the financial results of both the eastern and western divisions were in, they showed that The Home Depot's West Coast strategies of EDLP pricing and targeting of professional customers was working. These new aggressive strategies were now proven successful and would be the new direction for all The Home Depot stores.

Over the next year we began to roll out the California strategy into each of our markets across the country. This meant changing much of our initial pricing in all our Eastern stores. We used the retail method of accounting, which meant that any markdown initiated would hit our bottom line the month we reduced our price. To make the transition a managed evolution, we systematically lowered our regular pricing in these markets month by month over a full year and did not promote the *day-in/day-out* pricing concept until we had completely transitioned to the California strategy.

We accomplished this by continuing to run our monthly catalogue, which was the heart of our marketing program, with our exciting, reduced prices in our Eastern stores. However, the promotional pricing in each edition of the catalogue did not return to regular prices at the end of the advertised month. In effect, the sale that began each month simply lasted forever.

Over the course of a year, all the major seasonal items were advertised, which often were the most price-sensitive items. We were able to bring all price-sensitive items into EDLP compliance by the end of the year. We had now established the right pricing that maximized sales and gross profit dollars. We could then begin to promote the *day-in/day-out* pricing message on a national basis.

MAXIMIZING GROSS PROFIT DOLLARS

Our pricing strategy from the beginning was always to maximize gross profit dollars, not gross profit percentage. This was a strategic concept that our competition did not understand or simply could not implement. We found the key to this strategy was to find that sweet spot where sales and profits were maximized. This meant driving down the prices on high-demand, price-sensitive items to increase sales and corresponding gross profit dollars.

In some cases, however, gross margin dollars were maximized by raising prices on products with low demand that were not price sensitive. This is where the knowledge and intuition of the merchants is invaluable. A good merchant understands the nature of price-elastic items, where a percentage change in price results in a higher percentage change in quantity demanded, versus price-inelastic items, where a percentage change in price results in a smaller percentage change in quantity demanded. Remember the goal is always to maximize gross profit dollars.

In essence, it is the not the procurement cost but the customer's perception of the value and the nature of their demand that must be the basis for the actual item pricing. This requires merchants who know their customers and understand the price elasticity of their products.

PRICING WITH CREDIBILITY

Most retailers price their products using a safe, well-established margin based on their current costs. But retailers would actually set much better pricing if they didn't know the cost—if they had to put themselves in their customers' shoes and understand their customers' perception of value and the alternative pricing options available in the larger marketplace. Instead, our competitors continued to base their retail pricing on past mark-up guidelines that were set by product cost instead of customer demand. Their eyes were on their calculators instead of their customers

They would then use high/low pricing in their advertising to keep their preset gross margin percentages on plan. They might even throw in the term EDLP, even though they didn't understand what it meant.

Most customers do not trust most retailers—and they shouldn't.

This inconsistent and confusing pricing strategy created doubts in the customer's mind, while we pursued and delivered on our *day-in/day-out* message. That consistency created trust. Our objective was to set the right price at the beginning. We wanted the right price to motivate the customer to buy today and to reinforce our value statement so they would come back the next time they needed home-improvement products.

Another typical pricing practice used by our competitors subtly reinforced their image as retailers, as opposed to wholesalers, which is what The Home Depot wanted. Here's an example:

Many retailers price their products by applying a percentage markup to their cost and then rounding up to a price that ends in nine. For example, their percentage markup formula might suggest a price of $1.86, so they would round up to $1.89 or $1.99. Conversely, if their formula ended up with a price of $2.05 they might round down to $1.99. This creates a very retail image to their pricing.

We at The Home Depot wanted the customer to realize that our pricing was truly wholesale pricing, not typical retail prices. A price of $1.86 or $2.05 worked fine for us, and we believed such non-retail price points gave customers confidence that they were not paying typical retail prices.

MAKING THE PRICE MESSAGE EMOTIONAL

We had fun with pricing in our advertising, to the humiliation of our competitors. Our ads depicted our cartoon character, Homer, smashing competitors' prices with a hammer or some other graphic description that made our commitment to having the lowest prices very clear in the customer's mind. The message was that our *day-in/day-out* pricing was the new normal, and our competitors' high/low prices were passé and, frankly, dishonest.

Our grand-opening message was simple: "Lower prices start today and last forever!" We shouted, "No more phony sales!" The not-too-subtle message was, *Are you tired of being ripped off by your favorite home center?*

The customers' experience of confirming that our EDLP pricing promise was true created an incredible trust in The Home Depot. Our success in communicating a new pricing paradigm generated brand loyalty. The day-in/day-out pricing promise led customers to become fans, much like those of a sports team. We knew we were winning when we heard a customer say, "That's my store."

Here are the key elements of The Home Depot day-in/day-out, EDLP pricing policy:

- You never pay high retail prices.

- There are no limited-time sales—it is always the right time to buy.

- There are no silly games or loyalty cards required to get the best deal.

- Everybody buys at true, professional, wholesale prices.

- We shop the market, so you don't have to.

- Our competitors' ads are our ads. We will not only match our competitors' prices; we will beat them by at least 10 percent.

- You can trust us to increase your standard of living by driving down the costs of home improvement.

The key to a credible pricing policy is understanding that maximizing gross profit dollars is not a function of margin. An appropriate EDLP policy may actually result in an exceptionally low or unusually high margin. But it is important that the customer sees the price as the best in the marketplace. If this is truly the case, then the margin percentage is irrelevant. In other words, EDLP does not require nor is it defined as low margin. Rather, it means that the price is right without promotional reductions.

NEW PRICING REQUIRES A NEW ADVERTISING STRATEGY

Eliminating the need for sale pricing changed both the message and the media chosen for our promotional efforts. Print is ideal for item/price advertising but not the most effective way to communicate image/brand messages.

We now had a truly *unique, sustainable, compelling, competitive advantage* that could be more effectively communicated with conviction and emotion through electronic media. We had a powerful new message of trust that every homeowner needed to hear. Television (this was in the 1980s, you remember) allowed us to reach customers with an emotional, believable message.

Print advertising is simply not the best vehicle for reaching a mass audience. Television and radio were far better methods for communicating our superior pricing to virtually one hundred percent of the target market.

Meanwhile, those competitors who were still locked into high/low limited-time advertising tended to continue using print media, which only reached a small and declining customer base.

When such a competitor would advertise items at below-market prices for short periods of time, we simply empowered our salespeople to meet that sale price and beat it by an additional ten percent. We never wanted our salespeople to have to say, "I'm sorry, we usually have the lowest prices, but this week we don't have the best price on that item."

It would be dysfunctional and confusing to the customers for us to adjust our EDLP prices up and down every time a competitor ran limited-time advertised special; it would violate the whole EDLP trust concept. In reality, very few customers were aware of any given competitor's current advertisement. Even fewer were interested in purchasing a specific item listed in it. There was little reason to adjust all the pricing in all our stores because of a competitor's advertising that had little real impact on the vast majority of our customers. The price guarantee was sufficient to respond to any customer's need for a price adjustment. On those occasions, we never hesitated to offer our price guarantee and give the customer the benefit of the doubt, even when the product comparison was not absolutely clear. Our only disclaimer was that we reserved the right to limit the quantity purchased to the normal requirements of our home-owner and professional customers. This assured us that we would always have product in stock to serve the project needs of every loyal customer.

WINNING THE PRICE BATTLE AT STORE LEVEL

Trust is the key word for successful promotion, and the first priority had to be securing the confidence of our own store associates. We had to make sure our sales associates would always be able to look the customer in the eye and proudly claim that nobody could beat our prices. The moment of truth for a customer's perception of our brand's validity was the sales associates' response when confronted with the price question by the customer. The battle is won or lost in the minds of the employees.

How they handle the price question is far more important to the customer's price perception than all the money and effort spent on paid advertising. In fact, the wrong response by a salesperson can negate the total promotional investment.

One outcome of understanding sales associates' importance is that we did not offer employee discounts. The reason was simple: We wanted them to complain if they ever found an item for their own personal need that was not the best price available. We had to be consistently right in our pricing to earn our own associates' respect. There wasn't a better employee price or a better pro price. There was the *day-in/day-out* right price. Pricing credibility must be earned.

ATTACKING THE COMPETITION WITH PRICE

Most retailers are consistent and predictable. They are constantly working against last year's numbers, so they tend to repeat their promotional activities. If you want to know what their promotions will look like this year, just review the previous year. When you know their pattern, you can devise a plan to ambush them.

Since we knew our competitors tended to be predictable, our strategy was to be unpredictable. One of the most important lessons we learned was that our response to a competitor's promotional program should always be bold. When you can shock the other guys, it tends to paralyze them.

Timid responses to price competition would simply create more competitive challenges and lead to future price wars. The competition will try to read your resolve in regard to your pricing commitment, so it was important for us to leave no doubt that we would respond to any price challenge with a vengeance. That is how to prevent, stop, and win pricing wars. We wanted to keep our competition wary of engaging us in a price war by letting them know we were a little crazy and unpredictable.

The Home Depot's entry into Central Florida was a good example. We entered that market in 1983 with our first two Orlando stores. Soon we added our first store in the Tampa market. The leading traditional home center in Central Florida was a firm called Scotty's. With more than fifty stores, this was considered one of the premier traditional home center companies in the country. They were not ready for The Home Depot's zealots, who were about to blindside them.

Scotty's published a semiannual full-color catalogue of their entire product assortment. We gathered hundreds of Scotty's catalogues and hung them with chains off every counter in our stores. We wrote in felt pen on the covers: *"Our Price: 20% Off Any Identical Item in This Catalogue."*

This was the beginning of the end for Scotty's. The message was, *Hey folks, Scotty's prices are 20 percent too high.* They never published another catalogue. Their management was immobilized. Two years later Scotty's was out of business. Their price/value image had been destroyed.

The Costco Stare-Down

The competition needs to understand that you will challenge their pricing and not blink, even when the situation is uncomfortable or painful. Here is how that played out when Costco decided to challenge The Home Depot in Washington State.

We had a group of stores in the Seattle market and were surprised when Costco added a 30,000-square-foot annex devoted entirely to home-improvement products to their Kirkland store. Costco typically prices its merchandise at a low margin of around 11 percent, and these home-improvement items were no exception. The items they chose to stock were, of course, our best-selling products.

Our response was to identify every item in Costco and reduce our price twenty percent below theirs on an EDLP basis. This meant we were selling many of our best-selling products about ten percent below our cost. We put signs in our stores saying, "Why pay for Costco membership when their prices are 20% too high?"

Clearly, we lost money on every sale. This went on for months. It was painful, but it had to be done.

The Costco membership is perhaps their most important asset, so this is where they were vulnerable. The membership fees are the key to Costco's ability to use a cost-plus method of selling their products with an eleven percent margin. This is a significantly lower margin than is typical in the retail industry, either online or off-line. The resulting low prices create sales volumes that make Costco the most efficient big-box retailer. Costco had no choice but to protect the value of their membership and the trust relationship with their customers. Within months, Costco stopped their home center experiment and closed the home-improvement annex.

Costco is a great company with incredible customer loyalty. For the record, I am a Costco member and love shopping in their stores. They consistently offer top quality products and the lowest prices. They are the quintessential big-box model when it comes to efficiency and productivity.

But had The Home Depot not ambushed Costco and turned the tables on them, there would probably be home center annexes in most Costco stores across the country, and The Home Depot would have a powerful competitor, much lower margins, and far less market share.

CUSTOMER PERCEPTION: THE ONLY THING THAT MATTERS

Our objective was to always intimidate the competition—which we developed into an art form. However, the real important issue in pricing is to develop that trust relationship with the customer.

Most retailers fail to achieve this and resort to all kinds of sales and gimmicks that confuse the customer. It becomes a game. Retailers feel they have to run limited-time sales because customers expect a bargain and will otherwise wait to purchase. The customers feel they have to wait for the sales and compare advertising to make sure they buy at the right price. This is circular logic, where one bad assumption leads to a decision based on another bad assumption.

The result is a mutual lack of trust between the customers and the retailer. This high/low pricing tends to distort the demand and the timing of customer purchases, leading to inventory imbalances that can disappoint customers or, conversely, to costly overstocks. Retailers are often afraid to not run a weekly sale because they know their competition will. This is actually the best reason not to run limited-time sale advertising. Why bring yourself down to the competition's level? Why advertise that your prices are not dependable?

The Home Depot promotional message let the customer know there was now a better way to buy. This was not an *item/price* message; it was a *brand/image* message. The only thing that really matters in pricing is the customer's perception of their pricing alternatives. Perception is reality, and there was a new awareness that The

It's hard to win a war when everyone has the same weapons. Dare to be different.

Home Depot's message that Low Prices are Just the Beginning was actually true. We had established a clear impression in the customer's mind that we had a convincing *unique, sustainable, compelling, competitive advantage* over the traditional high/low competitors. The good thing about this process was that as the customers bought more and more product, our buying power increased, while our competitors' status decreased. EDLP was both a tactical and strategic win for us.

This aggressive EDLP pricing policy continued to be a pillar of The Home Depot for fifteen years, beginning in 1985. Then, in 2001, the founding management team of The Home Depot transitioned to a new CEO from outside the company. This would prove to be the end of The Home Depot's price leadership. But that is a story we will tell a little later.

5

BECOMING THE CHANNEL CAPTAIN

The Home Depot was changing the market far faster than the supply chain could adjust to the new realities.

As already mentioned, during the early years we found it difficult, and sometimes impossible, to obtain all the product lines and brands our customers wanted. Many potential vendors maintained a policy of restrictive distribution for their products, wrongly thinking this would protect their market share. They were production-oriented, not market-oriented. They didn't understand what was happening with the ultimate user of their product at the other end of their supply chain.

Fortunately for us, the DIY homeowner felt remarkably little loyalty to the traditional home centers and even less to most of the national brands of home-improvement products. The brand-name vendors tended to confuse *brand awareness,* which is important to most customers, with *brand insistence,* which is rare with the DIY customer.

We were making customers aware of new products and innovative brands. In many cases, we simply created our own brands. We could now impact the degree of brand awareness in the marketplace and turn it to our advantage.

GENERAL ELECTRIC LEARNS A HARD LESSON

A case in point was our introduction of the Phillips brand of light bulbs. General Electric was the number one brand of light bulbs in the United States, and The Home Depot was its number one retailer. Phillips, on the other hand, was a dominant brand in Europe but essentially unknown in the North American market.

Phillips approached us with an offer that was hard to refuse. They could provide us with light bulbs having the exact specifications of General Electric bulbs at a savings of around thirty percent on identical items.

We invited the national sales manager of General Electric light bulbs to our office and made him aware of the Phillips offer. We asked him to re-quote GE's prices to lower our costs. His answer was a resounding no. He explained that General Electric was the dominant brand in the U.S. and that the customer had brand insistence for its products. He asserted we had no choice but to continue to feature General Electric light bulbs.

Since this was a big deal involving millions of dollars, I went to Bernie Marcus, our CEO, for guidance on how hard we should push GE. Bernie immediately called Jack Welch, the CEO of General Electric. We explained the situation. Jack replied that he understood the issue, but he would have to back his guys and not compromise on price.

At that point we decided to move half of our light bulb volume to Phillips and promote the brand among our customers. Our sales results proved that our customers were *not* brand insistent on light bulbs. Because The Home Depot had established a reputation for offering the most complete selection of light bulbs in the marketplace, along with having the best prices, our customers trusted us to offer quality products—even ones they weren't familiar with.

This single move changed the pricing and brand paradigms on light bulbs in North America. GE ultimately had to recognize this new reality and adjust prices, while losing market share. More recently, General Electric completely exited the light bulb business.

PURSUING THE REAL BRANDS

The multiple-channel marketing system in the U.S. meant that manufacturers sold brands traditionally preferred by the professional customer exclusively to professional specialty shops and wholesalers, while home centers were offered similar products but with DIY brands.

For example, the Masco Corporation manufactured and sold Delta brand faucets to plumbing wholesalers but designated their Peerless brand to the DIY stores. Kohler sold their brand only to traditional plumbing dealers through plumbing wholesalers, but their Sterling brand was available for the DIY stores. Sherwin Williams sold their namesake brand in their own specialty paint stores but used the Dutch Boy brand for the DIY stores. Many other examples could be added to this list.

This dual branding was acceptable to most traditional DIY home centers, which agreed to purchase these second-tier brands. It did not work for The Home Depot. Unlike homeowners, who tend to have only brand awareness, the professional customer has strong brand insistence. After The Home Depot established EDLP pricing and began to target the pros, we needed to carry the preeminent brands that were known and trusted by them.

We relentlessly pursued those preferred brands. In some cases, such as Purdy paintbrushes and Klein electrical tools, we had to wait for top management to pass to a second-generation team before these old-line companies would risk selling their brands to The Home Depot. However, we persisted and were able to obtain these key brands over time.

DEVELOPING QUALITY PRIVATE LABEL PRODUCTS

We often found there was no alternative source for a key product category within the U.S. market. We, therefore, developed the ability to source products on a worldwide basis. In many cases, this meant developing our own private-label products that were designed and built to our specifications.

We did not originally have a quality line of mechanics tools. The number one brand in the U.S. was Craftsman, which was owned by Sears and not available to us. The second most important brand was Snap-on, but this company only sold to professional customers through its own fleet of franchised mobile van retailers. A third professional brand was Proto, but it was only available through industrial wholesalers.

So, with few options available to us, we developed our own brand, which we named Husky. We ensured the Husky brand specifications could match quality for quality with any of the name-brand products. This allowed us to put a lifetime guarantee on the product line.

During Husky's introduction to the world, we invited customers to bring their old, damaged Craftsman products to our stores to exchange for new Husky tools. This provided us with a huge bin of old or defective Craftsman tools to display in our stores. This was a powerful visual reinforcement of a message we wanted our customers to get loud and clear: The products of our primary tool competitor (Sears) were subpar. Husky went on to become a major brand with a wide range of quality tools at The Home Depot.

INVENTING BEHR PREMIUM PLUS

We had an outstanding private label success story with Behr Paint. Today Behr is a well-known popular brand of paint in the U.S., but it wasn't always so. The number one brand of exterior stain in the 1980s was Olympic. We could not obtain the Olympic stain line, so we marketed the Behr exterior stain program.

Behr was a small producer of redwood stain in Southern California. Most of the patio furniture in California was made of redwood. Behr supplied the clear finishes to protect and the stains to refinish faded patio furniture. Then they expanded their product line to include stain for wood trim on houses.

Behr's products were appropriate, given their western U.S. production facilities. The company was not too interested in the East Coast, where most of our stores were located at the time. Homes in the East had different product demands. In addition, Behr would face the cost of shipping a heavy can of stain, which is mostly water, across the country.

On the paint side of the aisle, the number one brand in the U.S. in the 1980s was Glidden Spred Satin. We sold the Glidden Spred Satin paint in our stores, but it was a very low-profit product. The retail price per gallon was around ten dollars and, in some markets, we were selling the product below our costs. This aggressive pricing strained our relationship with the Glidden Company.

We began to think seriously about offering our customers a private label paint line where we could control the specifications and the pricing. We began a discussion with Behr.

The Behr management team had a can-do culture similar to our own *Bleeding Orange* culture. They were up to the challenge. We learned that Behr could not produce paint that was price competitive with Glidden's Spred Satin, due to Glidden's economies of scale. However, they showed us how they could make a superior product in regard to color purity.

Together, we developed and introduced the Behr Premium Plus brand, which we co-branded and marketed at a premium price. We introduced Behr Premium Plus paint at fifteen dollars a gallon, which was 50 percent higher than the Glidden Spred Satin product. We used TV advertisements to establish the brand and tell the quality story of better color choices. We educated our expert salespeople to the advantages of offering our customers a premium product.

Within three months, Behr Premium Plus was our highest selling paint in units and dollars. The Glidden paint company lost their dominant market share, and Behr is now a nationwide major brand name in quality paint with both homeowners and professional customers.

THE QUEST FOR THE TOP BRANDS

Whether it was breaking down the door of a professional brand like Halo Lighting, as described in chapter one, developing our own private label tool line, as we did with Husky, or taking market share from a consumer product brand such as Glidden paint, we learned we had credibility with our customers. We now had the marketing power to impact brand market share in the North American marketplace. The winning strategy was to carry the major brands when possible and, when these brands were not available, to make an end run around these hesitant vendors and bring new products and better prices directly to the consumer.

The leading name brand vendors almost always dragged their heels until they saw their customers eagerly buying competing products in our stores. Then it dawned on their management teams that they really needed us and that The Home Depot's express train was pulling out of the station without them on board.

When they finally crossed that threshold and realized they must sell to The Home Depot, they typically found their fears of losing market share were unfounded and that selling to us expanded the market and created a larger market share for them. The Kohler Company was a great example.

KOHLER OPENS DISTRIBUTION AND WINS

Kohler was, and probably still is, the most important brand of sanitary ware in the country. Sanitary ware includes toilets, sinks, bathtubs, faucets, and bath accessories. Kohler did not want their brand in The Home Depot's stores. They were terrified this would cause their traditional wholesale distributors and specialty stores to boycott Kohler products.

Kohler wanted home centers to stock their Sterling brand. We had held many meetings with Kohler's top management to try to change this policy, but we seemed to be at an impasse. We needed the famous Kohler brand, and Kohler did not want their brand in our stores, even if we purchased the product through wholesale distribution.

After many discussions, we asked the company's CEO if there was any regional market in the U.S. where they were not pleased with their market share and were not getting the support they desired from their traditional distribution channel. The answer was yes: San Diego, California.

This was a perfect opportunity to prove to Kohler we could positively impact its market share. We initiated a test program in our San Diego stores. It produced incredibly positive results for the Kohler brand.

The Home Depot began selling truckloads of Kohler products in the San Diego market. This was incremental to Kohler's business, since the traditional dealers did not respond with the feared boycott. Instead, they renewed their commitment to the Kohler brand in order to defend their own market position. Their dealers improved their in-stock inventory positions and enlarged their showrooms to compete with The Home Depot. It was a big win for Kohler. This story was repeated over and over as other recognized name brand manufacturers realized that selling to us was accretive to their market share.

Another example of a company fighting to maintain their dual brand distribution policy was the Bosch tool company. Bosch is a German maker of power tools that is absolutely dominant in Europe. For years they sold green tools to the home center market and blue tools to what they considered the more legitimate professional tool suppliers. Bosch had very little market share in the U.S. before the 1990s. However, they decided to make a major push into the American market, and The Home Depot was considered a key piece of this strategy.

My merchants approached me with the good news that Bosch had contacted them and that this famous high-quality line of tools could now be available at The Home Depot. I had been to Europe and was aware of their two-color approach.

"What color are the tools?" I asked.

My merchants were not sure; they had not asked the question.

They soon let me know the tools being offered were green. To the great disappointment of our merchants, I vetoed the Bosch deal. Subsequently, a senior Bosch executive from Germany sat at my desk and told me what a bad decision I had made. The conversation got a bit heated, with some fist pounding on the table as I was told that Bosch Tools would become a major brand in the U.S., with or without The Home Depot. I told him the answer from us was, without.

About nine months later, I received the good news from my merchants that Bosch had reconnected with them and was now happy to sell us their blue line of power tools. Another manufacturer had seen the light!

Many manufacturers are myopic and seem to think that market growth is a zero-sum game, where market share can only be moved around, not expanded. The Home Depot knew we could expand the market by inspiring our customers, showing them how to do the project, and then making the project affordable. We did not accept the proposition that the market for a product had a fixed capacity. Our goal was to expand the market so it represented a bigger pie; then we would work to get a very big piece of that pie.

THE CUSTOMER MUST WIN

Even today, four decades after this whole thing started, a few branded product lines are still not available at The Home Depot or any big-box home-improvement store. This relatively small group of vendors still wants to believe they, rather than the final customers, are in charge. These production-oriented manufacturers have yet to learn the customer is in charge and the supply chain must accommodate their desires. Boycotts never work in the long run. When customers have a desire or need, it will be fulfilled.

We did not always have the exact brands we wanted, but we always found a way to provide the customer with the right solution for their project. Reluctant vendors found that turning down The Home Depot created a new, dynamic competitor they could not control.

THE EVOLUTION OF SPECIALIZED DISTRIBUTION CENTERS

Because each of our stores was a warehouse, our original business model did not include central distribution centers. The first change in this thinking was in the lumber category.

The government grades lumber to facilitate trade and control quality. The government grade has to do with strength and other factors; it does not consider the appearance of the individual pieces of lumber. Most construction lumber in the U.S. is number two grade and may have visual imperfections that do not degrade the government rating.

The deal you turn down today is the deal you will have to compete with tomorrow.

In traditional lumber yards, the store personnel would pull a customer's lumber order, load it on the truck, and often deliver the shipment to the jobsite—without the customer having yet seen the lumber.

However, every DIY customer in our stores would pick up each piece of wood and inspect it carefully for any flaw. The wood might be going inside a wall, never to be seen, but to the customer selecting the lumber, each piece had to look good.

To assure that our lumber could meet the customer's expectations regarding appearance, we established relationships with lumber mills that would set an additional grading criterion. These mills would sort their lumber first by government grade. Then they would do a second selection by appearance.

Direct sourcing at these mills meant we needed to take responsibility for transportation and distribution to our stores. Much construction lumber is produced in mills in the Northwest U.S. or Canada. To drive down transportation costs, the first leg of this journey had to be by railroad cars. These freight cars would go directly into our flatbed distribution centers located in each major metropolitan market. A flatbed distribution center is a facility designed only to move commodity products in full units by forklift, with a minimum of manual labor. There mixed truckloads would be put together for shipment to our stores. These lumber units were then side-loaded onto flatbed truck trailers for delivery to the stores or jobsites. Our direct sourcing and efficient flatbed distribution centers gave us a consistent quality advantage as well as a cost advantage over competitors who purchased primarily from local lumber wholesalers and trading companies, with quality and price constantly varying by mill and shipment.

Because we managed our own flatbed distribution centers, we also had the flexibility to ship to our stores at the ideal times. We could distribute lumber and building materials to be ready for the weekend homeowner business and then restock Sunday night for the professional business Monday morning. This provided a service level, price level, and quality level local competitors could not match.

LOGISTICS FOR WORLDWIDE SOURCING

We began bringing in our first containers of private label manufactured products from Taiwan in the early 1980s. Our first success story was in the category of ceiling fans. We took a product that had previously been seen in commercial applications like restaurants and provided the style and pricing to make it a great practical and decorative item for the home. This was followed by private label hand tools.

These products first came from Taiwan; China was a closed market at that time. We later migrated much of our sourcing to Hong Kong, which gave us entry to the lower-cost manufacturing base in the New Territories zone of southern China. Ultimately, China fully opened the doors to all the mainland producers, which provided an expanded manufacturing base for us to grow our private label product assortment.

This created numerous opportunities for sourcing outdoor furniture, lighting, window blinds, wool rugs, tools, flooring, faucets, wood flooring, sanitary ware, stone products, and pottery, just to name some of the many options available from China.

CARTON GOODS DISTRIBUTION CENTERS REQUIRED FOR IMPORT SUPPLY CHAIN

The long supply lines to Asia required us to establish distribution centers, to allow direct sourcing from foreign manufacturers with full container shipments. These distribution centers used high-cube racking to hold cartons of imported product. They served as a bulge in the supply chain to assure the constant availability of import product to the stores.

Imported private label products quickly provided over 20 percent of our sales and 30 percent of our gross profit dollars. This was a win-win for our customers and for us. Worldwide sourcing skills provided lower-priced products, often with extra features and benefits for our customers, while we earned higher gross margins.

The other advantage of our new global distribution was that it made the domestic vendors sharpen their pencils when it came to pricing. Proving to the domestic manufacturers that we had the competence and infrastructure to source quality products on a worldwide basis was a reality check that forced all the providers to rethink their own pricing policies.

Competition is a wonderful thing and a great benefit to the ultimate consumer. The average American has benefited greatly from the world-wide sourcing of consumer products. Any attempt by the government to inhibit the customer's ability to obtain the best value available as a result of global sourcing is an anti-customer initiative that will result in significantly higher prices to the consumers and eventual lowering the standard of living.

Private Label Echelons

We learned that each private label brand needed a clear positioning statement that defined how the product should be marketed and priced. Different products required different strategies.

We defined three classifications for marketing private label products:

- **Generic or Opening Price Brands:** These are commodity products sold strictly on price. The quality statement is that the product will meet your expectations.

Examples at The Home Depot: HDX

- **Departmental or Mainstream Brands:** These are products that match name brand products in quality but sell for less than the branded product.

Examples at The Home Depot: Glacier Bay, Commercial Electric

- **Equity or Power Brands:** These products meet and often exceed the name brands in terms of quality and features/ benefits. These products can be sold at or even above the name brand product price.

Examples at The Home Depot: Husky Hand Tools, Hampton Bay Fans and Lighting, Behr Premium Plus Paint, and Ridgid Power Tools

WORLD CLASS LOGISTICS

An investment in proper logistic facilities, integrated systems, and an in-house traffic department was necessary to assure that products purchased at low *first costs* in a foreign market could be delivered to our stores at the lowest *landed costs*.

First cost is the cost at the end of the production line at the manufacturing facility. Landed cost is the total cost, including product and logistic costs, when the goods ultimately reach the store. When purchasing offshore, purchasing at true first cost is normally a possibility and must always be the objective. This is often referred to as buying on net-net terms, which means all distribution and marketing expenses are netted out of the costs.

Purchasing at first cost requires eliminating the intermediaries who perform much of the distribution function. However, these functions are still required, and it is up to the retail buyer to manage these functions and absorb the costs involved. These costs might include quality control testing, customs duties, inspection fees, freight charges, warehousing expenses, import department overhead, and, in some cases, private label marketing. The proper internal infrastructure must be in place to efficiently perform these functions. Applying all these logistic and distribution costs to the first cost of the product defines the landed cost.

The Home Depot made the necessary investments to be competent in worldwide sourcing and to perform these logistic and marketing tasks efficiently. We, rather than the manufacturers, were now the channel captain for many categories of goods. This gave us great leverage to assure we could bring outstanding values to our customers and secure our position as the EDLP price leader.

Now we could expand our sourcing to go beyond China and truly source internationally. This allowed us to import ceramic tile from Italy, rugs from India, plastic toolboxes and organizers from Israel, ladders from Mexico, lumber from Canada, pottery from Vietnam, stone flooring from Turkey, wood moldings from Chile, light bulbs and batteries from Korea, and other categories from various countries. As a result, we could give our customers better value and new, unique products for their home and lifestyle.

The ability of The Home Depot to source directly on a worldwide basis became a core competency. Imports sometimes filled a void left when domestic vendors refused to supply; at other times they provided unique products simply not available in the U.S. Often the advantage was simply great pricing that could expand the market by lowering the selling price in our stores. Our desire to find new ways to delight our customers drove us to travel the world in search of great values.

The Home Depot product shipments were always purchased *ex-factory*. This means The Home Depot accepted responsibility for selecting the transportation carrier and paying the freight charges. It did not matter whether the shipment was a full container from a foreign port, or a special-order item sourced from a domestic vendor; the terms were always specified *ex-factory*. This allowed The Home Depot's traffic department to negotiate freight contracts that leveraged the total buying power represented by the continuing flow of shipments. This assured the lowest possible transportation costs while encouraging increased service levels as a premier freight customer.

The vertical integration of The Home Depot's private label supply chain prevented middlemen from using The Home Depot's volume to subsidize procurement for their own customers who were The Home Depot's competitors. This assured that The Home Depot would have truly unique products at great prices. It was a win for The Home Depot and, even more important, a double win for the customers.

6

BUYING RIGHT

The continued growth of The Home Depot, combined with investments in logistics, distribution center facilities, and systems, gave us ever-increasing procurement power. By the early 1990s, our bargaining position shifted dramatically. Before we had been begging vendors to sell to us. Now we had leading name-brand vendors begging to be preferred growth partners. The industry skeptics had capitulated; now they vied for preferential positions in our merchandise mix.

Delta was the number one brand of faucets in the United States at that time. It was a division of the Masco Corporation, a major plumbing industry conglomerate that owns some of the top brands important to plumbing wholesalers. This was the channel of distribution to the professional decorator and installation contractors in the kitchen and bath business. Masco finally determined that, to grow their market share, they needed a presence in The Home Depot. This meant finding a way to begin selling us faucets branded with Delta, the crown jewel in Masco's stable of brands.

This was a big problem for the Delta division, which was committed to selling the Delta products only through two-step wholesale distribution. They were not about to change that policy and risk their relationship with the major distributors in the plumbing industry.

We began a dialogue with Masco's executive vice president of national accounts. We wanted to carry the Delta brand in our stores, and the Masco corporate management wanted to make this happen. The EVP could see the big picture. He realized Masco needed to find a way to partner with us, yet he also understood the concern of the Delta division in regard to upsetting the status quo in the industry. How could the restrictive distribution policy of their Delta division be diplomatically overridden?

We settled on a rebate program. The Home Depot would purchase Delta products from the wholesalers designated by Delta. Masco then would provide a corporate rebate that would allow us to net our cost down to the factory-direct pricing.

This compromise provided a workaround that allowed us to sell the number one brand of faucets while obtaining our products at the right net costs. The end result was that we increased the market share of the Delta brand, while the wholesalers saw no dilution in their own Delta volume to their customers.

SUCCESS WITH DELTA BREEDS FURTHER SUCCESSES

Before long other Masco divisions bought into the corporate rebate program and Masco became our largest corporate vendor. This provided us with a number of the leading brands in the plumbing industry, a major breakthrough for our prestige. The feared industry boycott simply did not occur.

This sent an important message to the rest of the home-improvement industry. We had once again proved that The Home Depot could expand the market for manufacturers who allowed us to promote their brands.

The fact that the market had stabilized to this new reality ultimately allowed us to completely bypass the wholesale distributors and purchase Masco products as a direct account. The barriers were dropping quickly. Major new brands were beginning to show up in The Home Depot stores.

As described in the last chapter, we were now becoming the channel captain for the home-improvement business. This meant we could impact the brands, products, and prices that would define the market for home improvement.

PRIVATE-LABEL GROWTH

We were proud of our growing assortment of name-brand products and were able to show our customers they could come to The Home Depot and buy the top brands at a discount. At the same time, we had developed many of our own private-label products, which allowed us to offer the customer an alternative choice. This dual track was the best of both worlds in terms of quality and price.

Our strategy was to promote the name-brand products. That would generate customer traffic to our stores. At the same time, we trained our people how to sell our private-label alternatives. This meant our private-label products had to be quality products with features and benefits we could point out to our own associates. This could not be done with inferior products. It was critical that our sales associates believed in the quality and performance of our brands. They needed to know they were doing the customer a favor by recommending our own brands.

The good thing about purchasing private-label products on a worldwide basis is that it is possible to define product specifications in order to assure unique feature/benefits for the customer and define quality standards. Another benefit was our ability to determine the packaging design and specifications, focusing on package size to lower logistic cost and impact labeling to enhance the point-of-sale presentation.

After these specifications were defined with an offshore manufacturer, we could negotiate on a *first-cost, net-net basis*. This means that the net costs are defined and agreed upon with no allowances built in to cover logistic and marketing functions. This is the best kind of relationship to have with a vendor, provided you have the infrastructure and systems to manage the total flow of product from the factory to the ultimate customer. Fortunately, we did.

NEGOTIATING WITH DOMESTIC VENDORS

However, it was generally not possible to establish the same kind of candid negotiations and product flexibility with domestic name-brand vendors. These vendors were not likely to open their books or produce to The Home Depot's specifications. They certainly were not interested in establishing net-net cost pricing with us. In these cases, we used other methods to peel the onion, in an effort to identify allowances and discounts we could obtain from these domestic vendors that would allow us to drive down costs and maximize the benefits of our buying power.

Domestic-branded vendors tend to build logistic costs, marketing funds, and customer allowances into their published cost prices. Their marketing and sales people generally have some leeway in being able to move a portion of these allowances and funds around to key customers at their discretion. Our goal was to tap these discretionary funds to the maximum. These are some of the ways we accomplished this goal:

PEELING THE ONION TO REDUCE COSTS

Product Line Reviews

We would systematically conduct a "product line review" of each category of products. Every current or potential vendor in that category had the opportunity to make a presentation with the intent of remaining or becoming a supplier to The Home Depot. The analysis was done at the line item level, referred to as a *SKU* (stock-keeping unit).

The reviews were conducted and completed in one day. Each vendor would make a presentation and stay in the vicinity until they received a phone call asking them to return for final negotiations. The rule was that final commitments from both the vendors and The Home Depot would be signed, sealed, and delivered by the end of the day. There were to be no pre-meetings and no further negotiations post-meeting.

During these vendor presentations, we obtained all the marketing information the vendor possessed on their category of merchandise in regard to total sales, market trends, competitors' pricing, and innovation. The vendor would, of course, present their suggested product mix and their best net pricing on those items. These presentations and negotiations focused strictly on the prices for the items under consideration. Discussions of promotional allowances, rebates, or other discounts were for other meetings at other times. Our focus in a line review was on item (SKU) pricing.

Once all the vendors had made their presentations, we would combine all this data on items and pricing with our internal data, considering pricing, margins, and quantities being sold. A revised *model stock matrix* was then developed that defined all the features, benefits, and price points that would be required to offer a comprehensive range of choices to our customers with a minimum of redundancy and duplication in our inventories. Each vendor's proposed product mix and pricing would be positioned in our matrix to determine the vendor's competitive advantages on an item-by-item basis.

At this point, in addition to pricing, we would consider our relationship with each vendor to ascertain with which vendors we preferred to grow our business. The chart shown shows an example of the qualitative issues a merchant might use to evaluate the status of a vendor, on the basis of at least four categories:

Shared compatible strategies

Proven service performance

Product quality and innovation

Cost issues

Defining a Advantaged Vendor

Shared Growth Plans & Goals
Transparent Business Plan

In-store Service
Ship Complete & On time
Accommodate Packaging Request

Strategy | **Service**

Cost | **Production**

Annual Rebate Promotional Funds
Store Opening Discounts
Participate in Line Reviews

New Product Innovation
Exclusive Introductions
Offer Real Brands
Offer Private Label brands

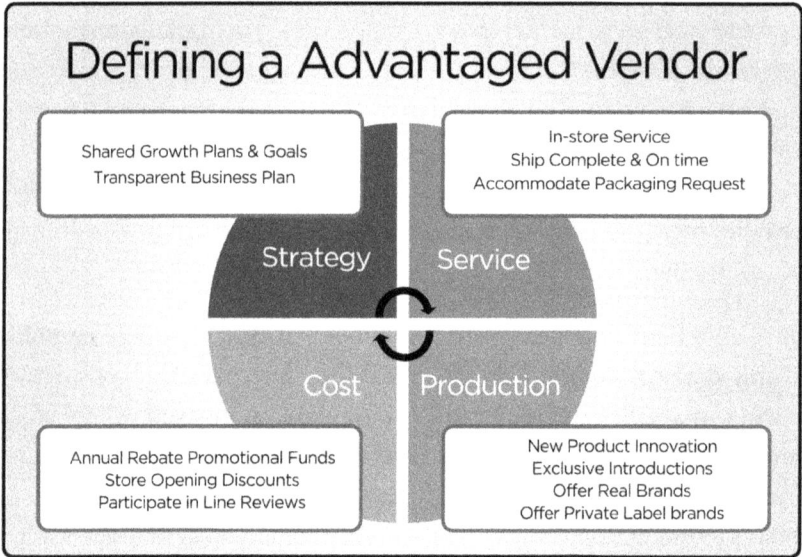

Taking a systematic approach to defining what you want and expect from a vendor relationship provides an insightful guide for negotiation. First we defined the criteria for being chosen as an advantaged vendor. Then we were ready to evaluate vendors to determine their compliance toward the ideal standard.

Evaluate Vendor Status

Advantaged

Neutral

Disadvantage

Disadvantaged - Seek a replacement
Neutral - No incentive to grow business
Advantaged - A mutual desire to grow

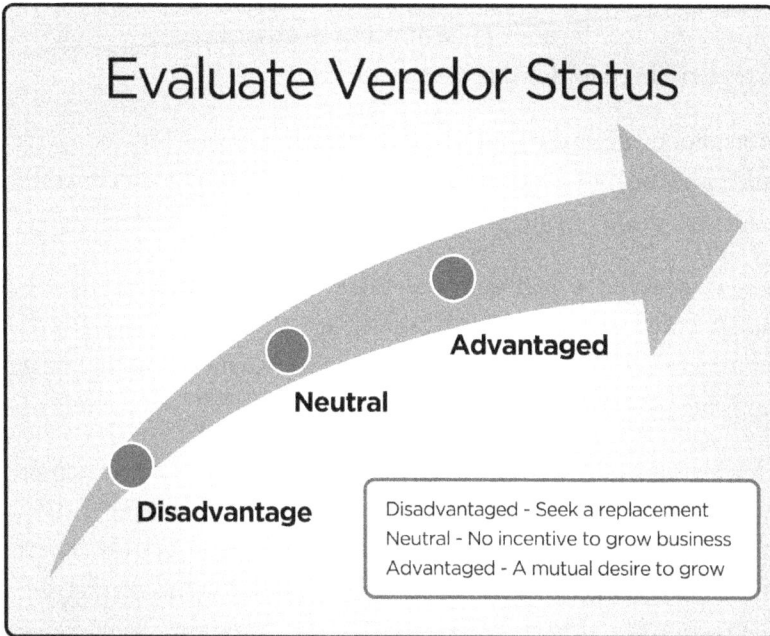

The next step in the product line review process would be to put together a counteroffer to the pricing the vendors had offered in the morning session. The counteroffer would be presented to our advantaged vendors.

During this step, we looked at our current product mix in terms of features, benefits, and price points, with an eye toward designing a revised product mix with new lower cost and new retails designed to achieve increased sales volume. Since we now had the proposed prices from all the vendors, we could make a tough but reasonable counteroffer. It was then time to call our most preferred vendor back to our meeting so we could present a new product listing that would increase this vendor's share of our product mix and significantly increase their total sales volume with us. This offer was predicated on the vendor's accepting our counteroffer on price.

The vendor winning the largest market share increase had to accomplish this by working on lower gross margin but betting that increased sales would generate more gross profit dollars. If the offer was accepted, a handshake finished the deal. If the vendor did not agree to a deal, that company opened the door to having a competitor become our number one preferred vendor for that category.

The vendors essentially walked away from the meeting knowing they would either be hiring more people and increasing production or cutting production and laying off people.

After we secured a deal with our most preferred vendor, the other vendors would be brought back into the meeting by turn and given an offer for a revised SKU listing, once again dependent upon accepting our counteroffer prices.

As a growing company we needed vendors with a strong vision and potential for growth. It was difficult for the vendors to simply stay in neutral or strive for only their fair share of the market. As a result of the line review process, some vendors would gain SKUs and market share while others would lose. It was possible that a disadvantaged vendor score and indifferent pricing could eliminate some vendors completely.

Vendors did not relish these reviews. They always had to face the hard decision to gamble on gaining more market share while significantly reducing their gross margin percentages. We were, in effect, educating our vendors to consider how to grow their profitability by gaining more gross profit dollars through higher sales volume. The alternative was to lose market share while attempting to maintain their fixed historical margin percentages.

For many production-oriented vendors, this was a difficult, if not impossible, proposition. For the more growth-oriented vendors, it was a reasonable chance to take market share. This model of driving down prices to increase gross-margin dollar generation was our approach to the business, and we expected our vendors to embrace the same logic. We needed a profitable but also efficient supply chain. This needed to be a win-win-win outcome for The Home Depot, our preferred vendors, and, of course, our customers.

The result of the product line review for us was the guarantee of a lower net cost for a specific and agreed upon time frame going forward. It would define some new, lower retail prices that would help us gain market share. In the process, we would have removed redundancies from our merchandise mix, and we would now have a more streamlined store inventory. We were often able to establish a more consolidated vendor base. All of this would work towards generating a higher GMROI.

ANNUAL REBATES

A key factor in determining that a supplier was an advantaged vendor was the company's willingness to reward growth with an annual rebate to The Home Depot, thus sharing a portion of the increased profits generated by their increased production. As a vendor's sales volume increases and production ramps up, long-run average costs decline. The savings from these declining costs tend to fall to the bottom line as economies of scale

When all vendors get their fair share of your product assortment and shelf space, you cannot possibly be buying at the lowest cost.

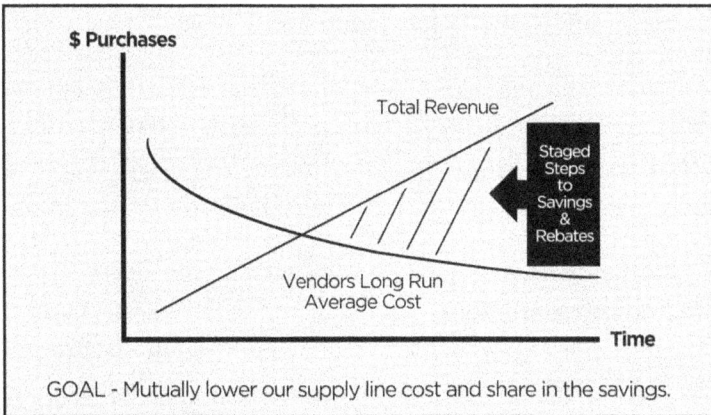

Rebate Justification

$ Purchases

Total Revenue

Staged Steps to Savings & Rebates

Vendors Long Run Average Cost

Time

GOAL - Mutually lower our supply line cost and share in the savings.

are generated. Our goal was to identify stages of incremental revenue growth and to establish rebate allowances that would allow The Home Depot to share in a portion of the increased profits as our purchases hit each of these preset mileposts.

These agreements were not negotiated during a line review. They were more likely to be negotiated between the senior management of our vendors and an officer of The Home Depot. This was a top-level discussion regarding the criteria for being an advantaged vendor. The result would be a mutual commitment to growth, based upon shared market objectives.

PROMOTIONAL FUNDS

Most name-brand manufacturers have promotional funds built into their cost structure and will offset retailer promotional expenses either by paying for a share of the media cost for advertising their products or providing a discretionary fund based upon a percentage of sales. The Home Depot did not accept either of these methods.

Each fall we conducted a market tracking survey to determine our market share in each of our ten major product categories. We set a new market share goal for each of those ten departments for the following year, along with a promotional program designed to achieve that goal. Each of these promotional programs had a specific budgeted cost which, when combined, became the corporate promotional budget for the company.

The rationale for the marketing expenditures was a commitment to grow market share. The merchants for each of these departments would sign off on their department's promotional program and accept responsibility for funding the corresponding promotional budget.

The merchants for each of these categories would then identify the vendors who would most benefit from the new sales plan for next year. Their representatives would be invited to a marketing presentation, where the merchandising plans, target market share, and advertising budgets would be shared with them. Each vendor would then attend a private meeting with the departmental merchants, where their share of the next year's advertising budget would be determined.

A significant portion of the next year's advertising budget was off-loaded to the vendors before the start of each year. These funds went into a general marketing fund to grow the sales and market share of each department per the annual plan. The funds were totally flexible regarding how The Home Depot spent the money.

The point was that we were committed to increasing market share and each contributing vendor could expect a corresponding sales increase in the coming year. The idea was to think of each vendor as a sailing vessel on The Home Depot wave. The message was the old adage, "*A rising tide lifts all ships.*" Smart vendors wanted to be on the crest of that wave.

NEW STORE AND PRODUCT LINE ALLOWANCES

Our compounded growth rate of twenty-five percent per year ultimately led us to a point of opening more than a hundred stores a year. This was a huge capital investment. Each of these stores represented an increase in market share for our vendors and the potential for a long stream of new income. Therefore, it seemed appropriate and logical that the vendors would support our growth by providing opening-store discounts and store set-up support. The amount of the discount varied by vendor. Our objective was to purchase these goods at their net production cost, if possible.

This same type of negotiation was initiated whenever a vendor was involved in putting a new product line into our stores. Often this meant some items in the store had to be deleted to make space for the new product assortment. In some cases, the vendor would buy back existing inventory at our cost. However, when the discontinued merchandise was price sensitive, the preferred method would be to buy the new products at a significant discount and often at no charge, which would provide a margin cushion to allow us to mark down the discontinued product and offer special clearance price reductions to our own customers.

The Home Depot had now proven that we could significantly impact a vendor's brand in the marketplace. We needed vendor support to accomplish our objectives. The vendors, in turn, were willing to offer their support as long as they could see the promised benefit of increased market share. Constantly peeling the onion to reduce costs enabled The Home Depot to enlarge the market, obtain a larger share of that market, offer better value to our customers, provide increased wealth to our investors, and create great career paths for our associates.

SPECIAL RELATIONSHIPS WITH KEY VENDORS

A good example of offsetting costs with vendor support was The Home Depot program for sponsoring the Olympics. The Home Depot was one of the major sponsors of the 1996 Olympics, held in Atlanta. Our management felt it appropriate for us to support the Olympics in our hometown, despite the forty-million-dollar price tag, which was a lot of money to us—and definitely not in our promotional budget.

Olympic sponsorship is a four-year commitment through the winter games and then the summer games. We entered an agreement with the International Olympic Committee (IOC) that allowed us to place the Olympic logo on the packaging of special promotional items from vendors we would designate as part of The Home Depot's Olympic Family. We offered our advantaged vendors the chance to become part of our Olympic Family program by sharing a portion of the promotional cost. This let us off-load the cost of sponsorship while generating some exciting promotional offers for our customers.

These Olympic commitments were in excess of a million dollars per vendor and often required senior management and board approval within each of the sponsoring vendor companies. While this was a lot of money, it also guaranteed a preferred vendor relationship with The Home Depot and special product promotions over a four-year period. This would include periodic Olympic Family meetings with our merchandising and marketing team at various Olympic training venues, which was seen as an incredibly positive opportunity for the vendors to enhance their relationship with The Home Depot's senior management.

All of these supporting vendors were betting that this investment in The Home Depot would pay off over the course of the Olympic campaign and, hopefully, beyond. They saw a company that was rapidly growing and grabbing more and more market share. This was a bet they simply had to make.

DEVELOPING A WINNING SUPPLY CHAIN

The Home Depot had become the most important retailer in the North American supply chain of the home-improvement business. We were a force that every vendor had to consciously determine either to support with inventory or to compete against. This was not achieved overnight, but once we had growth momentum, the writing on the wall became evident to most of the vendor community.

We now had the power to determine the winners and losers in the home-improvement market. We could put our thumb on the scale and impact sales by determining which stores would stock a particular product, how often it would be promoted, how much shelf space it would receive, and what other products would be available for the customer to select. This was a hard charging and demanding business. We did not dwell on past successes but always challenged the vendors to help us find new ways to delight our customers.

Our goal was to increase market share; our vendors needed to have the same vision. We had to work constantly to make sure our channel of distribution was the low-cost lane. It was a matter of making sure our supply chain was more efficient than our competitors' supply chains. This required a unique, symbiotic relationship, based on trust, between us and our vendors to grow our mutual market share.

It was important to realize that the final deal made with our vendors had to be a win-win solution for us and for the vendor. It would serve no purpose to cut a deal that would bankrupt the vendor and cause us to lose an advantaged vendor. Yes, we needed price concessions, but we, in turn, were obligated to increase the vendor's sales and market share. Our whole supply chain needed to consist of winners.

MANAGING GROWTH

The challenge for The Home Depot as we grew across the country was staying ground-engaged with our stores. We needed to be sensitive to the local product requirements and make sure we were priced right against the local competition.

It was vital to keep our merchants interfacing with the store operations staff in their market and in their stores. The stores couldn't be allowed to simply become numbers. Person-to-person interaction between store management and the merchandising group was crucial. Both groups needed to be on the same wavelength in regard to delighting the customer with the right product, assortment, service, and price.

Therefore, the country was divided into geographical regions. A complete merchandising and store operational management team located in each market had the responsibility and authority to adapt the model stock, pricing, and promotions to the local market. However, this created a dilemma: How to negotiate corporate programs with preferred vendors that would apply on a nationwide basis? We needed to be able to establish corporate policies and negotiate on a corporate basis when it was to our advantage, but also to be able to have local flexibility to accommodate local market situations. We had to be as centralized as possible but, conversely, as localized as necessary.

Our solution was to establish a matrix within our organizational chart with straight lines of authority on a geographical basis but with dotted-line authority to corporate officers in Atlanta. In regard to the merchandising groups, the dotted line to Atlanta connected to me.

In the mid-1990s The Home Depot was operating four geographical divisions. Each division had a division president, a vice president over store operations, and a merchandising vice president who had line responsibility for all product departments in the geographical division. Each geographical division could establish relationships with local vendors to serve the stores in that area. Once a vendor was established as a basic supplier to more than one division, though, they became a "corporate vendor," requiring integrated chain-wide negotiations and relationships. However, there were no corporate merchandisers or a buying organization at the Store Support Center in Atlanta.

As executive vice president of merchandising, I assigned each of the four divisional merchandising vice presidents with responsibility to manage an assigned portion of our ten major product categories, with authority for corporate programs in those departments. When a vendor qualified for a corporate relationship, the appropriate merchandising vice president would assign a captain position to one of the divisional merchandisers. The captain would negotiate costs and terms on behalf of all the divisions. The local divisions maintained control of the actual model stock for their market and the retail pricing, but the vendor procurement costs, terms, and allowances were negotiated on a chain-wide basis.

This may sound a bit complicated, and it was. The advantage was that it kept the merchandising decision makers close to the stores, both physically and mentally. This decentralization was the "*better good*," as opposed to concentrating all the decision-making in the Atlanta corporate office. It was consistent with, and a key part of, keeping the *Bleeding Orange* culture of pushing decisions down and out through the company. We needed corporate coordination, but even more, we needed local ownership and initiative.

This matrix management worked well most of time. The divisional merchants within a department would meet regularly to compare notes and to make joint decisions on future programs under the guidance and direction of the appropriate divisional merchandising vice president. They would also schedule joint departmental line reviews.

Every quarter we would bring together all the merchants in the company to develop corporate promotional programs and share merchandising success stories and failures. This created many opportunities for our merchants from the four divisions to interact. Of course, being The Home Depot with its many type A personalities, competition grew between the divisions as they worked to create the absolutely best stores. This was healthy as long as we remembered that our common enemy was external.

The matrix management allowed The Home Depot to operate—particularly in the areas of merchandising and store operations—as a decentralized organization. More centralized direction and authority was, of course, required in areas such as finance and accounting, where uniform discipline and control was essential. However, even in these areas, there was a need and willingness to be ground engaged with the front-line workers and a certain bias against central overreach.

This could be seen in the way the information technology (IT) group was organized. The IT systems design and programming staff was divided into functional groups, such as finance, store operations, logistics, and merchandising. The managing directors of each of these functional groups had to be former frontline workers, as opposed to career system analysts. So the IT merchandising group was headed by a past merchant. Likewise, the IT store operations group was headed by a past store operations manager. This same logic applied to each of the IT system design teams, whether they focused on logistics, finance, or any other work group. This assured that the systems would be *ground engaged* and that the processes would be truly functional for the various work groups.

The Home Depot was, by design, a very decentralized company, which played well into the *Bleeding Orange* culture. Things were going great. The Home Depot was the clear winner in the home-improvement business, and everyone was getting rich. It was the start of a new century, and everything was about to change—for the worse.

PART II

FOUNDATION CRACKS:
STRUCTURE FATIGUE

7

CRUSHING THE ORANGE CULTURE

By the year 2000, The Home Depot had been in business for twenty years under the original management team headed by Bernie Marcus and Arthur Blank. The Home Depot had stores coast-to-coast and border-to-border and had become the largest retailer of home-improvement supplies in the world. Their successful model of home-improvement retailing was emulated and feared by building material retailers both at home and around the globe. Momentum should have been on The Home Depot's side. But the *Bleeding Orange* culture was about to be challenged externally and, even more, internally.

The Home Depot had surpassed the 1,000-store goal and was now quickly running out of new markets. This had the effect of cannibalizing existing store business, which resulted in declining sales in existing stores and more marginal returns on investments in new stores. The decline in top-line sales per store had a negative impact on the individual stores' operations and the resulting return on investment.

In the past, the company had been able to leverage cost factors via economies of scale on a store-by-store basis. However, falling revenue store by store created negative reverse leverage. Cannibalization was essentially a self-inflicted injury.

The Home Depot had previously entered the Canadian market (see chapter 2), but this alone could not provide enough new store opportunities to fuel long-term growth. An initiative was needed that could profoundly move the growth needle. The challenge was to find some combination of domestic and international growth that could continue this phenomenal growth story. It was important to show Wall Street that The Home Depot was still a growth vehicle worthy of their investment.

DOMESTIC RETAIL DIVERSIFICATION

The company was a creative learning machine. Therefore, new formats were designed for specific target markets not fully exploited by the big-box warehouse home-center stores now reaching into every major metropolitan market. Three experimental formats predominated:

The Crossroads was a superstore for the farmer and rancher, aimed at the rural market. A handful of these stores were opened in test markets in Illinois, Iowa, and Missouri.

The Villager was a super hardware store aimed at the small neighborhood market, competing with hardware chains like Ace Hardware and True Value Hardware stores. These stores were tested in New Jersey.

The Home Depot Expo was targeted for the upscale home decor market. This went beyond a test and was rolled out to multiple locations across the country.

While these formats had some limited success, they were ultimately not able to generate the return on investment of the core big-box warehouse home-center stores, and these business ventures were terminated.

INTERNATIONAL OPPORTUNITIES FOR GROWTH

The Home Depot had previously considered international growth outside North America and had explored a number of alternative opportunities in both Europe and Asia. Leading home-center operators in Europe were beginning to model themselves after The Home Depot.

This included, most notably, the Kingfisher Company, which had begun to open B&Q Warehouse stores in Britain, and the Hornbach company in Germany, which was opening large Hornbach Baumarkt stores in multiple European countries. Big-box stores in France emerged under the banners of Castorama and Leroy Merlin.

The management of these companies admired The Home Depot. At the same time, they feared we would enter their markets and easily capture market share.

Merger discussions with selected European companies took place during the mid-nineties. Unfortunately, a lack of clear, strategic, international vision by our own management and a lack of sophistication in merger and acquisition protocol resulted in the termination of these negotiations. In the case of Kingfisher, the discussions halted when we insisted on purchasing only the big-box warehouse stores instead of the entire company. The negotiation with Hornbach broke down over the issue and timing of majority ownership.

Our very senior management had differences of opinion as to the advisability of a European versus Asian expansion. This created a stalemate of sorts while we searched for a breakthrough growth strategy. Our research showed us we would need to consider acquisitions in some country markets and greenfield operations in others.

We knew growth outside the U.S. would always be more difficult and costly than continued domestic expansion. In some countries, many of them in Asia, we would need to create costly new infrastructure to serve the stores. Conversely, in most European markets, we would have to fight the entrenched infrastructure of existing competition and much stricter governmental controls.

CHINA BECKONS

Then the Chinese government invited us to open the first western-style home center in China. Keep in mind that in the mid-1990s, China was emerging as a potential economic powerhouse but was still backward and basically underdeveloped. The Chinese government had issued goals to its governors and mayors to help China take giant steps forward.

The Communist party leaders instructed the government of Tianjin, a city of about eleven million people that is essentially the seaport for Beijing, to bring modern retail distribution to China. This resulted in the Chinese government assisting a private entrepreneur to establish the Home World group. This company's primary objective was to first open big-box retail stores in Tianjin and then to expand throughout China.

The first goal set by the Home World group was to bring The Home Depot to China. A delegation of the Chinese government and the Home World management team showed up at our Atlanta office without an appointment and demanded an audience with senior management.

At that moment I was the highest-ranking officer in the building, so I asked my assistant to go to the lobby and suggest that they make a formal request for such a meeting and come back at a better time. They responded that they had come a long way from China and had no intention of leaving until they could meet with the boss.

I finally relented and had the visitors taken into our executive conference room. The group was led by the vice chairman for building material production for the entire country of China. The spokesman for the group was the entrepreneur, Mr. Du Sha.

Once in the conference room, they rolled out an impressive series of large topographic maps and building plans and explained through their interpreter that they had built the first Home Depot store in China, and we now needed to become joint venture partners and run the business.

A quick review of the plans they presented showed that they had, indeed, built an exact duplicate of The Home Depot store. They had sent a team of architects to California to visit our stores and take detailed measurements and drawings. They had actually built a store that met our specifications, and it was now sitting empty in Tianjin, China, ostensibly waiting for us to merchandise it!

THE CHINA DEAL

I advised the group that we had given no serious thought to opening stores in China and that we did not share their priority to bring The Home Depot to China. They could not believe it. Here they were, showing genuine interest; how could we not jump at the opportunity?

They did not come to Atlanta to get no for an answer. They continued to argue why we should make the big jump to China. I finally conceded that on my next buying trip to China I would visit them in Tianjin and discuss this matter further.

Eventually, I did, visit the store site in Tianjin and, sure enough, the store was standing there, tangible evidence of their commitment. I was then invited to Beijing to again meet with the vice chairman of building material production, whom I learned was a high official in the Communist Party. After some preliminary discussions in the government offices, the vice chair hosted a grand dinner, and the details of their offer were spelled out.

An interesting sidelight to our story is that the Chinese preferred to negotiate deals at formal dinners, where the entire entourage could gather around a huge, round table for a lengthy dinner with many courses and constant-flowing liquor. Each time a person would take a drink of liquor, it was appropriate to identify a dinner guest, offer a toast, and drain your glass (which would quickly be refilled by one of the attendants) to show your sincerity. At our dinner the terms of a proposed deal were outlined, But when the vice chair gave a heartfelt toast to The Home Depot, to our surprise, a different man on the other side of the table stood up and pronounced "Ganbei!" and drained his glass. Our host was so important that he had a designated drinker!

The terms offered to entice The Home Depot to enter China were head turning. For a small equity investment, we would have majority control of the joint venture. That was unique since at that time it was technically illegal for a foreign company to have majority control of a joint venture in China. We quickly learned that although many things were illegal in

China, the key to doing business was developing relationships that could grant exceptions to the law. We were also offered an agreement that we would be the only foreign home-center company allowed to operate in all the Chinese provinces.

The real plum was an offer to grant us license to export products from China without going through a Chinese trading company, as was currently mandated. We were already importing millions of dollars of private-label product from China, so the value of this license would more than offset the initial investment involved in the joint venture. My team took this proposal to our corporate board of directors. The board turned the proposal down.

The main reason we rejected the deal was the concern that doing business with the Chinese would be a public relations nightmare in America. At that time, it was assumed in the public media that a joint venture with any business in China was simply doing business with a company that was a front for the "Chinese Red Army." This was still a huge political issue for many Americans in the mid-1990s.

We advised the Home World group that we could not proceed with the joint venture. However, we did not want to create a hostile relationship with the Chinese government. China was supplying more and more products for our stores. Our counteroffer was to provide assistance to the Chinese home-center project, but without making an equity investment in a joint venture. We would be helpful but remain officially at arm's length.

A team from China was invited to intern in our West Coast stores to learn the business. We essentially opened a window into our processes and procedures and introduced the Chinese team to many of our American vendors. A big orange box store called HomeWay was soon opened in Tianjin, China, followed by twelve more in Northern China.

We had passed on Europe and now were taking an arm's-length approach to China. There was, nevertheless, still a window of opportunity for The Home Depot to expand internationally and become the dominant building material retailer on a global basis. We appeared to be invincible to the international players in our industry, so we were in a position to negotiate very favorable deals if we wished to acquire foreign companies. Of course, we also now had the advantage of a strong balance sheet if we deemed it better to enter a specific international market alone.

However, all these advantages would not last long. The success of The Home Depot was known, and the big-box concept was being duplicated by numerous building material retailers in Europe, Asia, and Australia. The world was changing, and the clock was ticking.

NEW GROWTH DILEMMA

This reticence to move aggressively outside North America was not characteristic of The Home Depot's *Bleeding Orange* culture, which had been so bold in the past as we marched across the North American continent. However, quickly acquiring sites and developing new stores in the business-friendly environment of the U.S. was relatively easy, compared with the complexity of entering foreign markets.

Great success and corporate size can shift even a dynamic company like The Home Depot onto a more conservative path. The past increase in corporate value had come primarily from new-store growth, but there was no longer a clear consensus on where new-store growth should be focused.

This more conservative strategy regarding growth began to impact the *Bleeding Orange* culture. Continued growth meant career opportunities for the orange-blooded associates. You might say that new markets and new-store growth was in our blood. The culture was still in Attack, Attack, Attack! mode. The Home Depot needed a target market on which to focus its momentum for growth.

THE SOUTH AMERICAN DISAPPOINTMENT

As part of the North American focus on growth, we recruited a small team of Spanish-speaking home-center veterans to put together plans to open the Mexican market. I was in charge of that initiative. However, the Mexican peso was devalued in December of 1994, and the corporate board of directors ultimately decided to terminate the Mexican project.

The decision to hold back was, of course, the wrong move at the wrong time. Before this downturn, acquiring Mexican property had been remarkably difficult and expensive. This temporary financial distress could have provided the best window of opportunity for market entry at the lowest cost. However, our board did not see it that way and ordered the abandonment of the Mexican project.

Soon thereafter, I decided to get off The Home Depot train, after experiencing thirteen years of incredible growth and accomplishment. I had devoted much of my time and energy into developing an international strategy for growth but had hit a number of brick walls which was frustrating. I had broken through many brick walls in the past; the Mexican wall was a tough one to leave standing. I, therefore, resigned from the company in 1996. This ended my career at The Home Depot, which ultimately led to a new, twenty-year career advising other—and sometimes competing—international home-improvement retailers.

To my surprise, the team that had been set up to open the Mexican market subsequently made a job-saving proposal to the senior management to enter South America via Chile. One of the merchants on the Mexican team had been employed by Sodimac, the primary building-material merchant in Chile. He was obviously persuasive, as he convinced the company to make the international leap to Santiago, Chile.

This would be The Home Depot's first step outside North America. The Home Depot entered the Chilean market in 1998 in a joint venture with the Chilean department store retailer Falabella and subsequently also opened stores in Argentina.

The Falabella partnership seemed to bring many advantages to The Home Depot's entry into South America. Falabella was the largest department store retailer in both Chile and Argentina. Their private-label credit card was the most widely used form of retail credit in Chile. Such a joint venture with one of the leading retailers in South America would give instant credibility to The Home Depot's plans to enter Chile.

However, the South American initiative did not go well from the start. The Home Depot had greatly underestimated the task of opening these stores. By 2000 the project was clearly missing projections and struggling.

DIFFICULTIES EMERGE

The Home Depot was finding it exceedingly difficult to bring the *Bleeding Orange* culture to South America and to duplicate the incredible success it enjoyed in the United States. The North American business model and culture was not fully transferable into South America.

An example is the very different perception between North Americans and Chileans of The Home Depot's cartoon mascot, *Homer*. To the U.S. customer, Homer was a friendly guy-next-door doing DIY projects. He is the Do-It-Yourself stereotype. However, the South American public saw imperfections. First, Homer was seen as overweight, which meant he was lazy. Secondly, his baseball hat was covering his eyes, which meant he was dishonest. Finally, he wore a plaid shirt, which showed he was a foreign *gringo*. *Homer* did not make a good first impression. The Home Depot's cartoon mascot was just one of the cultural idiosyncrasies that did not transition well into South America.

Many other variables also played out differently in South America. North American homes are built primarily of wood, while South American homes are primarily built with cement. This makes a major difference in terms of building materials, tools, and costs.

Also, the South American customer, unlike his or her counterpart in North America, did not perceive the warehouse concept as an efficient, cost-saving format. They were already shopping in *bodegas* that resembled warehouses. The Chilean impression of the big orange box was that the stores were old and dirty, instead of clean and modern, which is what the Chilean customer associated with the quality and value they expected in a modern store.

Understanding the culture is essential when you leave your home country. Manual labor in Chile is incredibly cheap by U.S. standards. Many affluent homeowners have their own staff of household help. Most remodeling and maintenance is performed by *maestros,* which are similar to but less sophisticated than a U.S. "handyman." This availability of low-cost labor and a culture that does not consider DIY work a hobby created a limited DIY market.

The income levels in Chile and Argentina are much lower than in the U.S., and a significant portion of the population lives below what is considered middle class in the U.S. The average income today in Chile is $25,879 per year, contrasted with a U.S. average income of $43,241. This income difference is exaggerated even more by extremes of income and wealth, which vary significantly across most of South America. There is a growing middle class, but it is relatively small, compared to that in North America.

Other issues: The Home Depot *Bleeding Orange* culture that expected the employees to give 100 percent effort to the company, with long hours of work, conflicted with a culture where family time is highly important. The company loyalty of The Home Depot's U.S. associates came close to religious devotion. This was simply not the case in Latin America. In fact, employees in other cultures considered the cheers and testimonies of the typical store meeting at The Home Depot strange.

American stores were non-union, while unions are mandatory in Chile. This requires a whole new management perspective and style of dealing with employees. Labor relations was one of the obvious areas where there was a true clash of cultures. The Home Depot's orange-blooded management found this very confusing.

The relationship between store employees and management is different in Chile than in the U.S. The U.S. culture is less hierarchical, with rewards based on achievement. The Chilean management style is more paternalistic, creating a different kind of relationship and compensation system. A U.S. store would have fewer employees and pay them well, while a Chilean store tended to have far more employees who were paid much less. It was a quality-versus-quantity conundrum. There is a strong perceived social value of hiring multiple employees in South America.

THE PROBLEMS MULTIPLY

There also were huge system issues. The Home Depot IT systems were legacy systems that had been developed over time and could not easily be adjusted to new tax laws, currency issues, and a new language. An alternative IT system had to be designed and implemented, which did not go well. In some areas the new IT system simply didn't work, which created some big gaps in reporting during the early, critical months of operation. This left management often running blind in regard to the numbers necessary to evaluate performance.

The logistic problems were also significant for The Home Depot's vendors. Chile does not have a huge manufacturing infrastructure. For The Home Depot to maintain its normal width and depth of stock, a high percentage of the product mix would have to be imported. Many key products were simply nonexistent in the Chilean market. The Home Depot encountered significant transportation, warehousing, and working capital costs unique to establishing a business in a part of the world almost 5,000 miles from home. This was complicated by the fact that Chile itself is a narrow country 2,700 miles long.

There was a certain naivety to thinking a North American home center plopped down in Santiago, Chile, could expect the metrics to work the same as they did in Atlanta, Georgia. This tendency to see the market through U.S. glasses led The Home Depot to often ignore the advice of their partner, Falabella.

There was also a certain arrogance that led to underestimating the acumen of the domestic Chilean infrastructure at both the vendor and competitor level, both of which were well established in their home market. The Home Depot received a much more reserved response from the local building material vendors and a far more dynamic response from the primary retail competitor in Chile than it experienced when entering domestic markets in North America.

There are many differences between doing business in Santiago, Chile, compared with San Diego, California, even though they are both named for the same saint! South Americans are more used to dealing with dramatic market changes and react much more quickly than do competitors in the U.S.

South American business is strongly impacted by relationships. The senior management of all companies need to interact and develop a trust relationship. However, the senior management of The Home Depot was thousands of miles away from the local market. The Home Depot marched into Chile without investing time in the one-on-one relationship building that was required to become *simpatico* with the local power players in the industry. This was often seen as arrogant and wrong by the South American vendors.

STRONG LOCAL COMPETITION

The U.S. Home Depot stores had a much more esoteric product mix than typical home centers in South America. The U.S. model is specifically focused on building materials and tools for home improvement. However, the better model in South America proved to be an eclectic product assortment more like a general store, with categories such as housewares, pet supplies, automotive accessories, and camping supplies, in addition to the core home-improvement departments.

The Home Depot's main competitor was the Chilean Sodimac Group. I was invited to serve as an advisor to the Sodimac board and established a twenty-year relationship to help them maintain and grow their business in Chile and throughout Latin America. Sodimac did not operate big-box stores in 1998 but had a viable, traditional home-center business in one format and a drive-through building material specialty business in another store format. They quickly combined these two formats into one big-box home center to compete with this new existential threat to their position in the Chilean market.

This created a new combination store that was simultaneously *softer* and *harder* than The Home Depot's model.

On one hand, the Sodimac combination store proved to be more friendly to the female homeowner, with a much broader assortment of household and decor items. On the other hand, these new Sodimac stores featured a drive-through building material section that offered superior convenience and inventory depth for products like cement, rebar, steel, and lumber.

This new combination store format, combined with a native understanding of the local culture, allowed Sodimac to successfully protect their market share. In fact, this new format became a growth vehicle to actually increase market share. The Home Depot entry into Chile proved to be a huge benefit to Sodimac as they changed their business format to adjust to the new competition. In the process, Sodimac not only protected their Chilean business but also now had a proven, successful category-killer concept they could take to Peru, Columbia, Argentina, Brazil, and Uruguay.

Like Dorothy in the Wizard of Oz, The Home Depot began to realize *they were not in Kansas anymore.* The Home Depot would learn how to deal with Latin American culture later, in Mexico, but at that time the orange machine was producing red ink in Chile and Argentina.

In 2001 The Home Depot vacated the South American market, selling their majority interest to their joint venture partner, Falabella. This was a huge defeat to the *Bleeding Orange* culture. The Home Depot was not accustomed to failure.

THE LOWE'S FACTOR

The Home Depot continued its rapid growth in North America and continued to deal with the predictable problem of cannibalization and lower sales per store. This resulted in a dramatic decline in average store sales. It marked the end of an era.

The business model had to change as the average store sales volume fell. This lower sales volume per store impacted staffing, depth of inventory, operating expenses, and, ultimately, prices. The resulting changes negatively impacted the customer.

To complicate matters, The Home Depot was not alone in the North American market. The Lowe's company had belatedly developed a big-box home center model and was now emulating The Home Depot by rapidly opening stores across the country. Every new Lowe's store further cannibalized the market. Lowe's had sufficient size and critical mass to go head-to-head with The Home Depot and take significant portions of market share in cities across the country. The Home Depot could outperform Lowe's in sales and profits but could not eliminate them.

The Lowe's story starts way back in 1921 in a mountain village in North Carolina, where Lowe's was a small hardware store. It evolved into a traditional lumberyard in the late 1940s and expanded to multiple locations in the 1950s. These were large, drive-through lumberyards with a sort of small general store in the rural communities that Lowe's tended to serve.

Lowe's continued to expand its number of locations and ultimately became the highest volume building material retailer in the United States. Their primary target customer was the professional homebuilder. Then, in 1988, Lowe's watched as The Home Depot passed them in total sales to become the highest volume home-improvement retailer in the country.

This was a wake-up call for Lowe's. The board decided to diametrically change strategy and refocus on the DIY homeowner, transitioning to the big-box home center format. Lowe's had been primarily located in rural locations but now began to bring their new big *blue* boxes into The Home Depot's urban markets.

HEAD TO HEAD WITH LOWE'S

The Home Depot subsequently attacked Lowe's in their North Carolina home base, where they were dominant. The intent was to stop the company's growth in its tracks, just as The Home Depot had done with so many other competitors. A price war was initiated and, for the first time, The Home Depot's competitor did not blink.

In fact, Lowe's not only matched Home Depot prices but made further reductions that ultimately drove prices below cost on key commodity items like lumber, roofing, and concrete mix. The Home Depot responded tit-for-tat but found itself in the most difficult price war it had experienced.

The Lowe's price war was not on total categories, as in the earlier battles with Scotty's and Costco, but on specific high-volume commodity items. The rapidly spiraling downward price war had no bottom. This devolved into a typical no-win price war. The quantities sold of these negative-margin items skyrocketed as contractors and dealers came from all over the southern U.S. to take advantage of these unbelievable and unsustainable prices.

This time the competitor was more capable and stubbornly determined. The price war was too much for The Home Depot's resolve. Past boldness evaporated. The Home Depot blinked, prices were raised, and the war was over.

Thereafter, a pattern emerged. The Home Depot tended to set the prices and not react when Lowe's would match them. The Home Depot and Lowe's now had an oligopolistic position in the market and avoided direct price competition. They would compete with other's product and service variables, but the world had changed.

COAST-TO-COAST COMPETITION

The Home Depot's confidence and ability to use price as an offensive weapon was now in question. The Home Depot had allowed a competitor to survive. That changed everything. The Home Depot had become a paper dragon in regard to pricing. This affected strategy and had an even bigger impact on the *Bleeding Orange* culture.

Pricing policy must always consider the customer's perception and work to develop a long-term trust relationship. Certainly, the customer's willingness to drive past a Lowe's store to shop at The Home Depot was greatly reduced when there was no perceived price difference. Pricing is an important tool for gaining market share and needs to be used intelligently. The Home Depot had lost the ability to use price as an aggressive tool. This resulted in a weakened value image for the brand.

Lowe's was weak on the West Coast, where The Home Depot was well established, especially in California. However, a new big-box competitor based in Washington State called Eagle Hardware was proving capable of taking market share in The Home Depot's Northwest marketplace.

Eagle Hardware had established thirty-two stores in nine western states, including the lucrative California market. When Lowe's acquired Eagle Hardware in 1998, it established Lowe's as a viable coast-to-coast competitor to The Home Depot.

I traveled to Spokane, Washington, three years before the Lowe's acquisition to meet with Eagle's CEO at his corporate office. He made it clear that his main purpose in establishing the Eagle Hardware stores was to be a perfect acquisition target for The Home Depot. He invited us to negotiate a deal.

Our senior management team met to discuss whether we should acquire Eagle. The issue was whether to buy Eagle or to kill Eagle. We decided, as was typical with our *Bleeding Orange* culture, to *Attack, Attack, Attack!* Eagle had a strong brand image for product variety and superior in-store service in the Northwest. Beating Eagle would take more than just an aggressive pricing policy. The Home Depot did establish a strong price gap with Eagle, but Eagle proved to be a tough competitor. Victory did not come as quickly as expected.

MORE COMPETITION

Then, before The Home Depot could accomplish the goal of stopping Eagle in the marketplace, Lowe's bought the company. In retrospect, the decision not to purchase Eagle was wrong. We had not seriously anticipated this bold move by Lowe's. In fact, The Home Depot's aggressive pricing policy was probably a factor that created the impetus for the sale of Eagle to Lowe's.

This was another blow to The Home Depot's image of invincibility. It further damaged the *Bleeding Orange* culture, which had morphed from a vision of dominating the market to the reality of sharing the market with Lowe's.

Pricing between The Home Depot and Lowe's stabilized but, in doing so, created an opportunity for specialty retailers to operate under The Home Depot's price umbrella. In some cases, specialty retailers, such as Floor & Decor in flooring and Harbor Freight in tools, were able to become the price leaders in their specialized product categories. The Home Depot and Lowe's were now both vulnerable to a new breed of low-overhead, specialized *category-killer* retailers. This was another element, in addition to cannibalization, that would impact potential store revenue at The Home Depot.

CHANGE ACCELERATES

The retail world is ever dynamic. The Home Depot had even more new challenges to address.

The Home Depot needed to aggregate a larger assemblage of target markets in both the homeowner and professional marketplaces. New products and new services would be needed to reverse the downward individual store sales trend. The existing model was not working as well as in the past, and a business-as-usual attitude would not create the changes needed for healthy, comparable year-on-year store growth. A quantum jump was needed in logistics and systems, driven by technology, to create increased productivity in the brick-and-mortar stores as well as to capitalize on the new opportunities emerging in the area of e-commerce and digital marketing.

It was the start of a new millennium, and with it a perfect storm was brewing that would challenge the *Bleeding Orange* culture and perhaps the very future of the company. Bernie Marcus, the company's chairman, was about to retire. Co-founder Arthur Blank was Bernie's apparent successor, assuring some continuity going forward. However, that picture would soon be obliterated by a whirlwind of change.

8

NEW CEO, NEW GAME PLAN

A new threat to The Home Depot's culture was the board of directors' December 2000 decision to hire Robert ("Bob") Nardelli. They apparently felt The Home Depot had become stagnant and needed new leadership. They hired Nardelli, who had recently left General Electric, and made him the CEO as well as chairman of the board.

This meant founder and CEO Arthur Blank would leave the company. Thus, in a very short period, the two founders of The Home Depot—Bernie Marcus and Arthur Blank—departed, and a huge part of the *Bleeding Orange* culture left with them.

I had left the company five years prior, so the rest of this story is from my observations outside of the company.

A certain aura of success surrounded anyone coming from the "Jack Welch School of Business Success." GE was the darling of Wall Street, and CEO Jack Welch was considered to be the ultimate business guru. Nardelli's GE resume imparted a certain halo effect of ultimate competence. Unfortunately, putting a dynamic retail company in the hands of someone with absolutely no retail experience, let alone any real understanding of The Home Depot culture, was a big gamble.

Nevertheless, Nardelli was given total authority to bring General Electric thinking and processes to The Home Depot. He would be on a mission to change the company's strategies, tactics, and culture, with devastating results.

A CLASH OF CULTURES

The company's board naively underestimated the importance of The Home Depot's decentralized organization, believing General Electric's highly centralized manufacturing culture was superior and transferable to The Home Depot's systems and culture.

The Home Depot had a proud history of success and thousands of dedicated employees still devoted to taking ownership and delighting the customer. This was the essence of the culture. There was a feeling of personal responsibility to make sure the customer had no reason to ever shop elsewhere. Unfortunately, this army of orange-blooded zealots would soon find themselves in confrontation with a new regime that came from a vastly different school of thought.

The new Nardelli-led management team was diametrically opposed to the pillars of The Home Depot's *Bleeding Orange* culture that had proven successful over the preceding twenty years. Decisions would now be made in the executive suite. They would soon give the customers some very good reasons to shop elsewhere.

The Home Depot did have challenges to its own growth. The competitive and technological changes in the marketplace required a new, larger vision and major investments in systems and logistics as the company entered the digital age. Change was needed.

However, Nardelli's 180-degree cultural change did not build on the past success and sought to redefine the very essence of The Home Depot.

NARDELLI'S DEAL

How did this come about? In preparing for his retirement from General Electric, Welch had groomed three people as possible candidates to succeed him as CEO. Nardelli was one of those candidates. When Jeffrey Immelt was chosen in 2000, Nardelli left GE.

Nardelli was able to market himself to The Home Depot board as the embodiment of the brilliant business acumen of Welch and General Electric. Because the board was just as enamored with the GE success story as the rest of the business world, Nardelli negotiated an incredible contract that gave him total control of the company—and one with hefty compensation. The sheer size of the package shocked the business community. According to a 2007 Bloomberg article in *Business Week*, Nardelli's last yearly contract netted him $38.1 million. He was guaranteed a $3 million annual bonus. (He also received a severance package of over $200 million that would ultimately embarrass the board.)

NEW PRIORITIES AND MEASUREMENTS

The Home Depot culture was pervasive for the moment, but times were changing. The seeds for destruction of The Home Depot's valued *Bleeding Orange* culture were sown the day the company founders left and the General Electric culture arrived. I might add that the seeds of General Electric's decline were also in place but would not appear for a number of years.

As we've discussed, the *Bleeding Orange* culture was based on a decentralized organization structure, with decisions purposely pushed down and out to the stores. This created an impetus for taking personal ownership at every level of the company. It was a celebration of creativity and a willingness to learn that created a unique environment focused on serving the customer's needs and desires. It was okay to try something new and fail. In fact, such an initiative would be applauded if it promoted creativity and innovation.

The message from the top of the company had always been that decisions would not be made simply to impact the numbers for the immediate quarter. Rather, the focus would always be on doing what was right for the customer, with the belief that being customer-centric would always pay off and create the right long-term results.

The General Electric structure and philosophy were the antithesis of *Bleeding Orange* culture. In fact, the culture of The Home Depot was anathema to the new management group. Its model was a highly centralized manufacturing organization where directives flowed from the top down. This apparently worked well for a manufacturer with large central manufacturing plants, inherently different from The Home Depot.

The new regime was very numbers driven. The focus was on processes and systems that needed to be precise. The numbers drove the business. The rule was that quarterly financial budgets would be achieved and earnings per share would increase every quarter, regardless of the impact on the stores or the customers' shopping experience. Earnings per share was the *holy grail* and would increase every quarter or heads would roll. Customer satisfaction now took a back seat to the numbers.

CENTRALIZATION

The new regime wasted no time dismantling the matrix organization that placed the merchandisers in their geographical divisions close to their stores and customers. The divisional merchandising offices were closed, and all merchandising decisions were centralized and dictated out of the Atlanta headquarters.

Atlanta is a long way from Seattle, San Diego, Boston, and Miami, and there were significant variations in the local climates, home construction materials, lifestyles, preferred brands, and relevant competitors. The South can experience spring weather while the North is still experiencing winter snow. It can be wet in the Southeast while drought conditions exist out West. The variables across a continent are immense.

A huge communication gap grew between the stores and the centralized merchandising group in Atlanta. The sign in front of the headquarters building still read Store Support Center, but communication now flowed down instead of up.

Processes, systems, and standardization became the order of the day. When veteran company officers tried to explain how some of these new policies were dysfunctional to The Home Depot *Bleeding Orange* culture and the *esprit de corps* of the company, senior management did not understand or appreciate these concerns.

As a result, a large number of The Home Depot's vice presidents and directors left the company. (Fortunately for those departing executives, they had been part of The Home Depot during the amazing growth years. They had the personal wealth of the company's stock and could walk away from the disaster unfolding around them.) This was a huge brain drain for the company, leaving it with a new management team that had no corporate memory and no real understanding of the magic of the *Bleeding Orange* culture. The Home Depot now had corporate amnesia.

NEW CRITERIA FOR SUCCESS

You have to understand the General Electric mentality. It produced airplane engines. Jet engines require a zero-failure rate. You don't want airplanes to fall out of the sky. But retail is a dynamic business that must adjust to constantly changing variables. Innovation and experimentation are necessary. Trying to grow a retail business with zero failures is impossible. Without trial and error, you will never push the envelope. You will never think outside the box. Creativity and innovation will die. The *Bleeding Orange* culture simply could not survive long under this new corporate environment where any failure was considered fatal.

"One area where I think we are especially distinctive is failure. (We have had plenty of practice.) Failure and invention are inseparable twins."
— Jeff Bezos

Experimenting, by definition, involves success and failure. However, failure of any project was now unacceptable and would result in dismissal. Individual initiative and creativity were suppressed. The new company policy was that the bottom ten percent of performers, as defined by achievement to budget, would be automatically dismissed each year.

One of the very best regional managers, who ran the highly successful Northeast division, was transferred to the lagging Midwest division to help turn it around. He had proven to be an effective and outstanding manager in past assignments but could not turn the Midwest around in only one year. Therefore, at the year-end review, he was in the lower ten percent and out of work. The company lost one more superstar.

The *Bleeding Orange* culture that created a cult of believers who could achieve the impossible through personal creativity and initiative simply could not coexist in the new centralized world of rigid General Electric processes. Experimentation and risk taking were no longer part of the culture. The dynamic nature of the business had changed, to the detriment of the employees and the customers.

STRATEGIC MISTAKES, TACTICAL NIGHTMARES

The Home Depot's new imperative was the rigid rule that earnings per share must increase every quarter. There could be no variation. Wall Street needed to be impressed every three months. Policies and directives had to be implemented that would force the quarter's financial results.

Pricing: *The Old Home Depot* was clearly the price leader in the marketplace, and EDLP pricing was the philosophy and the rule. The customers could always count on finding the lowest prices for home-improvement projects at The Home Depot. The simple rule was that we would always win the price battle.

Now, however, pricing became a tool to force quarterly increases in earnings per share. The shortcut to fix any quarter's shortfall in earnings per share was simply to raise prices, regardless of customer demand or competitive offers. The retail accounting system pushes profits to the bottom line when prices are raised. Therefore, increased prices would immediately drive profit results up for the current quarter. A stroke of the pen could greatly improve this quarter's results. Earnings per share would increase—that was the rule.

Quarterly profits did increase, but so did The Home Depot's retail prices. Of course, as prices increased, sales became sluggish and sales trends began to turn negative. This led to a new promotional policy.

EDLP: *The Old Home Depot* was a pioneer in establishing Everyday Low Prices. This created a trust relationship that made limited-time, i*tem/price* advertising unnecessary.

Now prices were raised with no concern for the market or the competitive status. This negatively affected sales, which then led to the need for weekly advertised sales to create store traffic. This was the end of the successful EDLP pricing policy that the sales staff had embraced and the customers had trusted for fifteen years.

The Home Depot had succumbed to the *high/low* pricing practices it had defeated so often in the past. The previous trust relationship no longer existed. There were good times to buy, and other times were not so good. The Home Depot priced some items right, and other items were priced better elsewhere.

The Home Depot was quickly becoming a high-priced retailer with constant promotions to give the illusion of value to the customers. Customers are not stupid; in fact, with the Internet as a tool, they are pretty darn smart! The Home Depot was destroying its price image, which had always been a key strength.

Six Sigma Nightmare: *The Old Home Depot* was customer focused. The new Home Depot was black belt focused. The Six Sigma process-oriented management system was implemented to control cost and eliminate errors. Six Sigma is a system of process improvement that has been used by many companies to reduce defects and increase profitability. It was a central tool of management at General Electric under Jack Welsh.

Six Sigma may have some worthwhile applications to the work process in a controlled manufacturing environment, but it can be detrimental in a retail store application. Whole teams of people can become hyper focused on one variable at the micro level of the business, while thousands of variables in the macro business that are impacting the business in detrimental ways are ignored.

Thousands of employee hours were spent evaluating minutiae instead of taking care of customers. The big-picture problems, like the out-of-stock situation or prices that were no longer competitive, were not the focus. In fact, they really were not even on the radar screen. The employees spent hours in lectures and projects to get their Six Sigma black belts, while the customers were being ignored and enduring Six Sigma Hell. The bureaucrats loved spending hours working on their black belts, while the orange blood was draining out of the company.

Inventory Position: *The Old Home Depot* had a fetish about being in stock on all products all the time. We knew the customers wanted to save money and time. We knew if we abused the value of their time by being out of stock, we would anger the homeowners and lose the professionals' business.

Now the push was for lower and lower inventories, to minimize the amount of working capital required. This helped achieve ROI goals in the short run—until the customers lost confidence that they could obtain the products needed for their projects and began to feel coming to the store was a waste of time. The big picture was that the stores were desperately out of stock, which made project selling virtually impossible. Empty counters fail the customer. This is the unpardonable sin at retail stores in general, but even more in a project-oriented home center.

Instead of taking action to refill empty counters and peg hooks with merchandise, there was a Six Sigma practice of identifying out-of-stock items and placing yellow tags to show that the condition had been acknowledged. Soon every store looked like it had broken out with a severe case of yellow measles. The solution should have been to fix the problem so there would be no reason to put yellow tags in the store. Instead, being out of stock became institutionalized.

People: *The Old Home Depot* insisted on hiring the best people to give competent advice to customers. Our store managers sought experienced people and paid them what they were worth.

Now fixed pay ranges were designed to lower the average hourly pay in the company. The old Home Depot drove down cost intelligently, but these ill-advised cost reductions were destroying the business. Before long most of the old-time experts on the sales floor began to leave the company. Customers found their trusted friend in the plumbing department was no longer there. Good people left the company both in the stores and in the Store Support Center; and it wasn't just money—the troops felt unappreciated and demoralized.

New-Construction Fiasco: *The Old Home Depot's* target markets were both professionals and homeowners involved in repair, remodel, and maintenance of residential buildings. These were synergistic target customers in a relatively non-cyclical segment of the building material industry.

However, The Home Depot now purchased a multitude of wholesale businesses focused on the new-construction business. This is a highly cyclical business that has very little synergy with the core repair, maintenance, and remodeling business of The Home Depot. These acquisitions included plumbing wholesalers, lumberyards, and other businesses dependent upon new construction.

The underlying issue was that The Home Depot had lost its first love. It was no longer working to improve the in-store shopping experience and delight customers with new products and better values. The focus of the company's capital investment was not on improving the big-box home center but on chasing business outside of the stores. The focus and direction of the company was now on the growth of the wholesale new-construction business, which was in an economic bubble that was about to burst.

E-Commerce: *The Old Home Depot* focused on constant improvement within the big-box stores. The new regime initiated a major jump into e-commerce, focused outside of the stores.

You might say it was good timing and great vision to embrace the digital world, and you would be right. However, the problem was not with *what* was done but *how* it was done. An autonomous e-commerce business was established that reported directly to the CEO and was completely separate from the core brick-and-mortar big-box warehouse business.

This required a new team of e-commerce experts with little or no retail background, let alone any orange-blooded experience. This was an expedient way to move quickly but was detrimental to the overall organizational structure. This new business had virtually no synergy or interplay with the stores. There were no hooks to create an interconnected business with the core physical stores, which led to major confusion for the customers, the employees, and the vendors.

The physical store and e-commerce entities began to compete. The store staff had a completely different background and perspective from the digital staff, who came from outside the company. Lowe's was no longer the enemy—the enemy was internal. The brick-and-mortar group wanted to be the best home-improvement store, while the e-commerce group wanted to be Amazon.

A vendor who sold e-commerce could be blocked from selling in the stores and vice versa. A customer who purchased on the Internet was *persona non grata* when attempting to return the product to a store. The immediate impact was to incur incredible new incremental costs and only marginal sales, which created an online business with significant red ink.

The Home Depot's new focus was on growing business outside the stores, with a lack of investment in the core, big-box business. The checkbook was apparently open to fund the 3-percent-of-sales-penetration online business, while the physical stores that represented 97 percent of the business starved for attention and investment.

Store Maintenance: *The Old Home Depot* was not a pretty store. However, it was functional. It may not have always looked good, but it always worked good [sic].

Now if the company was not on track to increase quarterly earnings per share, investments in store maintenance and improvements would just have to wait. This created a situation in which the stores slowly sank into physical distress.

THE NEXT TRANSITION

The company was now in trouble. The stock price had fallen. The trade journals speculated that the company might be ripe for a hostile takeover. The company had accumulated significant assets, but the value of the company on Wall Street was declining. The Home Depot magic had dissipated, and some people would argue it was time to break up the company and redeploy those assets.

> *"Innovation can't be forced, but it can be quashed."*
> — Mat Ridley

It was time for another quantum change, starting again at the top. As the investors saw The Home Depot's stock price stagnate, they became very vocal about the generous compensation package the board had given to Nardelli. The board asked him to take a reduction to calm the investors. However, Nardelli showed little flexibility and had an incredible severance package available. He elected to take it and leave the company.

A new and much more positive chapter in The Home Depot's story was about to begin. Frank Blake would become the next CEO, and he would devote his energies to rejuvenating the stores and reestablishing much of the *Bleeding Orange* culture

PART III

RECONSTRUCTION:
REBUILDING DOMINANCE

REVIVING THE ORANGE CULTURE

In 2007 Bob Nardelli was out, and Frank Blake became the new CEO of The Home Depot. Nardelli had recruited Frank to join The Home Depot, where he focused on mergers and acquisitions. Like Nardelli, Blake did not have a retail background. He was a lawyer and had been the general council for General Electric before becoming deputy secretary for the U.S. Department of Energy. Fortunately, Blake had a completely different management style than Nardelli.

Blake was an excellent listener with an open mind. He saw that the current strategies were not adding value to the company. It helped that his son was one of The Home Depot's store managers. Blake listened to The Home Depot's remaining veterans and gained an appreciation for the *Bleeding Orange* culture of the company's first twenty years. Then he committed himself to reestablishing many of the business practices that had worked so well in creating The Home Depot.

Once again, serving the customer became critical to the company culture. This led to a renewal of the *Bleeding Orange* values. This can be best explained by a picture of The Home Depot's inverted pyramid.

The inverted pyramid is a triangle that puts the customers at the base but then turns the triangle upside down. The base—the customers—is now at the top of the chain of command. Next come the store associates, followed by middle management. The CEO is in the peak of the triangle but at the very bottom.

This is a restatement and reinforcement of the philosophy that called the corporate office *the Store Support Center*. It puts the priority on serving the customer and empowering the employees closest to them.

REVIVING THE CULTURE

Reviving the *Bleeding Orange* culture was a huge task. The Home Depot was a very big enterprise that had truly lost its way; its brand was tarnished. The bigger the ship, the harder it is to turn, and The Home Depot was an exceptionally large ship.

Blake wasted no time implementing changes that would enhance the vitality of The Home Depot's big orange box. The focus would once again be on improving the customer experience in the physical store.

Of course, the past was the past, and many of the orange-blooded veterans were gone. The company had changed, as had the market. Things would never again be the same as in the first twenty years. But at least now many of the recent errors were being corrected.

NEW POSITIVE TRENDS

The period of lost culture had been a temporary gift to Lowe's. The ancient Dutch philosopher Desiderius Erasmus is credited with saying, "In the land of the blind, the one-eyed man is king." Certainly, for a period of time, The Home Depot had lost its customer service crown, and Lowe's appeared to be royalty, in comparison.

The following chart from Wolfe Research, LLC, shows the change of market share, as measured by comparable store growth, between Lowe's and The Home Depot. It clearly marks the year in which The Home Depot lost its way and how Lowe's gained market share for nine years as a result of the changes initiated by the Nardelli regime. But the policies and actions of Frank Blake and his team eventually turned the advantage back to The Home Depot.

We can see how sensitive the customers are to receiving good service versus bad service and how quickly they respond. While this chart only takes us through 2014, The Home Depot continued to increase market share for many more years.

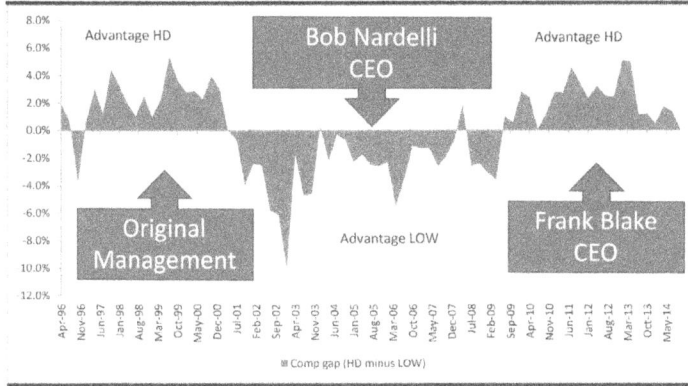

History of Market Share Growth Lowes Vs. Depot

Exhibit 4: The comp gap over time

Source: Wolfe Research, Company filings

It is revealing to see just how quickly the customers moved away from The Home Depot and then back again, based on their in-store experience. The customer is truly in charge. The impact of diminishing the *Bleeding Orange* culture of the company was felt first by the employees working in the stores and then by the customers shopping in the stores.

While the company's top line had grown, through new-store growth and acquisition of the wholesale business units, the price of The Home Depot stock on the New York Stock Exchange was stagnant. During the same period, the value of Lowe's stock more than doubled. The purposeful dismantling of The Home Depot's unique culture had an incredible impact on both companies but in opposite directions. But now a light shone at the end of the tunnel—a bright orange light!

REFOCUSING ON THE BIG ORANGE BOX

Blake was brought in by Nardelli to initiate a merger and acquisition initiative that would diversify The Home Depot into the new-construction segment of the building material industry. This led to establishing the HD Supply wholesale building material division, which cobbled together eleven wholesale businesses. This became a significant percentage of the company's overall business.

However, early in his tenure as CEO, Blake sold this division to refocus the company's efforts on enhancing the core big *orange* box home-center business. He understood that the strength and competitive advantage of The Home Depot was its focus on the repair, remodel, and maintenance business, not the new-construction business. (Home Depot would repurchase HD Supply thirteen years later after a much scaled-down HD Supply had spun off all the new-construction business and was focused on the repair and maintenance of commercial buildings.)

Blake's timing in selling the wholesale business at the end of August 2007 was perfect. The 2008 housing crash was about to create a depression in the new-construction industry.

Another huge move was to reorganize the relatively autonomous e-commerce business. The staff were told they would no longer be working for an autonomous entity and that their jobs would need to be integrated into the structure of the core big-box home-center group. The goal now was a new team effort committed to developing an interconnected retail business that was customer-centric; the customers would decide how they would like to buy, how they would like to take delivery, and how they would like to return products.

The Home Depot changed its digital marketing focus from that of a company with multiple isolated management silos to a more integrated company focused on creating a One Home Depot experience.

THE DEMISE OF THE HOME DEPOT EXPO DIVISION

Blake also closed all fifty of the Home Depot Expo stores. This division was a group of big-box stores focused on interior decor.

The idea for the Expo stores had come from an internal meeting in which we were asked to define the biggest threat to The Home Depot's big-box home-center business. We recognized that we operated a number of related businesses under one roof, including construction materials/ tools, home decor, and garden/seasonal. We concluded that the biggest threat would not be another home center but a specialist operating a big-box store that would concentrate on only one of these core businesses.

Around this time a piece of property in San Diego came up for sale. It was only one mile from our highest-volume West Coast store, so we purchased it to keep our competitor, HomeClub, from buying it. Now we needed to find a use for the property.

The answer was to test our theory by opening a store the size of The Home Depot focused entirely on interior decor. The Home Depot Expo Division was born. Since I was responsible for West Coast merchandising at the time, the Expo experiment became my special project.

The original idea was to democratize the home design business. Any number of interior designers and specialty retailers catered to the top five percent of the home decor market. But the Home Depot Expo aimed to bring these prestige products, brands, and services to the middle class.

The motto for the Home Depot Expo was *Expo Style—Home Depot Prices*. This experimental Expo in San Diego proved to successfully generate sales without impacting The Home Depot sister store nearby. Expo could pull business from the independent specialty stores but, more importantly, it expanded the market for interior design products by bringing design services to The Home Depot's typical middle-class customer.

Soon stores were opened in Atlanta, New York, and Dallas under the Expo banner. These new stores quickly changed the local market for home decor, and each generated sales of over a million dollars per week per location. This was a big-ticket project business requiring a high degree of customer service to coordinate project design, special order, assembly, delivery, and installation. It is not possible to offer these kinds of services with efficiency and accuracy without highly sophisticated IT systems. Unfortunately, the company did not have adequate systems in place to manage this complex business. This created growing problems, due to the sheer size and volume of the Expo business. This led to a series of tactical and strategic changes ultimately caused the Expo to lose its vision of serving the middle class.

New stores opened across the country, often in markets characterized by middle-class demographics. But these stores did not do as well as planned.

There is always a tendency when dealing with the design community to become too *avant-garde*, which is dangerous for a mass merchant. Much of the Expo business became focused on the very top end of the designer market. It also became too dependent upon servicing the new-construction custom homebuilder. This market evaporated in 2008 with the housing crisis, which virtually shut down new construction. In January 2009 Frank Blake took the hit and closed all the stores in the Expo group.

GETTING OUT OF CHINA

Blake also decided to close the Chinese store division in 2012. This was one of the last acquisitions he had made under the Nardelli regime. It involved purchasing the Chinese HomeWay home-center chain in 2006 for a reported $100 million. (These were the same stores the board had refused to support with an equity position back in 1994.)

The American home-center model does not work in China for many reasons. All the American and European home-center retailers that entered the China market failed.

I can point out many of these obstacles from my experience as a board member of HomeWay's parent company. A brief list of reasons would include:

- Most middle-class Chinese lived in high-rise concrete buildings, not single-family homes.

- Labor was cheap, so there was virtually no DIY market.

- The supply chain was monopolized by domestic wholesalers, each of whom dominated the business in their city. They dictated prices at cost and retail, resulting in extremely low margins for the retailer.

- The retail workforce in China was very unsophisticated and unable to truly provide project assistance to the customers. In most cases the wholesaler supplied and controlled the retail workforce. Big orders were redirected to the wholesaler, cutting out the big-box retailer.

- The middle management of a retail business in China was most likely corrupted by the vendors.

- The laws and, more specifically, the exceptions to the laws regarding business operations and taxes were different for foreign-owned companies than for Chinese companies.

- The Chinese government channeled funds to domestic companies to determine the winners and losers in the marketplace.

- Import duties were high, but corruption made these imported products available in the marketplace. As a result, it was impossible for companies that followed the law to compete with key products and brands.

- A foreign company simply never plays on a level playing field in China, as business is relationship-based, not rule-of-law based.

- A wide gap exists between the cultural values of the West and the cultural values inherent in China, particularly as they relate to ideas of good versus bad or right versus wrong.

SETTING THE STAGE FOR FUTURE GROWTH

Blake at first put the China project on the back burner but ultimately closed the stores and left the Asian market. All the focus and attention of The Home Depot management would now be on the One Home Depot concept of enhancing the core, big orange box stores in North America.

Having removed all the distractions from The Home Depot's core business, Blake began to take the steps necessary to enhance customer service and reinvigorate The Home Depot brand. The focus changed from opening new stores to growing the year-to-year business in the existing stores by increasing sales per square foot.

This entailed selling more products and services to The Home Depot's current customers by enhancing the store shopping experience. It also required aggregating a larger number of market segments to reach new target customers. The company was now refocused and committed to enhancing the customer shopping experience both off-line and online. The DIY customer still constituted the core business, but the future growth would be focused on the professional-business segments, online sales, and installed sales services.

In the next chapter we will explore the ongoing initiatives that are taking The Home Depot to new levels of customer convenience and service. Specifically, we will explore innovations in the areas of store service, point-of-sale merchandising, logistics, digital marketing, e-commerce, installed sales, and pro sales.

10

HOME DEPOT REGAINS ITS DOMINANCE

In 2015 Frank Blake had put in five years as head of The Home Depot and was ready to move on. Craig Menear became CEO. Under Menear, a merchandising veteran of The Home Depot, the company has accelerated the revival initiated by Blake. Menear is committed to the *orange blood* idea of making customer service the focal point of store activity.

Many elements of the *Bleeding Orange* culture appear to be back in place, with the inverted pyramid (see chapter 9) guiding priorities for all decision-making. Here are some of the positive steps The Home Depot has taken that have helped to continue to grow sales, profitability, and return on investment—cementing the company's dominant position in the home- improvement industry.

RENEWING CUSTOMER SERVICE

In the early days, when Bernie Marcus would walk the stores, one of his first questions would be "How many people are on staff with gray hair?" Each store manager knew the answer for his or her store.

Many of these older associates were former tradesmen or had other professional industry experience. These mature folks had great product knowledge, usually combined with outgoing personalities. They came to be known as Bernie Boys, a term of endearment they wore proudly. It meant they were valuable and appreciated. And best of all: Customers could trust these experts with their projects.

After the Nardelli regime, it was critical for The Home Depot to restore the expertise that had been missing for seven years. Imposed wage controls and lack of recognition had chased so many great salespeople out of the company. The Home Depot worked hard to bring back many of the mature salespeople and restore previous levels of product knowledge. It's an ongoing priority.

ENHANCING THE STORE EXPERIENCE

The revival continued with a new commitment to increased self-service convenience throughout the store. This can be seen in the point-of-sale displays and signing throughout the stores. The stores are now *easy to stock, easy to sell, and easy to buy.*

This self-service convenience is complemented by trained staffing in specific areas of the store, where customers must be able to interact with expert associates one-on-one to have their questions answered and their projects designed. These knowledgeable salespeople offer personal project assistance in areas like millwork (windows and doors), kitchen and bath, interior decor (flooring and window treatments), and paint. Real experts are absolutely critical in two other areas as well: the customer service area at the entrance of the store, and the professional services area at the exit to the building material section.

Competence has returned to the sales floor, and gray hair is back in style.

SMARTER SERVICE

Product knowledge is even more critical now, as the information readily available on the Internet has made today's customer more sophisticated. The bar has been raised. In addition to enhancing the store experience with knowledgeable people, The Home Depot has given its sales staff state-of-the-art technology in the form of "smart" handheld devices and customer service terminals with access to the company's intranet and the Internet. Educational and training curricula focus on giving the sales associates the confidence to assist customers using the new digital tools, all in order to meet the customers' new expectations.

The new customer service goal ensures that 60 percent of all store personnel now focus on interacting with the customer in an *eyeball-to-eyeball* relationship. The key is to make sure every person wearing an orange apron understands that job number one is sales resulting from interacting with the customer. Knowledgeable people are once again appreciated, recognized, and rewarded. Customer service is celebrated!

STRUCTURAL CHANGES TO IMPROVE CUSTOMER SERVICE

To free sales associates to focus on customer contact, another group of employees has been put in place. Members of the Merchandise Execution Team (MET) wear orange shirts instead of orange aprons and report directly to the merchandising department.

MET is tasked with doing normal housekeeping, such as down-stocking inventory, maintaining signs, updating bin labels, supplying sales literature, and ensuring that every eight-foot bay in the store is in compliance with the approved merchandising planogram, to facilitate self-service.

These employees also implement the planned promotional strategies for the impulse areas of the store, such as end caps and the impact sales area at the front of each store. In these areas special buys are purchased by the merchandising group, programed into the annual promotional calendar and displayed for designated time periods. The MET group is also involved in the merchandising resets required time to time.

The objective of the MET program is to make sure conditions in the store are always *easy to stock, easy to sell, and easy to buy,* so the sales associates in the orange aprons can focus their full attention on serving the customers.

BETTER USE OF THE 24-HOUR CLOCK

A separate MET group rotates to the stores and performs major store resets, primarily in the dark hours, when the store is not open. This has given The Home Depot the ability to roll out new programs with full compliance to over two thousand stores with remarkable speed.

Nighttime receiving of incoming merchandise is handled by a dedicated team so the incoming freight can be brought to the floor while the store is closed. This averts problems for customers in peak traffic hours. The Home Depot stores work on a schedule. Designated high-traffic periods are focused intensely on customer service; at other specific times the staff is focused on getting the store ready to service the customer.

SPEED OF SERVICE TAKES PRIORITY

Expediting the customer in and out of the store is another new focus. This includes self-checkout lanes, where one cashier can simultaneously serve multiple customers. The full-service checkout areas have been re-engineered to quickly move customers and products through the process. The cashier stands together with the customer, and the computer terminal screen facilitates a wide range of activities and information, so any need or request of the customer can be quickly provided.

Cashiers are trained in the mechanics of the job and in the importance of providing the customer with friendly, helpful, personal experience. This is important since the cashier is usually the last person to interact with the customer before he or she leaves the store.

BETTER AND FASTER SERVICE

Whenever interaction with a customer can be traced, such as in the process of checking out, or making home deliveries, or installing products in the customer's home, the customer's satisfaction level will be measured. Electronic surveys are used to determine voice-of-customer scores. The customer responses are constantly monitored and posted to keep everyone focused on job number one. The employees know their *voice-of-customer* score and work to always improve.

The objective is to always respond quickly to the customer's needs and desires. A premium is placed on being able to identify the customer's problem, solve the problem, and get them on their way quickly and competently.

The Home Depot website reminds customers, "Time is money, and we save you both." For many customers, time is more important than money. The goal on the website is for the customer to zero in on a desired product in three clicks. Speed is now a *unique, sustainable, compelling, competitive advantage* at The Home Depot. It is technology that provides the tools for speed and accuracy. The Home Depot's approach to disciplined capital allocation has kept this technology at the cutting edge.

LOGISTICS PLAYS IMPORTANT ROLE IN CUSTOMER SERVICE

The advent of the Internet has greatly changed customer expectations. As just one example, the customer has been offered a sea change in terms of home and jobsite delivery. The Home Depot has responded to this challenge.

Bulky high-cube, low-value products like cement and lumber are a major part of the home-center business. This creates challenges that the pure-play Internet providers have not and really cannot address. But The Home Depot is making massive investments in technology and facilities to bring these products into the store (upstream) at the lowest landed costs and then to deliver them to the customer (downstream) quickly, on time, complete, undamaged—when and where the customer wants them.

There is a new vision of offering the customer delayed or same-day service, depending upon the need. New systems and facilities to deliver what is promised when it's promised have been a major part of the capital investments during the Menear administration

CREATING DISTRIBUTION EFFICIENCIES

The upstream flow of products, from vendor to store, has been accomplished with a combination of specialized facilities, each of which serves a specific function. This includes:

- *Flatbed distribution yards* located on rail heads facilitate the flow of lumber and other full-unit, mixed-load shipments of building materials to stores. This minimizes freight cost by bringing products from the vendors to the major markets on rail cars and then building mixed loads of these full units for shipment to the stores by flatbed sideloaded trucks.

- *Import distribution centers [DCs]* are high-cube facilities to store imported products. They serve as a bulge in the supply line for imported products that have a long lead-time in the ordering and receiving process.

- *Rapid response cross-dock centers* strategically placed across the country. They receive full truck shipments from domestic vendors and then cross-dock to full trucks of mixed-vendor products for the stores.

- *Direct fulfillment centers* stock only products being offered directly to the customer via e-commerce. The products are then shipped directly to the customer—or to the stores if the customer prefers the store-pickup option.

Separating these upstream shipments by function allows the company to isolate the costs, design the most efficient facilities and equipment, and, in the process, drive down costs.

The downstream programs recognize that for many products the store is not the end of the supply chain but, rather, one more link to the customers' homes or jobsites. This repositions the store to be both a pickup depot for almost half the online orders and the facilitating point for most customer returns.

It also sees the store as a warehouse and shipping point en route to customers' homes or jobsites for much of the bulk building materials. In addition, the company is investing in specialized facilities that will allow faster service to the customer from direct fulfillment building material centers located strategically in the major metropolitan markets across the country.

The focus is no longer on building volume by opening new stores but on improving services to capture a larger share of the DIY homeowners' wallet while aggregating a larger market with both the do-it-for-me customer and the professional customer.

The primary function of a retail store is simply to be in stock when the customer wants a product. The Home Depot has made big investments in technology, systems, and facilities to assure that this job is done well, both for both off-line and online transactions, while constantly increasing inventory turnover.

One critical driver is that The Home Depot purchases its products on an ex-factory basis and can, therefore, totally control the logistic function of getting the product from the producer to the ultimate customer in the quickest and lowest-cost manner.

DIGITAL MERCHANDISING AND E-COMMERCE

The Home Depot website is now seen as the front door to the store. This recognizes that a project may start on the website, but the customer's journey may intersect with many different touch points. The touch points might include the Internet, the store, the call center, or an authorized third-party entity. In every case the customer needs to see one company, one mission, and one brand. Most likely, this journey will ultimately bring the customer in contact with the physical store.

The Home Depot is recognized as one of the most competent online retailers, with an ever-increasing percentage of their business coming though this channel. Over one million SKUs are offered, with perhaps thirty thousand of those in the store. Most of the remaining choices are stocked in vendor facilities but shipped to the customer in The Home Depot cartons with The Home Depot paperwork and packaging, so it is clear The Home Depot is selling and taking responsibility for each shipment. The majority of e-commerce orders are shipped directly from the vendors. The Home Depot does, however, operate a few dedicated direct fulfillment DCs for some specific categories of product that make sense to inventory and ship themselves.

E-commerce sales are credited to the local brick-and-mortar store, based on zip code analysis, to ensure store ownership of both online and in-store customers. Many online orders actually originate in the stores. The stores provide a significant piece of the e-commerce logistics; they are a convenient location for product pickup for orders placed online and shipped from vendors or The Home Depot fulfillment centers. The stores also serve as a source of building materials and other bulky products that can be delivered to the customer's home or jobsite. The customers' preferred method of returning products is via the local Home Depot store, even if they purchased online. Project sales are often accomplished through multiple touch points, both on the Internet and in the physical stores.

COMMUNICATION AND STORE CONNECTIVITY

E-commerce is only one piece of the digital strategy. The Home Depot website is the primary mechanism for communicating with customers.

Promotional offers are now primarily presented on the website; print media is extremely limited. Digital promotional items might include a local promotion catalogue, a feature story on the home page, or direct e-message communication.

The website also offers a vast library of inspirational and how-to videos. The goal is to establish The Home Depot as the go-to source for all home-improvement projects. In addition to e-commerce products, many services can also be accessed via the website, such as providers for installation projects.

The website connects the customer to the store by showing local store inventory levels of products the customer is interested in. A map is provided that takes the customer from the item on their phone or computer to the store, then to the aisle in the store, and then to the bay in the aisle where the product is stocked.

Customers can use *augmented reality* on The Home Depot app to show how products might look in their own setting. They can also use reverse searches to find items on the website to duplicate and replace current items in the home.

The Home Depot has mobile apps designed specifically for homeowners and for professional customers. These very helpful tools provide shopping ease and information that lead to customer convenience and loyalty.

The Home Depot is the largest retailer of home-improvement products on the Internet. Its online sales have grown at a faster rate than Amazon's. They are clearly the winning model in omnichannel retailing. This One Home Depot strategy is the essence of *interconnected retailing*. The Home Depot sets the pace for digital marketing and e-commerce for the home-improvement industry.

IN-HOME SERVICE

The Home Depot has the ability to sell and install numerous project categories with competence. They have simple programs through which customers can obtain quick, professional installation on products purchased in the store. Expert sales associates in the store and at the call center can design more complex projects; an entire room, such as a kitchen, can be designed, procured, delivered, and installed.

Another program that is managed via the call center facilitates design and installation service on more complex projects that require home visits. In many cases the store merely displays a project and invites the customer to contact a call center, which will then send a qualified vendor to the jobsite to design, quote, sell, deliver, and install a product or project.

Pro Referral is a service offered via the Internet through which The Home Depot acts as a broker to unite people who need a home service with service suppliers. The wide range of available services goes far beyond simply installing a product purchased in the store or on the website. The customer can go to The Home Depot website to select a service provider and then set an appointment.

The Home Depot has the processes, systems, and supply chain to take a customer from project design all the way through the process to installation and total satisfaction. Does this mean installed sales projects never encounter problems? No, there will be occasions when a service goes wrong. The key is having processes, systems, and a culture of urgency to correct the situation. In fact, the systems in place track each step in the customer satisfaction process in an effort to discover problems and fix them before they become customer concerns.

Homeowners in need of professional services can contract with their own professional contractor, have The Home Depot take over the entire job, or use The Home Depot's website to find qualified service providers. No matter how the homeowner wishes to pursue his or her project, competent programs are in place to assure fulfillment within each of these three alternatives.

SELLING THE PRO

The great success of The Home Depot, compared to its nearest rival, Lowe's, is largely due to the amount of business it does with the professional customer focused on repair, remodeling, and maintenance. The Home Depot consistently proves its ability to save them time and money.

Some of The Home Depot's pro-friendly practices include:

- Stores are located near the customer's home, which is the jobsite.

- Prices are comparable to—and sometimes better than—the prices offered by specialty wholesalers.

- The stores are open longer hours, seven days a week, which is a great convenience and time saver for the tradesman.

- The Home Depot offers most major brands preferred by professionals.

- Multiple credit programs offer both a revolving credit program, with payments over time, and a sixty-day, interest-free program, depending on the professional customer's need.

- Excellent in-stock availability and an easy return policy save the professional customer time and money.

- Home and jobsite delivery are available, often with same-day service.

- The Home Depot pro app offers the professional an incredible database of information, making it easy to buy products and manage their business.

- E-commerce allows the professional to purchase products and services on a 24/7 basis.

- Highly qualified salespeople are available to serve the professional on the sales floor and in the customer service checkout area.

- Special events at store level celebrate the professional customer, with vendor demonstrations and other rewards to show appreciation.

- There are special prices on selected items when purchased in quantity, cumulative discounts on paint, and special pricing for large projects.

THE COMPETITIVE ADVANTAGE OF TECHNOLOGY

The Home Depot offers a comprehensive app designed for the professional to research product, order merchandise, check credit data, get tips on doing jobs correctly, check inventories, find products in the store, and research past purchases. Investing in this technology has provided a huge competitive advantage.

In 2015 The Home Depot acquired Interline, an e-commerce supplier of maintenance supplies for the commercial business community, with distribution hubs across the country. This maintenance, repair, and operations (MRO) resource has been rebranded The Home Depot Pro and now provides the total product and service offering as part of its professional customer program. This allows The Home Depot to provide building materials, repair items, and maintenance supplies to both residential and commercial business establishments.

EXPANSION BEYOND THE BOX

The Home Depot does operate some businesses outside its core big-box business. These include Home Decorators, an online furniture and accessory store, and The Company Store, a complete online source for domestics such as bedding and towels. It also operates Blinds.com, an online window-coverings retailer.

These online businesses would seem to be a natural core for a new omni-channel opportunity, bringing them together into a decor-based physical store that could take market share from IKEA and Bed Bath and Beyond. A new physical store format that incorporated the company's existing e-commerce entities and aimed at the middle-class mass market could be a winning combination, with multiple-store potential both domestically and perhaps internationally. However, nothing indicates that such an initiative is imminent.

The Home Depot does operate two decor-focused stores known as The Home Depot Design Center. These stores target the extreme top percentile of the home decorator market and have little synergy with the demographics of The Home Depot core customer. This is a high-end, finite market that is relatively well served by decorators and specialty retailers. This is somewhat surprising, considering the past experience of exiting this market when closing the Home Depot Expo stores.

INTERNATIONAL VISION

The Home Depot, while being the dominant home-improvement retailer in North America, has no announced plans to grow beyond this geographical boundary. However, the worldwide retail market for home-improvement and building materials is larger outside the North American continent. The super cities of tomorrow will be outside the United States.

The company got a black eye in South America, but that was twenty years ago. The Home Depot today is a stronger and smarter company. It is by far the premier retailer worldwide in both online and off-line retailing of home-improvement products and is more advanced in terms of technology and logistics than most of its international counterparts.

The Home Depot states that one of their strategic pillars is "Disciplined capital allocation driving productivity." This puts the growth focus on sales per store, as opposed to depending on new stores to drive increased sales. This has worked well for the company over the past ten years. The question remains as to whether the opportunity and need exist to implement these same productivity gains though acquisition of existing home-center groups in the global market.

FUTURE CHALLENGES

The Home Depot is once again the gold standard in the home-improvement retailing world. Its customers are clearly indicating this with their dollar votes at the cash register. The company continues to grow its business, primarily by increasing average ticket sales. This indicates their ability to gain a larger share of the homeowner's wallet by making complete project sales, while also growing the share of business being done with the professional customer.

The current incredible success of The Home Depot has been accomplished with major commitments to technology and logistics. These investments have provided increased customer service, while driving down costs and greatly increasing the company's profitability. The merchants now have great tools that were not available in the past to better serve the customer.

Has The Home Depot been able to completely reinstate the *Bleeding Orange* culture of the first twenty years? No. The days of the Grim Reaper advertising or Homer walking his pet piranha to eat high prices are gone forever. In fact, the Homer mascot seems to be gone. The Home Depot is now an operationally driven company, which has created incredible efficiency and productivity that have had a very positive impact on the company's bottom line. The Home Depot is the dominant home-improvement retailer in North America, and it has established this position by being able to serve both the homeowner and professional at a high level of satisfaction. However, The Home Depot does not appear to have the same cult following with homeowners that it had in the past, when it seemed to be everybody's favorite store.

Over the past few years the J.D. Power Company has conducted surveys to determine the favorite store of homeowners for home-improvement products. The top scores did not go to The Home Depot; they went to Ace Hardware.

In recent surveys, homeowners gave slightly higher scores to two other big-box home centers: Menards and Lowe's. Keep in mind that these are scores from homeowners. The bottom line is that The Home Depot does not seem to have reestablished its most-favored status with homeowners. But it does occupy a unique position as the best store at *simultaneously serving the homeowner and the professional customer*. This synergy gives The Home Depot its dominant market position in the home-improvement and building material markets.

THE PRICING DIFFERENCE

These customer preference scores indicate that The Home Depot still has top-line growth potential to increase market share with homeowners— or, conversely, to lose market share to competitors with better homeowner ratings. The challenge to The Home Depot of today is to more fully embrace the *Bleeding Orange* culture that created a fanatical customer base in the past. This would require the company to recommit itself to being *merchandising driven* and implementing changes aimed at delighting the homeowners, just as it has so successfully expanded its programs for the professional customers. This would require again embracing a culture that abhors having homeowners standing in competitors' stores.

Why are tool customers standing in the Harbor Freight stores? Why is Lowe's the largest seller of major appliances? Why is Floor & Decor the category killer for flooring projects? Why does Best Buy dominate the smart home category and high-end appliances? Why are batteries, trash bags, and light bulbs cheaper at Costco? Why does IKEA sell so many kitchens? Why is Ace Hardware rated number one in customer service? Why does J.D. Power rate other big-box home centers more highly? Why do Home Advisor and Angie's List monopolize the airways for installed sales?

Pricing policy is one area in which The Home Depot may be forfeiting leadership in some key product categories. While the official company line is that The Home Depot continues to have everyday low prices, their promotional policies more often resemble a high/low pricing policy with limited-time sales. The Home Depot's pricing is good, but do all customers believe they will *always* get the best deal at The Home Depot?

The original tagline used in conjunction with The Home Depot logo was *Low Prices Are Just the Beginning.* This later evolved to *More Saving, More Doing.* Today the tagline is *How Doers Get More Done.*

Let's take a look at this evolution. The first tagline made pricing the key point. Low prices were implied in the second tagline. Price and value are not stated or implied in the current tagline. Is there a reason for this change in message?

Once a brand loses the customers' confidence, it is hard to regain their faith. The days when nobody could beat The Home Depot's price leadership died during the Nardelli regime two decades ago. The current practice of running limited-time sales will never reestablish a trust relationship. In fact, it promotes the idea that there are good times and not so good times to purchases products at The Home Depot.

Price and value image are key to the brand image of any big-box operator. At one time, EDLP pricing was the primary value message to the customer. Today it is more likely to be a "special buy" or

> *"To ask is to grow."*
> —Rabbi Lord
> Jonathan Sacks

other limited-time sale message. Pricing is just one example of asking strategic questions in regard to customer brand preference and loyalty.

The main point here is *not* pricing. The question that must be asked is, if the customers are at the top of the inverted pyramid, why are they often standing in a competitor's store for home-improvement products?

STILL KING OF THE HILL

Perhaps another wild-and-crazy upstart company with low margins will recognize the window of opportunity to establish a new value brand. It might not be a *Bleeding Orange* message; perhaps there is a Bleeding Green or Bleeding Red somewhere over the horizon. The wheel of retailing rolls on!

Today's world is not the same as it was thirty years ago, and The Home Depot is not the same company. As we have surveyed its history, we have seen how The Home Depot grew and prospered when the culture focused on delighting the customer. We also saw how the company became inwardly focused on processes and numbers and nearly destroyed this all-important culture, with detrimental results.

Today we see that The Home Depot is revived and growing. This is a credit to Craig Menear and his team. He has recommitted the organization to the idea of the inverted pyramid that once again makes customer satisfaction the primary merchandising goal. Putting customer satisfaction and loyalty at the top of corporate priorities will further increase sales and improve the numbers on the bottom line. The Home Depot is executing their business plan with precision, and their continued increases in sales and market share prove the point.

The Home Depot deserves to be proud of its past and current accomplishments. The remaining question is whether another quantum jump in market share going forward is possible. Will The Home Depot of today take on competitors with a vengeance and regain cult status with the DIY homeowners?

The Home Depot certainly has the assets and momentum to redefine the market (again!) and create new paradigms that can shape new standards for excellence in the home-improvement industry. For the record, I am a happy stockholder of The Home Depot, as are my children and my children's children.

The Home Depot is once again a model of the high-performance retailer. When you look at the history of The Home Depot and consider the increased value of the company and the dividends paid out over the years, it is one of the truly iconic success stories of America. How rewarding it has been to be a part of it!

We have undertaken a forty-year overview of a dramatic American success story, from my personal viewpoint as both an early participant and a later observer. The story line was not inevitable. It was not even likely. There are many reasons why The Home Depot shouldn't have been so successful. It took an incredible company culture to survive the challenges, to persevere, and to win.

When I was with The Home Depot, the trade journals, investors, and other home-center operators always asked: "What is the secret of your success?" The questioner might follow up with, "Is it the low pricing, the size of the stores, the breadth of assortment?"

These are understandable assumptions. But success was never dependent upon the pricing, the product assortment, or the size of the store. It was always about the people and the secret ingredient that turned these people into winners. That powerful elixir was always one thing: *the Bleeding Orange* culture. The Home Depot story is far from over. It will be interesting and exciting to see how Craig Menear and his orange-aproned associates continue to build on this base.

What have we learned from forty years of The Home Depot history? What are the principles that guided the company to incredible success? What can retailers learn from this story about creating and running a high productivity retail business? Those principles will be outlined next in Part 4.

PART IV

BLUEPRINTS FOR SUCCESS:
PRINCIPLES FOR ANY RETAIL OPERATION

11

THE ART OF MERCHANDISING
PRINCIPLE 1:
MERCHANDISING IS AN ART EMBRACING CHANGE.

We have spent the first three parts of this book looking at the history of The Home Depot. We've seen how its *Bleeding Orange* culture focused on delighting the customer. This fostered incredible growth and prosperity for the stakeholders while driving down the cost of home-improvement for its customers—and ultimately revolutionized the home-improvement retail business. We also observed how the company became inwardly fixated on processes and short term numbers, which took the focus off delighting the customer and damaged its brand image.

Real, viable, long-term success demands a perpetual pursuit of the customers, in order to gain and maintain their loyalty. That is the essence of being a *merchandising-driven company*.

Now we'll draw upon the history of The Home Depot to identify *ten universal principles* any retailer can apply to become a successful merchandising-driven company.

I would like to add that the principles we will look at hold true not only domestically, but they also work on an international basis.

Two years after leaving The Home Depot in 1996, I was fortunate to establish a consulting relationship with some of the leading home-center retailers in the world. This led to working twenty years with the Hornbach Company, based in Germany, which operates stores in nine European countries, and with Sodimac, based in Chile, which has stores in seven Latin America countries.

I have advised the Komeri Company, which operates over 1,200 stores in Japan and worked with Bunnings, the dominant home-improvement retailer in Australia. I served on the board of Home World, which operated multiple shopping centers, including twelve HomeWay home centers in China.

While these markets are all unique, with their own idiosyncrasies, the core principles are valid and transferable worldwide. But let's start with the basics.

CHANGE IS THE CONSTANT IN RETAIL

Before we talk about the first of the ten principles, we must remember that it is absolutely critical for a growing company to be *merchandising driven*. In chapter 1 we saw example after example of once-great retailers that no longer exist because they lost their passion for delighting their customers. Think of past giants such as Woolworths, A&P, Kmart, Circuit City, Sears, Sports Authority, Toys'R'Us, and RadioShack. Mall-based department stores are current prime examples of retailers that have lost the pulse of their customers. Consider the bankruptcies of Neiman Marcus and JC Penny. We could add many other names to the list, now and in the future.

What's the pattern? It's a revolving scenario. The birth, growth, maturity, and death of once innovative, merchandising-driven companies can be called the *wheel of retailing*. The wheel of retailing has a lot of versions. But the stories of constructive destruction, where old precepts die and give birth to better solutions, all tell how companies dealt (or didn't deal) with change.

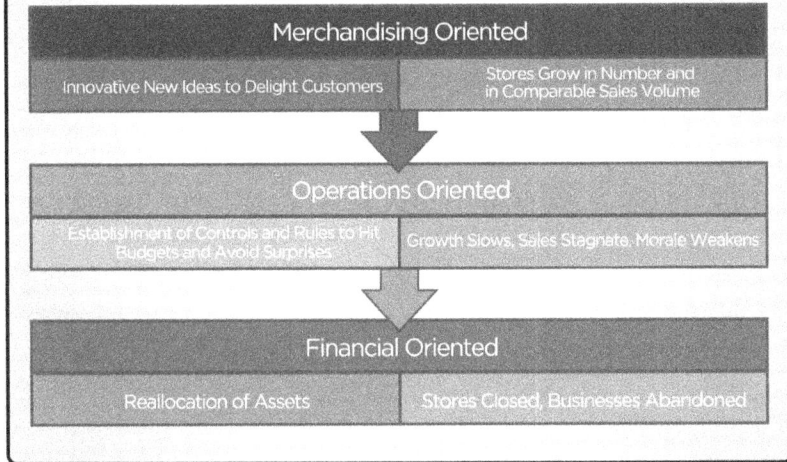

History of Retailing Failures
Bankrupt Past Leaders: Woolworths, A&P, Kmart, Circuit City, Sears, Sports Authority, Toys-R-Us, RadioShack

Merchandising Oriented

Innovative New Ideas to Delight Customers | Stores Grow in Number and in Comparable Sales Volume

Operations Oriented

Establishment of Controls and Rules to Hit Budgets and Avoid Surprises | Growth Slows, Sales Stagnate, Morale Weakens

Financial Oriented

Reallocation of Assets | Stores Closed, Businesses Abandoned

How to Kill an Innovator

Every exciting new retailer starts as a *merchandising-driven* organization. When they lose that orientation, they lose their customers. Modern history is filled with examples.

Think of market innovators we previously mentioned that ultimately went bankrupt. Consider the many large retail chains that have recently closed their stores forever. Each of these companies defined a winning retail format of their time, only to lose the game in the long run.

This scenario is sadly repeated in an almost predictable cycle. The biggest winners seem destined to become the biggest losers. But this does not have to happen.

All these once great retailers invented a breakthrough, innovative way to serve their customers. However, every business must constantly reinvent itself as the customers change and the competition adjusts to the new challenges. This results in internal changes, which tend to be resisted within the company, as the store operations group typically is preoccupied with the time and money required to implement such changes. There is always blind resistance to change. Internal arrogance can cause past policies and procedures to be regarded as sacrosanct and unchangeable. Merchants become restrained, and the business becomes more orderly, more predictable, and more easily managed. The company transitions from being a *merchandising oriented* business into a company that is *operationally driven*.

At this stage the status quo becomes very comfortable—and creativity stops. The crazy, creative merchants are gone or at least controlled. Of course, the seemingly smart course creates stale and out-of-date stores. The excitement goes away, as do the customers. The company opens more stores based on the same static formula and can't understand why the return on investment (ROI) increasingly shrinks as each new store is added.

This negative ROI trend leads to the next stage, in which the company now becomes *financially driven*. The new focus changes to redeploying assets. This, of course, is another way to describe cutting back on investments—and ultimately closing stores. This path ultimately leads to a dead end.

The demise starts the day a company takes their eyes off the customer, focuses on the numbers, and embraces the status quo.

RAPID CHANGE REQUIRES QUICK DECISIONS

Retailing is a dynamic business. Thousands of variables change daily: multiple products, in a multitude of stores, against numerous competitors, with various vendors. The list is endless, as the *wheel of retailing* relentlessly turns, bringing change after change.

As retailers adjust their tactics to address market conditions, the market changes in response. That, in turn, alters the metrics, requiring new tactics and perhaps new strategies. At the same time, the *product life cycle* is ongoing. New vendors and brands are emerging, while other established brands weaken and disappear. Speed to market with innovations becomes a strong competitive advantage.

These constant changes demand agile companies to make decision after decision on the run. There is often a desire to crystalize the retail experience into a science. It's understandable to seek predictable formulas that ensure successful decisions and avoid past failures. Books have been written, speeches given, and consulting fees paid to uncover the magic formulas to describe and unlock these formulas promising perpetual success. However, there really is no silver bullet. Packaged theorems ultimately fail because great merchandising is not a science. It's an art. It is the merchandising artist that can sense the market trends and make innovative changes on the run.

MAKING SMART AND TIMELY DECISIONS

The art of great merchandising requires great merchants. Merchandising talent consists partly of experience and partly innate proclivity. This unique group of people have keen insight into the market and their customers. They create the right mix of products, services, prices, and shopping environments to excite the customers. These artists feel comfortable making merchandising decisions based on their knowledge and feel for the business—acquired by experience—as opposed to others who rely on reams of data and search for formulas to guide their decisions.

Good merchants make decisions based upon their intuition and feel for the market. They have intricate knowledge of the products and insight into the customers' feelings and attitudes. A good merchant can walk into a store and smell success or failure.

"All of my best decisions in business and in life have been made with heart, intuition ... not analysis. If you can make a decision with analysis, you should do so. But it turns out in life that your most important decisions are always made with instinct and intuition, taste, heart."

— Jeff Bezos

That seemingly innate knowledge is based upon a real understanding of the customer. This customer intimacy comes from personal interaction with customers in a real-world store environment. Merchants must be able to walk in their customer's shoes and see the world as their customer does. These are the people who can create solutions for the customer's needs and desires.

Sure, some consultants and advisors are happy to oblige the unsure by expounding the latest popular business formulas. However, the *wheel of retailing* rolls on and once-popular precepts become passé. Meanwhile, the competitor that has mastered *speed to market* wins the battle for the customer's dollar. Change doesn't wait.

That's why great merchandising embraces change. It doesn't resist it. Every successful merchant must be an agent of change. Great merchants hear the beat of a different drum and respond with urgency. They need change to keep from boredom. Their natural tendency is to ask, "Why not?" instead of, "Why should we?"

Change is, in fact, the only constant in retailing. Long-term demographic changes alter customer attitudes. Technological innovations lead to new channels of distribution. New competitors arise while others fail. The retail world never stands still.

The key to long-run success is to make the *running changes* required to remain relevant, while keeping the company's compass on true north, which is, always, *delighting the customer.*

We saw The Home Depot evolve from a purely DIY-customer focus at the beginning to a business that now generates almost half of its total revenue from the professional customer. That is testament to the need to respond to market changes. In that case, the demographics of an aging population made the DIY business mature and the professional business a growth opportunity.

Today the entire retail business is going through a digital revolution driven by customers who have learned they can demand and receive more service in the procurement of their purchases. The Internet has enabled and accelerated rapid change in the retail industry. The retail business will remain strong, but ... who loses and who wins will depend on how they manage change.

THE INEVITABLE PRODUCT LIFE CYCLE

It is said that opinions are like belly buttons—everybody has one. When it comes to how to best merchandise a store, everybody is likely to have an opinion. But only a few have the keen insight required to be an innovator who can create new paradigms to further delight the customer.

This creativity is not common. Most people can't see new opportunities that are hiding in plain sight. Conversely, a good merchant can zero in on today's good idea while anxiously peering over the horizon to envision the next quantum jump.

A great merchant is driven and motivated by the customer's positive response to a new product, service, or program. This gratification stimulates further creativity and innovation.

Real merchants understand they are only as good as the next new idea. Every existing product will transition though a *product life cycle*. The following is a visual image of the process a product goes through from development, through introduction, growth, maturity, and finally to decline. All products will ultimately go through this life cycle. The irony of the *product life cycle* is that profits are only maximized in the *growth stage*—and it is downhill after that.

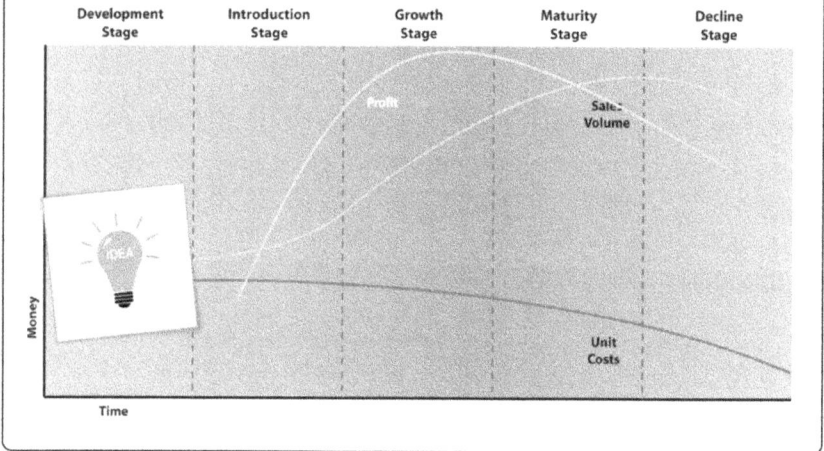

Innovation Maximizes Profitable Sales

Development Stage | Introduction Stage | Growth Stage | Maturity Stage | Decline Stage

Profit

Sales Volume

Money

Unit Costs

Time

The development stage of *the product life cycle* involves a lot of "blue sky thinking," resulting in a few breakthrough ideas and a lot of other notions that turn out to be dead ends. Here is where merchant artists must exhibit initiative and drive to stay on the cutting edge in an industry. Much of this requires developmental effort that will not show real results until sometime in the future. Creating a reservoir of new ideas is, therefore, a critical step, to enable the flow of innovative products and services that will bring future sales and profits.

The introduction stage requires an up-front investment of time and money. It's necessary to incubate and then market the new product. The growth stage is where all the efforts pay off in sales and profits. Revenue climbs and profits are maximized as the uniqueness of the product provides pricing power and early adapters reward the retailers who are the innovators.

The next step is the maturity stage, where competitors now duplicate the product or service. Prices begin to fall, and the demand tends to become saturated. The final stage is decline. The product has become a low-margin commodity sold only on price; profit is minimal.

Innovation is what keeps a store fresh and allows it to aggregate new customer segments. Innovation separates the retailers that are unique and at the cutting edge from those that are simply duplicating proven practices and becoming stale and obsolete. Every product ultimately goes through the life cycle. The cycle may be six months or sixty years, but it is inevitable. Successful retailers must constantly foster new products and services while terminating others.

SELLING THE NEW IDEA

Having developed a new product or program, the merchant's job is not finished. The next step is to sell the program—first internally and then externally.

There will always be resistance within the organization toward the *new* and a tendency to hold on to the *old*. Internal marketing of new ideas must precede external marketing to the public. Most people do not readily accept change; they need prodding. People naturally cling to familiar, mature programs, even when those programs are becoming obsolete. Dead inventory on items that should have been deleted is a malady that infects many retailers. The *why?* crowd can often slow down and impede the *why not?* innovators. Unfortunately, these nabobs of negativity often rule the day and harm the company while shortchanging the customer.

> *"The essential ingredient for success is a steady stream of innovation."*
> — Peter Drucker

Blind resistance to change is a common human attribute. It results in overestimating the effort and cost required for a new initiative without comprehending the potential upside. The company may need *why?* people in the finance or auditing departments, but they must not be allowed to be bad apples in the merchandising group.

Some retailers find it hard to make a merchandising decision without piles of data. After they have it, though, they find themselves afflicted

"Rules and models destroy genius and art."
— William Hazlitt

by analysis paralysis. Critical decisions are delayed. The troops beg for decisions that never come or arrive too late.

Other people look for easy formulas for retail success and are the ones who tend to ask which book they should read. The better question is, "In which store should I be working today?" [Exception - Breakthrough Retailing!] Experience is always the best teacher.

Of course, if secondary data is available to help make a merchandising decision, by all means, use it. Study good models operating in the market. Evaluating secondary data that is well researched and actionable can be helpful. However, real-world dynamics can rarely be consolidated or distilled into a simple slogan or set of numbers.

A merchant must be able to digest the available data and then integrate it with the intuition, insight, and natural talent that comes from truly knowing the products and the customer. *Speed to market* is essential, and critical decisions cannot wait. We need a timely answer to the question of how to next delight the customer. It is most often the merchant who can deliver that insight; it needs to be the merchant!

PROVIDING THE BEST SOLUTION

Every successful retailer must be able to clearly define the company's *unique, sustainable, compelling, competitive advantage.* Why? To enable internal focus on the right priorities and to effectively communicate these advantages to the ultimate customers. This requires a clear vision and understanding of the target markets.

This sounds obvious, yet one of the world's largest consulting firms advises its home-center clients to establish a policy they call *Win, Place, or Show.* In this model, clients are advised to develop certain departments or categories of merchandise that are clearly superior to the competition's.

Then they define categories within the product mix that are simply on a par with the competition's. Finally, they determine which categories can be offered to the customer that are actually inferior to the competition's offerings.

How completely absurd! This theory can only lead to mediocrity and defeat. Every merchant involved in category management should have one clear imperative: *To be the best and win!*

A successful big-box store must be seen as a destination and a complete solution for the customer's project. It must be able to pull traffic *past* its competitors by expanding its catchment area. Every merchant in every department must therefore strive to define how his or her mix of products and services provides a *unique, sustainable, compelling, competitive advantage* that makes the store or website visit imperative for the customer.

The "Godfather Rule" of merchandising: Make them an offer they can't refuse.

We must never accept any goal except winning the competitive battle. *Win, Place or Show* is a catchy slogan that might look good on a PowerPoint presentation. Consulting firms can provide excellent financial analysis and help identify benchmark goals. But if you are going to win, this must be balanced with the good judgment and common sense that comes from actually running a retail business and knowing your customers intimately. Retail expertise requires a sense of empathy with the store and customer that can only come from the store experience.

MAJOR ON THE MAJORS

The product mix at The Home Depot has significantly changed over time. During the first five years, a significant part of our store was devoted to furniture. In fact, everyone in the early days wore many hats, including Bernie Marcus, who was both the CEO and furniture buyer!

As sales volumes continued to grow, every department strived for more space, in order to expand assortments and increase dominance in each category. The total store size was capped at 100,000 square feet, so something had to give. We had to define which would be the core departments would help us to excel and dominate in the marketplace, versus those that had less merit to the repair, remodel, and maintenance customer.

We decided to eliminate the furniture department so other, more important departments could expand. It certainly could be argued and documented that there is a huge market for furniture and that many people would continue to buy furniture at our stores even if we were not number one in this category. It took a certain amount of common sense and customer insight to look at our stores and our brand from the customers' viewpoint to determine what combination of products would create the most project synergy and reinforce our competitive advantages. This was certainly a judgement call by The Home Depot's management.

AVOIDING THE TESTING TRAP

In today's changing world, a key competitive advantage is *speed to market*. Today's retailers need merchants who have the confidence to move forward with urgency while others dither.

Speed to market is often frustrated by endless tests. Often tests are simply an excuse to not make a decision. A poorly designed and implemented test may provide little value for a final decision. In fact, such a test can result in a fallacious decision. A test may be implemented without putting the necessary thought and effort into obtaining a genuine measurement of the real-world demand. Testing mistakes might include putting a new product in a small group of test stores without the point-of-sale aids, the employee training, or the marketing efforts that would really be required for success. Perhaps there were no success metrics determined prior to the test. This could be further complicated by not setting a reasonable deadline for measuring results.

In the end, the test goes on without a decision to either kill the idea or roll it out to more stores. These incomplete tests are like zombie programs that hang around and complicate the business with lingering unanswered questions. It may be true that tests are easier, and perhaps less costly, to initiate in new stores. However, the best and more reliable tests are made in existing stores. Baseline data of the prior situation can be measured after the test to evaluate the incremental return on investment.

Good tests are important; they must be actionable so winning programs can be rolled out and poor programs eliminated. Tangible evidence must demonstrate that *the juice is worth the squeeze*. This demands that a fair test be implemented and clearly measured to assure reliable data. While it is important to have merchandising talent capable of predicting customer behavior, good data that corroborate results is critical to confirm the merchant's hypothesis and overcome resistance to change.

DEFINING "BEST PRACTICE"

There are many management fads that become the management tool *du jour*. While most new management concepts have elements of logic and truth, there is a danger in trying to make the business more objective and scientific than it can be. In the process, we may inadvertently take the spontaneity out of the business and stifle innovation.

Once again, we must state that merchandising is an art, not a science. A classic example of trying to use science to run a retail business was the Six Sigma program at The Home Depot during the Nardelli years. While the associates spent hours and hours studying minutia at the micro level, the business was suffering at the macro level.

One of today's fads is lean management. This tool has proven to be particularly useful to companies such as automobile producers. In this case, a manufacturer may use the lean management process, which gets buy-in from the frontline staff in each factory in regard to eliminating waste. Lean management helps this group derive a series of practical policies and procedures that are unique to and beneficial for their working unit, since they are in the best position to identify the inefficiencies of their own work unit. This is all good.

However, retail is not manufacturing, and it is difficult to adapt the lean management concept into the more complex and decentralized retail business that may have hundreds or thousands of locations and where it is much harder to control the many changing variables. It becomes a time-consuming exercise to redefine processes for every working unit in a multi-store company.

In fact, it is counterproductive and actually impossible to have every store and functional work group unit define its own unique set of lean management processes. In the first place, there is simply not enough time to hyper-study every process in each department in every store while running the day-to-day business. Further, too many unique processes can lead to lack of coordination between work units and can become barriers to the workflow. Another fact of retailing is that the business environment can change quickly and decisions need to be made, leaving little time to go through the formal lean management process.

There is, of course, a benefit to ascertaining the *best practice,* and the lean management evaluation processes can help with this. Management's goal should be to identify the *best practices* and integrate them into the standard operating procedures for the company's multiple locations. These *best practices* should simultaneously drive down costs and improve customer satisfaction.

When a new and better process is defined in a multiple-store business, a conclusion must be drawn and a rollout plan established. This judgment call requires a management team that is ground engaged, understands the business, and can make intuitive decisions with confidence based upon the data at hand. This confidence comes from a deep understanding of the target customer, combined with experience in the business itself.

Business situations demand decisions and actions that involve some risk-taking to move forward in a timely way. Every business needs movers and shakers who can demonstrate this kind of dynamic leadership. The troops get frustrated when the management team fails to make smart and timely decisions.

THE PROBLEM WITH KEY PERFORMANCE INDICATORS

Another misused management tool involves KPIs (key performance indicators). Too often, human resource and finance groups use KPIs to micromanage the company's departments and facilitate year-end reviews. KPIs create the aura of objectivity while avoiding the subjective evaluations required to judge job performance and determine incentive rewards. In addition to the appearance of objectivity, these KPIs allow the *people up there* to micromanage the *business down here*.

"Now turning to our objective of balancing the art and science of retail, whenever I talk about balancing the art and science of retail, I'm careful to emphasize that we will always start with the art."

— Ted Decker,
The Home Depot

KPI objectives for the various corporate departments are often in conflict with each other. In fact, this conflict is built into the system.

For example, the finance department may decide to make driving down inventory shrink (discrepancy in physical-to-book inventory) the metric for a KPI. This may cause the merchant to pay more for the product from the vendor to obtain a shrink allowance back at a later date. This is not smart, but I have seen it happen. It may encourage the store management to issue false shortage claims against the vendors to pad the shrink numbers, which may lead to later price increases by the vendor who learns the game being played. It may even cause fraud in the process of taking physical inventory, which can ultimately destroy careers.

The result of poorly thought through KPIs is that the planned numbers may be realized, but with unanticipated negative consequences throughout the entire organization.

KPIs for the logistics group may require driving down the cost of transportation for each shipping container. This could lead to routing the containers on ships with multiple harbor stops, creating an unnecessarily long lead-time before the products are received. The result at store level is to beef up inventory levels to accommodate the longer shipping window. This hoarding runs counter to the store's KPI of increasing inventory turns. This creates a hostile situation between the logistic department and the stores, not to mention creating a feast/famine inventory position that impacts the ability to serve the customer in a timely manner.

The various corporate departments tend to focus only on their own KPIs, which often will be in conflict with those of another department. This encourages each group to create its own silo or ivory tower, which must then be defended against the rest of the organization. Communication turns inward instead of reaching out to the rest of the company for cooperation and coordination. The enemy is now within the company, and the focus is no longer on fighting the real competitor outside in the marketplace.

Sadly, customers are neglected while the war wages, simply because the KPIs were never focused on serving them in the first place. Many companies today have independent, warring silos within their company, yet they continue to demand conflicting performance metrics that exacerbate the problem.

BALANCING ART AND SCIENCE

This is not to say that tools as *lean management* and *key performance indicators offer no benefits*. We could add to this list *management by shared objectives, creative listening, Six Sigma, 360-degree reviews,* and whatever new brilliant management insight becomes popular tomorrow. They all have elements of wisdom regarding the functions of management.

The problem is that once they become the religion of the company, they become the primary goal rather than a tool to achieve the proper goal of customer satisfaction and loyalty.

The movers and shakers within the company are often forced to turn their attention away from the customer to devote time and energy to meeting after meeting focused on misplaced priorities. Success is evaluated by metrics other than those driven by customer satisfaction. Creative momentum is obscured by mundane issues.

The administrators who embrace these management doctrines become evangelists tasked with spreading the enlightened gospel. They are bureaucrats who love contemplative introspection more than moving the company forward. They love contemplating their navels while the world around them crumbles. These are truly dangerous people.

The Six Sigma program was the religion of The Home Depot during the Nardelli administration. When the new CEO, Frank Blake, took charge of the company, one of his first actions was to kill the Six Sigma program. Previously the way to get recognized and promoted was to achieve "black belt" status in the Six Sigma program, which focused on process. Now recognition and promotion would be determined by results driven by customer satisfaction. This was the end of Six Sigma at The Home Depot.

ENCOURAGING THE INNOVATORS

Executive management must protect the worker bees from bureaucratic tyranny that detracts attention from job number one—delighting the customers. Sometimes corporate edicts need to be rescinded. Sometimes burdensome procedures need to be stopped. Sometimes someone needs to say "Whoa!" This is the essence of customer-focused leadership.

Retail requires merchants whose confidence is based on their own experience in the stores and with the customers, enabling them to make running decisions. These are creative people who know how to get the job done. They see their life's ambition as the constant pursuit of excellence in serving the customer. They are the innovators and the movers and shakers who must exemplify the company's culture.

Innovation is the mother's milk of merchandising. Implementing new ideas requires cooperation and integration of activities between store operations, merchandising, marketing, human resources, and logistics. Other departments could also be involved; the point is that when all the groups are willing to work together to find new ways to delight the customers, good things happen.

The customers vote with their dollars, so their evaluation is the only measurement that really matters in the long run. The management team and every corporate department needs to fully appreciate this fact of life.

The need is to break down the silos, cut the red tape, and eliminate the conflicting KPIs and *"gotcha metrics"* that stop progress. This is absolutely necessary to facilitate the free flow of creativity and assure constant progress. If the merchants are empowered and free to be artists, you will usually like the resulting picture.

The goal must be to assure that your brand is unique and irreplaceable in the customers' minds. This is not just a cosmetic marketing differentiation; this means truly being different. It demands innovation that allows the brand to stand out in the crowd. The retail world is full of sameness that needs to be challenged.

The following poem, written in 1895, points out how the human condition has always resisted change, to its own detriment. Playing *follow the leader* will not result in innovation and new ways to delight the customer.

The Calf Path
(Sam Walter Foss, 1895)

One day through the primeval wood
A calf walked home as good calves should;
But made a trail all bent askew,
A crooked trail as all calves do.
Since then three hundred years have fled,
And I infer the calf is dead.

But still he left behind his trail,
And thereby hangs my moral tale.
The trail was taken up next day
By a lone dog that passed that way;
And then a wise bell-wether sheep
Pursued the trail o'er vale and steep,
And drew the flock behind him, too,
As good bell-wethers always do.
And from that day, o'er hill and glade,
Through those old woods a path was made,

And many men wound in and out,
And dodged and turned and bent about,
And uttered words of righteous wrath
Because 'twas such a crooked path;
But still they followed—do not laugh—
The first migrations of that calf,
And through this winding wood-way stalked
Because he wobbled when he walked.

This forest path became a lane,
That bent, and turned, and turned again.
This crooked lane became a road,
Where many a poor horse with his load
Toiled on beneath the burning sun,
And traveled some three miles in one.
And thus a century and a half
They trod the footsteps of that calf.

The years passed on in swiftness fleet.
The road became a village street;
And this, before men were aware,
A city's crowded thoroughfare,
And soon the central street was this
Of a renowned metropolis;
And men two centuries and a half
Trod in the footsteps of that calf.

Each day a hundred thousand rout
Followed this zigzag calf about,
And o'er his crooked journey went
The traffic of a continent.
A hundred thousand men were led
By one calf near three centuries dead.
They followed still his crooked way,
And lost one hundred years a day,
For thus such reverence is lent
To well-established precedent.

A moral lesson this might teach
Were I ordained and called to preach;
For men are prone to go it blind
Along the calf-paths of the mind,
And work away from sun to sun
To do what other men have done.
They follow in the beaten track,
And out and in, and forth and back,
And still their devious course pursue,
To keep the path that others do.
They keep the path a sacred groove,
Along which all their lives they move;
But how the wise old wood-gods laugh,
Who saw the first primeval calf.
Ah, many things this tale might teach—
But I am not ordained to preach.

INNOVATION BARRIERS

The merchant must have the vision and motivation to take the company to the next level. However, no matter how talented and committed merchants are, they often face obstacles to creativity. When this happens transformation is stifled and the store finds growth much more difficult.

These eight traps inhibit innovation:

• *Lack of Real Expertise*

Sometimes the wrong person is in the wrong job. A common error is to assume that any employee who has performed well in other departments can be transferred into merchandising and become an innovative spark plug to grow the business.

Not everyone has the background and innate ability to become an effective merchant. Yes, we must search within the company for candidates who can ultimately assume the merchandising position; but at the same time, we must understand this will require a why not? Person. Further, this person must possess the product knowledge, store empathy, and customer intimacy only acquired by quality time in the stores and marketplace. Not everyone can meet these criteria. Without these qualifications, it is impossible to be the person to create change and take the category or department to the next level.

> *"There are three kinds of people: Those who make things happen, those who watch things happen, and those who wonder, What happened?"*
> — Nicolas Murray Butler

A second and equally serious error is to not respect the unique knowledge required for each product category and assume merchants can be moved around the organization like chess pieces. For example, it is wrong to think a merchandising expert in commodity products, like building materials, could have the right feel for style and color to serve in a fashion-oriented department, such as decorative lighting. This is putting a round peg in a square hole. Yet this kind of labor shuffling is common in the retail business.

Not only is it damaging to customer service, it is also a huge mistake to ask an unqualified person to negotiate with vendors who are experts in their category of merchandise. The result will always be vendor one, merchant zero.

The talent required to be a great merchant is unique and specialized. A viable retailer must have merchants who are uniquely gifted in their areas of expertise, who know customers' needs, and who are a group of *why not?* people who see what others cannot.

• *Endless Tests*

Too often tests become excuses for not making decisions. While this has already been mentioned, it is critical to understand how detrimental it is to the company's viability when tests become stagnant. A test of a particular program may be implemented in a specific store or market but then languish, without a response as to whether the program should be expanded to other stores or simply killed. This creates confusion and greatly increases the workload, as multiple conflicting programs continue to be administered.

Objective criteria must be established prior to testing and testing data evaluated in a timely manner to make a go/no-go decision. Then the merchant must have the drive, charisma, and chutzpah to push for implementation and compliance in a skeptical world. A good merchant must be a great salesperson.

• *Fear of Failure*

If a merchant has made no mistakes, he or she hasn't pushed the envelope. They do not know how high is up.

To use a baseball term, merchants need to have a good batting average. A baseball player who gets on base one-third of the time at bat can enjoy a very lucrative career. Merchants need to be right more often than wrong. But if their batting averages are perfect, they have not tested the upper limits, which means they have not maximized their opportunities.

Failure is to be expected and overcome. A company-wide fear of failure is the fault of a senior management that has not created the right environment for experimentation and innovation.

• Displaced Priorities

Everyone wants a piece of a merchant's time. It is far too easy for merchants to spend all their efforts on other people's priorities instead of their own, which should be delighting the customer and creating sales.

A hierarchical organization generates endless requests for data, memos, and reports. Needless meetings take valuable time. Too often the merchants remain chained to their office by internal issues that divert their focus and impede them from being in the stores and working on the next breakthrough. Merchants must be protected from unnecessary monkeys on their backs that divert them from their primary job of developing the next innovative product or service that will enhance the store or website shopping experience.

External suppliers pull on merchants too. Every sales representative wants to meet with merchants (perhaps just to put the meeting on their call report to show their boss they are working). Vendor meetings are important, but they must be with vendors that correspond to the next innovation. And the time would be better spent if the meeting took place in a store rather than in a corporate office.

Each merchant must have a vision and plan for new programs that will be introduced next year and even the year after. These opportunities must receive top priority in both internal and external meetings.

• Failure to Sell Up the Continuum

Good products with the lowest prices create the highest unit sales. But the better and best products, while selling lower quantities, may offer more total sales and higher gross profit dollars. Merchants may be influenced by unit sales volume and overlook the possibility of selling up the continuum to better and more interesting products.

This overemphasis on opening price-point products often results from reliance on computer reports that show low-priced products sell best.

This data is, no doubt, correct information, but the merchant is likely to use good data to draw the wrong conclusions. A merchant needs to understand that duplication and redundancy within the same category may add only marginal sales. Offering products that allow the customer to buy up the continuum can create many new sales at higher price points and aggregate a whole new customer segment to the business.

Another factor in developing markets is that the merchants may be low paid and relatively low on the social class scale. It is difficult for such a person to see the need and opportunity for higher-end products.

• *Narrow View of Job*

Merchants tend to focus primarily on buying and merchandising in-stock products for brick-and-mortar stores. They do not spend quality time on the full range of goods and services that need to be available to the customer. This includes assuring proper project design, delivery, and installation. They must also embrace and manage all the product choices in the long tail of online programs.

In order to be the complete solution provider for the customer's project, merchants need to consider all the products and services the customer requires. The many decisions involved in putting together a coordinated program must be made by and through knowledgeable merchants. Merchants must be enabled—and required—to make decisions that affect the customer shopping experience. These include:

- Determining the items to be stocked in store.

- Determining the products to be offered online.

- Setting specifications for the products.

- Setting specifications for the packaging of the products.

- Determining the vendors that will supply the products.

- Negotiating costs and terms of acquisition from the vendors.

- Setting retail prices in-store and online.

- Creating and controlling the promotional offers and special buys.

- Determining the related services that the customers require and setting performance requirements.

- Determining store layout and point-of-sale displays.

- Assuring that proper product knowledge is transmitted to store associates and customers.

Many of these merchandising decisions may be turned over to an internal department that usurps the authority of the merchants. Certainly, merchandisers need support groups to provide data in these eleven decision points listed above. They may need auxiliary groups to execute the decisions made.

However, make no mistake; the decisions in each of these areas must be made by the merchants, who take full responsibility for the sales growth and return on investment for their category and department. The merchants must bring together all the available data from the support groups and then make decisions that maintain a focused direction toward a clear goal. Ownership of the merchandising strategy by the merchant is essential for executing a comprehensive merchandising program with competence.

• *Following the Competition*

It is too easy to play follow the leader. Matching a competitor's product offer results in a pricing policy that gives the customer no reason to travel past the competitor to your store.

The result of homogeneity in the marketplace is to make convenience the only competitive advantage. This is a very weak advantage. It is easily negated as competitors grow or new players enter the market.

Another reason to not follow the competition is that they are not smarter than you. I have often been disappointed by a merchant who explains, for example, that they stock twenty-four different models of hammers because their competitor has twenty-three. That is really the blind leading the blind.

Following the leader may seem like a safe strategy, but the leader will still be the leader. It is never wise to play someone else's game. Instead, define and implement a value proposition that creates a *unique, sustainable, compelling, competitive advantage.*

• *Needless and Unending Negotiations*

New items or programs often die in the process of negotiation. Good programs require a win-win relationship between the retailer and the vendor. Otherwise, there is no mutual commitment to success.

Unfortunately, some merchants mistakenly feel the negotiation is not complete until they are sure the vendor cannot make any profit in the program. This is when the vendor walks away, and an otherwise promising opportunity is truncated.

EMBRACING CHANGE

The merchant's job is never ending. There are always new ways to delight the customer. Priorities must be set and pursued with vigor. A wise company empowers its merchants with the responsibility and authority to grow their business. In today's digital world, change happens fast and there is most often a crying need to speed new innovations into the marketplace.

Senior management either tolerates (or even promotes) barriers to progress or creates an environment that encourages innovation and speed to market. The need is for leadership that facilitates decentralization by delegating responsibility without fear of losing control and empowering individuals with authority to excel.

A dynamic company must demand that its merchants be agents of change. How can change be accomplished while staying true to the core principles? The principles never change, but the tactics do and must.

For example, the principle may be to always drive down the cost of procurement and pass most of these savings through to customers in lower prices. This might mean vertical integration of the supply chain in one situation and a strategic alliance in another. There might be multiple paths to the goal that could change over time, but the principle has not changed. The objective is still to drive down costs and pass the savings to the customer.

> *"Hierarchies were built for a slower, older time when we could all wait in line for an audience before the throne."*
> — Kevin Hancock

The merchandising department serves as the heart of the company. The store operations group are the arms and legs. The stores must live in a constant world of *today*. They must receive and stock *today*'s shipments. They must take care of every customer who is in the store buying *today*. The merchandising group has the mandate to look into the future.

If the business is to grow in the future, the customer must be given more reasons to shop at your store *tomorrow*. Therefore, you must have a vision of what products or services should be offered a year from now and then again the following year. The merchant needs to stay current on the trends and interact with vendors to define the future.

New products do not simply fall out of the sky. Innovation requires searching for vendors, defining specifications, testing for quality, designing packaging, developing marketing plans, setting prices, and distributing the products. The merchant must spearhead the future growth. If the merchants quit defining the future, the heart stops pumping. Companies with rapid growth are always *merchandising oriented*.

Change has been the hallmark of The Home Depot's merchandising DNA. Our first eight stores were 60,000 square feet, while most of today's stores are 75 percent larger. The original stores had no tool rental service, while this has become an important and growing part of today's business. The first stores had only limited special order programs, while today online sales are the fastest growing part of the business. There was no installed sales program in the early stores, while today The Home Depot offers in-home service to customers in multiple ways. Delivery service was not competent and had limited availability, while today The Home Depot is investing billions of dollars to offer the best home and jobsite delivery in the industry.

The original business was aimed exclusively at the DIY homeowner. Today the target markets still include the Do-It-Yourself customer, but also include the Do-It-For-Me customer and professional customers, such as remodeling contractors and even business establishments, such as restaurants, hotels, and other commercial buildings.

All these changes and more resulted from striving to be the best and only store to meet all the customer's project needs. It might have been tempting to look at these changes as requiring new systems, people, and efforts that would add prohibitive cost and complexity to the business. It could

"Behold the turtle. He makes progress only when he sticks his neck out."
— James Bryant Conant

have been argued that business is good, so the status quo is good enough. But the *Bleeding Orange* culture always drove the company to the next level of customer service. Successful progress required both art and science. The art of merchandising creates the vision, while the science of technology helps execute it.

CREATING LOYAL CUSTOMERS
PRINCIPLE 2:
YOUR BRAND IS YOUR MOST VALUABLE ASSET—
AND IT RESIDES IN THE MIND OF THE CUSTOMER.

The retailer's most valuable resource is its brand. The brand gives customers the assurance of future satisfaction based upon past experiences. Customers' preference for a brand can also be a result of their perception that they and the company share values. Brand preference can resemble the devotion a fan has for a favorite sports team.

That means the most important variable in understanding the future intent of your customers is to know their perception of your brand. As previously stated, *perception is reality.*

CREATING A BOND

Retailers must make sure the customer knows they exist, but this alone will not create loyalty. The only way to protect and grow your brand is to provide the customers with a reason to choose your store. This involves providing customers with a promise that you care and are relevant to their lives. Then all policies and interactions with customers must reinforce that promise.

Finally, you must clearly differentiate your brand as the only one that can consistently deliver on this promise. Successfully interacting with the customers as they complete this journey—from awareness to the ultimate goal of bonding—is a proven path to customer loyalty.

Establishing Loyalty

MEASURING CUSTOMER PERCEPTION

The smart retailer constantly measures the voice of customer. This is a discipline that obtains the customer's satisfaction rating for every interaction between the company and the customer. This might follow the customer's check-out process, or the completion of an installed sales job, or a home or jobsite delivery.

Many companies today use the Net Promoter [www.netpromotersystem. com] process to measure customer perception. The customer is asked to measure his or her shopping experience on a scale of one to ten, with ten being complete satisfaction.

Those customers indicating a score of nine or ten are called *promoters*— people who have bonded with the company and are likely to share their delight with their neighbors. Those indicating a score of seven or eight are passive customers who have not bonded. Those indicating a score of zero to six are *detractors,* who are not likely to return and are likely to spread negative impressions of the company's brand.

The Net Promoter score is essentially computed by deducting the percentage of people who are *detractors* from the percentage of people who are *promoters.* This creates an index to compare the ability of stores, departments, and individuals to delight the customer.

A program of constantly monitoring customer perception of the company and its brand can become a great motivator for customer service when the results are tabulated and published for all employees and service providers. The goal of every department and every employee must be to constantly improve their Net Promoter score.

There is also a need for *market track* surveys that systematically monitor customer attitudes and perceptions at predetermined, timed intervals. The questions asked must be distilled to queries that can directly lead to action steps, which can favorably impact customer attitudes going forward. The beauty of market tracks is that customer attitudes can be tracked and charted to illustrate changes in customer perception over time.

Market research is a valuable tool, but misused, it can also waste a lot of money. Often a market research company will ask an incredible number of questions, resulting in an impressive, thick binder of cross-referenced charts and graphs. However, the voluminous collection of information that is often either immaterial or already known tends to sit on the credenza, making little impact on the business.

At The Home Depot, we made sure every market track survey focused on need-to-know data that would lead to an action plan. We performed these market tracks annually to benchmark customers attitudes and our market share. The surveys then were reviewed each fall and became the base upon which we built our merchandising and marketing plans for the following year.

DISCERNING THE RIGHT QUESTIONS

Before launching a totally new concept we would often use focus groups. For example, a focus group was our first steps in developing our Crossroads stores, aimed at the farm and ranch segment of the market.

A focus group would bring together a group of ten or twelve people who shared common profiles. A professional moderator would ask open-ended questions to probe their beliefs and attitudes on specific subjects. We might have a group of full-time farmers who raised crops in one session and a group of ranchers raising animals in another. These sessions would be observed via a two-way mirror and recorded for future reference.

A focus group is not designed to provide predictive answers. Instead it helps to define the questions that can then be empirically tested in broader market track surveys that are statistically reliable.

The point of all of this is that the customers are in charge, and retailers need to know what is inside their heads. It is not sufficient to simply give lip service to customer service but rather necessary to go the extra mile to know and understand each defined customer segment of the market. Customer satisfaction must be consistently measured and progress charted to assure meeting and exceeding customer expectations. Clearly, serving the customers must be at the center of every decision and this requires specific customer knowledge

Management gets what management inspects.

LEARNING TO LEARN

Retailers must learn to question their assumptions of past practices in light of customer needs today. Here's an illustration of that point.

Because the lumber department offers high-volume, low-margin products, The Home Depot placed it at the back of the store in the early days. The idea was to manipulate the customers so they would be forced past more products and spend more time in the store, on the assumption that they would purchase more.

Later we extensively researched customer attitudes and observed customer shopping habits with video cameras and stop watches. The conclusion was that our core assumption regarding buying habits was wrong. We found absolutely no relationship between the time the customer spent in the store and the number of products they purchased. We also learned that repeat shopping depended on how fast people could get into the store, find the product they needed, and then get out.

This meant we had to reset the store model. We had to locate the most needed items conveniently closer to the front of the store. And our biggest opportunity was to speed up the exiting process at our cash registers. We already knew we needed high inventory turnover. Now we learned it was important to increase turnover of our parking spaces!

Customer accommodation is always better than customer manipulation.

MAKING IT EASY TO BUY

Store merchandising and operations must change over time as customers' needs and habits change. The key is to be a learning organization, always willing to acknowledge change and respond in a positive manner to the customers. Certainly, today's digital technology involving the Internet and logistics will force a redefinition of store functions, layouts, and sizes —and redefine customer service. Customer expectations aren't the same as in the past, and they won't be the same in the future. Change must be embraced.

The good news is that the digital revolution provides better tools with which to delight the customer. The warning is that these tools must be used wisely, not to implement a new policy or procedure simply because it can be done or because someone else is doing it. Not everything that can be done should be done. It is important to understand how the customer makes decisions and then orient store design, website, and logistics to facilitate an improved and rewarding shopping experience.

There is always the question in retail circles of how to best arrange the products on the store counters to increase sales and profits. Some advocate displaying the higher priced products at the start of an aisle. Others advise displaying products by brand. Another idea might be to arrange displays by style or color. The right answer is to understand how the customer would set these priorities, given the opportunity.

Customers using the Internet can often determine the order in which products are presented to them by prioritizing how search results will be filtered. It would make good sense in physical stores to arrange the merchandise according to the same criteria most customers would use to evaluate their choices if they were sitting at home using the Internet. This may vary by category, so in some cases it might be a matter of price, where in other cases it may be brand or perhaps color. The customers are in charge, and everything possible should be done to make their shopping experience easy, convenient, and enjoyable.

THE DIGITAL REVOLUTION CHANGES EVERYTHING

The world of retailing is constantly evolving, as new ways are discovered to reach and serve the customer. This has had a huge impact on supply chains. At one time the manufacturer had the power to determine what would be produced, how it would be distributed, and what the price would be. This power passed to the retailers as they grew and became closer to the customer and more in tune with customer needs. The trust factor began to move from the manufacturer brands to the retailer brands.

Now the evolution has become a revolution: the digital world has put perfect knowledge into the hands of the consumer. Smart customers are now in charge. Power is in their hands to determine the winning brands, the preferred channels of distribution, and the prices they are willing to pay.

The key influencers are the customers' peer groups, not the manufacturer or retailer. The customer is able to obtain peer group comments, endorsements, or defamations of products and brands under consideration. This makes creating the right buzz in the marketplace critical to creating the right brand image.

Social media becomes crucial. Word of mouth has always been the most effective promotion, and digital technology gives word of mouth a megaphone.

The Home Depot's first day of business in late 1979 was not an outstanding success. Yes, promotions had been launched, and the grand opening celebration had begun. The founders were out in the parking lot giving away dollar bills to create excitement, but traffic was light. It was only over the next few months that the store volume steadily grew to amazing new numbers.

What had happened? The few customers who had had a totally unique *Bleeding Orange* experience were motivated to tell their neighbors. This created a new wave of customers who also told their neighbors. This had a multiplier effect, greatly magnifying store traffic. Word of mouth was powerful then—without social media. Customer testimonies are now even more important as a result of technology, which spreads opinions quickly and efficiently.

Another impact on our brand acceptance came when we were endorsed by a local Atlanta radio celebrity named Ludlow Porch. Porch said he was so impressed with the size of the store that "people should bring their lunch and make a day of it." He had a great following; homeowners thought that if he liked the store, it was worth a visit. That was all it took—one visit.

The digital communications revolution has enabled the retailer to provide more and better information to customers faster than ever before. We can enhance the shopping experience by providing knowledge on how to use products or comparison data to help customers select the right product. We can inspire the customer with innovations to improve their lifestyle. Two-way communication with the customer can provide a bridge, so information regarding product data, service inquiries, and purchase activity can flow back and forth at the customer's convenience. These tools help the retailer bond with the customer.

BRICK-AND-MORTAR STORES ARE
SLOW TO INNOVATE

The key reason for the evolution and past success of the pure online retailer is that traditional brick-and-mortar stores did not take advantage of technology as it became available to enhance the store environment and shopping experience. The pure online retailer brought a new level of convenience and raised customers' service expectations. Omnichannel retailing was a defensive response to the realities of the digital world, when it could have been an offensive tool from the beginning.

Brick-and-mortar stores could have been the innovators, using technology and smart logistics to offer the same wide range of products that were ultimately offered to the consumer on the Internet. However, most of the *special order* programs of the past in physical stores were severely limited in assortment and very sloppy in administration. These programs were essentially manual programs that were often difficult for salespeople to sell and equally hard for customers to buy. Time frames for delivery were often undefined. Delivery to the home was not always available. Freight costs were not always clear. Brick-and-mortar stores often regarded home delivery as an expense to deemphasize.

The traditional stores put their heads in the sand and ignored how important these services could be to many customers. The bottom line is that the management of most brick-and-mortar stores before the e-commerce revolution were simply fat, happy, and lazy. This satisfaction with the status quo left a clear path for e-commerce innovators to discover and respond to the customers' desire for more choices and more convenience. Only after the pure e-commerce retailers showed they could take market share from the traditional retailers did the management of the brick-and-mortar stores began to wake up to the realities and the imperative of embracing digital technology.

E-COMMERCE BRINGS NEW CONVENIENCE

E-Commerce is essentially a modern phrase for *special order*. It has the added advantage of being easily transacted outside the physical store. The ordering process has become so simple that customers can place their own orders. Traditional *special order* processes did not offer immediate satisfaction, as they typically required long and inconsistent time frames for fulfillment. However, the e-commerce retailers changed the negative concept of *special order* into the positive connotation of *more choice—available now.*

More choice has an obvious consumer benefit, particularly when combined with quick shipment. The early e-commerce retailers realized they needed to ask for payment at the time of the order but could not do so without the promise of quick delivery. This resulted in responsive supply chains. They had to provide specific, accurate product information with good illustrations to avoid costly returns, so they set up customer-friendly databases. In starting with customer satisfaction and working backward to the supply chain, the customer was served better. Ordering had to be so simple that the customers could place the order themselves without a salesperson's help. This begs us to ask the question, Why should it be easier to buy at home than to shop in a store? The answer is that it should not.

This new paradigm of good service changed the customer's expectations of all retailers, whether online or off-line. The customer's desires will be ultimately fulfilled, if not from within the established channels of distribution, then by a disrupter from outside. There is no reason why the *special order* programs in the brick-and-mortar stores could not have been just as easy and customer friendly as the current online experience. The management of the physical stores were simply myopic and not genuinely concerned with enhancing the customer's shopping experience. As a result of this over reliance on the status quo, many previously successful retailers became increasingly irrelevant in today's marketplace.

VIRTUAL STORES VERSUS PHYSICAL STORES

The quick acceptance of e-commerce and its rapid growth is often attributed to the low prices available on the Internet. The assumption is that pure online retailers were virtual stores without the overhead. However, the real motivation was never price. It has always been convenience and service. The truth is, the assumption that e-commerce is a lower-cost channel of distribution has proven to be incorrect for most categories of merchandise. The cost advantage for many products is, in fact, with the physical store.

Name brand products that are high in price and low in cubic size are perfect for e-commerce since the cost of freight on such items will usually be a relatively low percentage of the total purchase price. However, when the product is low value and high cube or simply low priced, this advantage dissipates; the advantage falls to the brick-and-mortar store that can buy in quantity and drive down logistic costs.

Retailers may think they have responded to the Internet challenge by embracing omnichannel marketing. However, too often this has meant bolting an e-commerce arm onto their brick-and-mortar store without truly integrating the technology into the core business. This often creates an internal rival to the physical store, resulting in two separate organizations that do not share the same vision and mission.

In its worst case this rivalry creates a *death cycle* by increasing Internet sales while decreasing in-store sales. This is not necessarily a good trade-off. Internet sales will tend, on average, to maintain a lower margin than the same basket of products sold in the store, primarily due to the higher logistic costs inherent in e-commerce.

The retail community is just now recognizing the reality of the lower profitability of online sales. They are discovering unforeseen costs, including the working capital tied up in slow-moving products, necessary investments in software and hardware, warehousing costs in terms of both people and facilities, and transportation of products to the customer's home—and often back again to the retailer as a return. Customer acquisition costs for pure online retailers are increasingly expensive as more and more websites vie for the customer's eyes.

We can see this *death cycle* in the declining profitability of much of the retail industry in recent years. We are now in an evolutionary phase where many retailers must make significant modifications both off-line and online if they wish to maintain a sustainable business model.

The disjointed infrastructure that can occur between the core physical store business and the e-business arm often results in brand confusion at the customer level, a lack of customer focus at the employee level, and channel confusion within the vendor community. This lack of synergy and inconsistent branding strategy between online and off-line divisions of a company can negatively impact customers' perception of the retailer's relevance and their trust in the brand.

ONLINE/OFF-LINE SYNERGY REQUIRED

The customer does not distinguish between online or off-line purchases from a specific retailer's brand. A bad experience is a bad experience and damages the brand, regardless of how the customer interacted with the retailer. This often occurs when the new e-commerce group is intent on growing their sales to impress the management but does not secure the proper logistics and in-stock position to properly fulfill orders, resulting in customer disappointment. This impacts the trust relationship at the center of customer relations.

The new digital imperative has clearly added costs and complexity to the retail equation. The expedited path to digital capability has often led physical retailers to chase an Amazon model, with a self-reliant online supply chain, instead of using technology to build upon their unique strengths as a brick-and-mortar omnichannel retailer.

Treating both the online and off-line functions as a synergistic interconnected retailing experience yields benefits in terms of both cost and convenience. It requires integrating all systems, such as merchandising, marketing, IT, and logistics, into one comprehensive system with one vision, one mission, and one brand image. It involves doing what is smart for the omnichannel retailer instead of simply imitating Amazon. Imitation may be the sincerest form of flattery, but it is a really bad business strategy. It's never smart to play someone else's game.

Customers' choice of a goods or service provider is based primarily on their confidence that their source is sensitive to their needs and that they will consistently receive the right price, right quality, and timely fulfillment of their needs. Isn't this what every customer deserves from every retailer? Unfortunately, with most retailers today, the shopping experience and information available to the customer inside the store still compares unfavorably with the experience the customer can receive in the digital world outside the store.

If a specification or other piece of information is important for the customer shopping at home, the same information is equally important to the customer shopping in the physical store. However, much of the good information available on the Internet, such as product description, specifications, uses, ratings, and related products, is simply lacking in the physical stores. This data needs to migrate to the point of sale either manually or even better with digital electronic displays and signing.

We see, too often, that the retailer trying to embrace digital technology puts all the company's time, energy, and investments into e-commerce while ignoring innovations that would bring the store up to a par with the digital age. The physical stores, which tend to represent the lion's share of the total sales volume, are often starved for innovation and investment. Online retailers have been able to capture market share by capitalizing on the vulnerability of brick-and-mortar stores that have struggled or even abstained from offering a better alternative for their customers.

The response from the brick-and-mortar retailers has, too often, been a knee-jerk reaction to imitate these online disrupters instead of implementing a superior interconnected retailing model, building on the synergistic potential of the omnichannel model. This is not an either/or choice but rather a strategy and commitment to simultaneously grow both off-line and online revenues.

Customer-centric Commerce

We have discussed e-commerce, omnichannel marketing, and interconnected retailing. They all boil down to one concept that can be expressed as customer-centric commerce. This is putting the customer in control and making all our resources available to fulfill their wishes.

This requires embracing the following attributes:

• Interacting with customers in person, by phone, or by Internet—any way they want.

• Being open for business twenty-four hours a day, seven days a week—whenever they want.

• Providing inspiration and helpful guidance—however they want.

• Showing the customers all their options—whatever they want.

• Providing quick shipment —when they want.

• Delivering the product—wherever they want.

• Making returns easy and simple—the way they want.

• Installing the product—with the service they want.

• Communicating with the customer—the way they select.

• Integrating all the systems involved with merchandising, marketing, supply chain, and store operations is a prerequisite to providing these customer-oriented attributes.

ASSURING CUSTOMER LOYALTY

Being *customer-centric* requires that we constantly find new ways to serve the customer. In other words, the best loyalty program is simply to be the best store by anticipating customer needs and wants and providing customer-friendly solutions.

That seems simple, but retailers often seem to miss that point and fail to define and implement best practices. They want to keep their old methods in place, so they initiate a loyalty program based upon points, contests, or some other scheme to bribe the customer to endure a store experience they really dislike.

Most loyalty programs try to imitate airline frequent flier programs. Does anyone really love their airline and feel confident they are always getting the best deal? Customers are generally not loyal to a specific store, and most of them belong to numerous loyalty programs, often at competing stores. Customers generally do not regard these programs as super deals so much as hoops they must jump through to buy at the right market price.

Most of these programs do not achieve their loyalty objective and certainly do not stem the tide of customers going to the better physical store or shopping online. Most formal loyalty programs are offered by retailers who are not the value leaders and are trying to hold on to their customers with products, services, and prices that are no longer relevant.

It is a maxim that the more a retailer shouts about its loyalty program, the less likely it is to have a truly competitive merchandising offer for the customer. The most liberal loyalty program in U.S. retailing for many years has been the Sears program, and that says it all. Case closed.

THE CUSTOMER'S PERCEPTION IS THE ONLY REALITY

Every retailer must determine what their brand stands for that no other retailer can truly duplicate. What are they clearly the best at when compared to the universe of competitors? It is not possible to be all things to all people; every successful retailer must define its target market(s), determine the customer's needs and desires, and then provide a solution that is clearly superior to that of any other competitor.

We opened The Home Depot's first stores in Boston and Washington, D.C., simultaneously. The main competitor in Boston was Somerville Lumber. The main competitor in Washington, D.C., was Hechinger.

Before opening our stores, we did market surveys to discover customer attitudes toward each of these brands in their respective markets.

We found that customers loved Somerville primarily because the company had built their business on outstanding service, including free delivery. It was clearly perceived as the best store for service. Conversely, customers seemed to dislike Hechinger. It was not perceived as best in anything and rated particularly poorly in service.

Retailing is a race with no finish line.

This awareness caused us to develop two completely different messages for our own grand opening in the two markets. The competitive attack in our advertising was much more aggressive in the Hechinger market, as it was easy to capitalize on their weakness. It was a different story in Boston, where we had to perform at a much higher service level.

Fortunately, our *Bleeding Orange* culture was service oriented and could rise to the occasion in both markets, although it took a little longer in Boston due to the loyalty of the Somerville customer. While low prices enticed the customers to visit our stores, it was always great service. - Bleeding Orange service - that created loyalty.

The price-sensitive customers must have total confidence and trust that they will always get the best deal without having to shop the market. The prestige customers may be focused on having product or brand that is clearly superior in every way to any alternative. The project customers may be looking for the best service solution that solves all their problems from start to finish.

Every company must be able to offer an acceptable level of product or service at a reasonable price to remain in the market. However, just showing up and performing adequately is not a winning formula. Winners are perceived as being clearly the best available solution by the customer. This is what drives loyalty.

A retailer must determine the optimum *unique, sustainable, compelling, competitive advantage* for its target market and execute at a consistently superior level. Customers' loyalty to the brand is determined by their perception that the retailer is truly better than the competition.

Customer perception should be constantly on the mind of every manager as both strategic and tactical decisions are being made. Nothing is more important to strategic thinking than understanding the impact decisions will make on the customer's brand perception. To create the right brand image, retailers must ask these questions:

• What does the customer think of our brand and our stores?

• What would we like the customer to think about our brand and our stores?

• What must change to assure the right customer perception?

• What is the most effective critical path to dynamic change?

• How can we most effectively communicate the revised brand and value proposition to the target customers?

• How can we consistently monitor customer attitudes in order to respond quickly to further changes?

Having achieved success, the next priority must be to leapfrog toward the next innovation that will create another quantum jump in customer satisfaction. This is the essence of a *merchandising organization.* It requires a corporate ability to learn and a willingness to change. This is often a blind spot for market leaders who live in a status quo world, allowing past success to obscure their vision.

GROWING THE TOP LINE

How do retailers know they are making progress and meeting the customer's needs? By watching their comparable store sales grow from year to year.

Year-on-year sales increases indicate that a larger target market has been aggregated and/or that a larger share of wallet has been obtained from existing customers. This has to be job number one for every manager in the company. The responsibilities of a merchant include cutting costs as well as driving sales, but the primary responsibility must always be to drive sales.

The sad truth is that most merchants do not spend most of their time focusing upon delighting the customer and growing sales. Too often they act as though market share is a zero-sum game. Virtually all their attention is focused on negotiating with their vendors to obtain new discounts in order to lower net costs on existing products at existing sales levels. The goal, in this case, is to increase gross margin percentages in order to drop more profit to the bottom line through constant negotiations. There is little thought about expanding the market or getting a larger share of that expanded market. A reduction in cost is seen as a bonus to the bottom line instead of an opportunity to pass this savings to the customer, in order to increase sales and grow market share.

Merchants can choose how they allocate their time. The question is whether they spend the majority of their time reducing costs or growing sales. Let's consider a hypothetical example.

INCREASED SALES MUST ALWAYS TAKE TOP PRIORITY

Picture a department in a retail business that is doing one million dollars per year at a 40 percent margin. Assume that management wishes to increase the contribution of that department to the bottom line in the coming year by $50,000. One way to achieve this is to negotiate cost reductions on every single item in the product assortment by 8.3 percent. On the other hand, the same $50,000 could also be achieved by increasing sales by 12.5 percent. Which of these paths is most achievable?

This is not a difficult question. The most achievable alternative would be to commit to the sales increase. Driving sales up by 12.5 percent is, in fact, possible if we find new ways to delight our customers. However, negotiating an 8.3 percent reduction on every single item that is currently purchased and stocked is virtually impossible. No buyer should be purchasing so poorly that such discounts are already being left on the table. Vendors will almost always resist across-the-board reduction of prices but are generally responsive to strategies that can grow sales and increase their market share. Growing market share is the best tool to drive down acquisition costs. Achieving a $50,000 increase in profitability is simply not feasible if the model is a zero-sum game for market growth.

The good news is that focusing on growing sales and gaining market share can achieve double-digit growth in sales, and that growth will increase buying power, which does create the opportunity to drive down costs. Unfortunately, many retailers put the cart before the horse. They spend most of their time trying to achieve a range of cost reductions that are not possible, while spending a small percentage of their time creating significant sales increases, which are possible.

Part of this wrong-headed approach to improving business metrics is that management often puts great pressure on the merchants to increase their gross margin percentages. This is a sales-defeating strategy. Achieving such a goal can ultimately lower gross margin dollars by depressing sales and, taken to its logical conclusion, could eventually kill the business completely, as the customer rejects the higher prices.

On the other hand, driving margins down can often increase sales and gross margin dollars, while taking market share and profits away from competitors. You become stronger and they become weaker.

GAINING GROSS MARGIN DOLLARS VIA INCREASED SALES

Let's look at one more illustration. Assume you are starting with a business selling one million dollars of product at 40 percent gross margin. This means the company expects to generate a gross margin of $400,000. Now assume you lower your prices and, as a result, miss the forty percent margin by five points—but you exceed the sales plan by twenty percent.

This change results in sales of $1.2 million at 35 percent margin. The new gross margin dollars generated will be $420,000. You lost five points of margin but beat gross margin plan in dollars by five percent. This is a good outcome.

In many companies, the merchant would get beat up at the next quarterly review meeting because of missing the gross margin percentage plan. However, considering that sales increased and an extra $20,000 has now been taken to the bank, this is a win in profitability and a strategic advantage in gaining market share. The merchant should be complimented for delighting the customers and earning their dollar votes.

Growing sales must always be the top priority. This may often mean lowering margins on highly price sensitive products. When this is done wisely, not only sales increase, but the gross margin dollars generated increase as well. The financial direction in many companies tends to focus on the gross margin percentage column of the profit and loss report, as opposed to the gross margin dollar column. The merchant who increases gross margin percentage is patted on the back, while the company's price image and brand may suffer as a result. This can become a fatal downward spiral. Sales on the products that drive the majority of a store's business generally display an inverse relationship between higher margins and quantities sold.

PRICING TO WIN LOYALTY

At The Home Depot sometimes the smart pricing strategy was to make no margin. Hurricane Andrew, which hit Southern Florida in 1992, is a case in point. We had just opened our newest store in Homestead, Florida, on a Thursday. The hurricane destroyed the store the following Sunday. The result of a major hurricane is an insatiable demand for roofing, plywood, generators, batteries, and other supplies, which become scarce and are often scalped at above-market prices. We responded by making a list of the most-needed products and then announcing to the Florida customers that all these products would be sold at our cost until the community was rebuilt.

True to our can-do *Bleeding Orange* spirit, we immediately put up a tent in the parking lot of our destroyed store, and for the next two years, that tent was our highest-volume sales store. Yes, we sold a lot of high-demand products at no profit, but the store was profitable based on the total mix of products sold. Furthermore, customer loyalty to our brand was assured. We turned the natural disaster into an opportunity to make friends and serve the community while generating sales and profits.

MULTIPLE DATA POINTS REQUIRED FOR GOOD DECISIONS

It is important to keep your hand on the customer's pulse, using numerous tools. For example, comparable store sales data can be combined with Net Promoter and *market tracks* internal data. Then this data needs to be bounced against secondary data from vendors and the external data available through Internet searches. This is using *data analytics* to understand customer attitudes, communication patterns, and shopping habits. This use of *big data* can provide additional insight into specific existing and potential target market groups.

You can then predict purchasing behavior to better respond to the customer's changing needs. It is of critical importance to be fixated on the customer and make sure all decisions are, in fact, *customer centric*. The following chapter will address pricing policies from the standpoint of customer perception.

13

PERCEPTION IS REALITY
PRINCIPLE 3:
THE "RIGHT PRICE" IS SOLELY DETERMINED BY CUSTOMER PERCEPTION.

Many books are written about how to properly price products and services. This is perhaps the most controversial issue in developing a business strategy. Retailers often search for the magic formula to maximize sales and profits. They tend to use established formulas that may have worked in the past but are not relevant to the customer today. But there is a better way to identify that "sweet spot" to price a given product. The focus must be on understanding the customer's perception of your prices, in an effort to use pricing to gain long-term customer loyalty.

The pricing policy of The Home Depot during the time of its most phenomenal growth was always focused on constantly increasing gross margin dollar contribution. (This is the difference between the retailer's cost of a product and the retail price paid by the customer.) The best method to achieve this was to gain the customer's trust by pricing on an EDLP (everyday low price) basis. We would then measure our success by the increase in GMROI (gross margin return on inventory investment).

GMROI is an index that measures gross margin dollars generated in a specific time period, divided by the average inventory at cost. Smart pricing creates sales that impact both the generation of gross profit dollars and the rate of inventory turnover. Therefore, GMROI is a great tool to evaluate the effectiveness of pricing strategy.

VARIABLE MARGIN PRICING

Most retailers do not set prices based upon customer perception. Instead, they tend to rely on safe margins that have been previously achieved. They then apply these established margins to future purchases in the various product categories or departments.

For example, they may have decided forty percent was the safe margin for light bulbs. Therefore, once they know the cost, they grab their calculator and apply the appropriate margin to establish the retail price. The fallacy of this kind of pricing is that it only looks at acquisition cost. It assumes all the individual SKUs within the category have the same demand drivers and, therefore, should maintain the same margins.

This totally ignores the customer's perception of value of individual items, as well as the customer's options as to other sources for these products. This naïve cost-plus pricing is, frankly, lazy and stupid.

It may well be that the light bulb category has a margin of forty percent, but it could be that no individual SKU within the light bulb assortment is actually priced at that specific margin. The forty percent number is simply a mathematical average and should not become an automatic pricing shortcut. Keep in mind when you are dealing with averages that they are like the man who sleeps with his feet in the oven and his head in the refrigerator and on the average feels fine.

The truth is that using these previously established category margins would never result in maximizing sales or gross profit dollars. There are always items that are *price elastic;* prices on these should be driven down to maximize sales and gross margin dollars. Conversely, *price inelastic* items can be sold at increased margin without significantly impacting sales.

This once again points out the importance of understanding the customers and being able to see the value proposition while standing in their shoes. The customer's perception and what you want the customer to believe should determine your retail pricing—not costs.

Most retailers would make much better pricing decisions if they did not know their cost. They would then be forced to observe the market from their customers' viewpoint.

Let's use light bulbs as the example again. Say there is a specific SKU that is heavily used in recessed lighting in homes and commercial buildings. It is, therefore, highly price-sensitive. Perhaps a price below the forty percent margin could attract a larger target market, which includes heavy users such as janitors, property managers, and small business units, as well as homeowners who are sensitive to price. Dropping the price, in such a case, could result in a large enough increase in sales that more money will be taken to the bank, even though the percentage margin declined.

On the other hand, if you are buying right and searching the world market for innovative suppliers of light bulbs, it may be possible to find a breakthrough lighting product at the very start of its life cycle that can command a significantly higher gross margin percentage than the forty percent category average. The key is to find a truly unique product with a consumer advantage and be the first to bring it to the market, perhaps with exclusive distribution for some period of time. This could be a light bulb with a unique look or, maybe, an energy saving advantage. In such a case, the retailer can offer the customer a great value in innovation that can justify a higher margin. In fact, the retailer would be foolishly leaving money on the table to use an averaged category margin on such a new and unique product, when exclusivity provides pricing power. The challenge with an exclusive product is to experiment with pricing options to find that sweet spot where gross margin dollars are maximized.

In the following example, the gross margin percentage was lowered by fifteen points and resulting gross margin dollars per unit by 50 percent. However, because of the new lower price, sales increased from ten to thirty units. Therefore, the actual dollars of gross profit taken to the bank increased by 50 percent. This is a good outcome.

Maximizing Gross Profit Dollars
Price Sensitive Example

Previous Margin 40%	Revised Margin 25%
Item Cost $6.00	Item Cost $6.00
Item Sell $10.00	Item Sell $8.00
Gross Margin 40%	Gross Margin 25%
Gross Margin Dollars $4.00	Gross Margin Dollars $2.00
Quantity Sold 10	Quantity Sold 30
Total Gross Margin Dollars $40	Total Gross Margin Dollars $60

The key is to maximize gross profit dollars using variable margins based on customer perception. It is amazing that so many retailers simply do not understand the dynamics behind this relatively simple concept. Naive retailers lack confidence in their own cost structure and will not reduce margins for fear of initiating a price war they cannot win. The truth is that high demand items are already being priced at the lower right price in the market, and the high margin retailer is already losing the price war.

Historical margins are irrelevant when selling to today's knowledgeable customer. Using traditional margins as a shortcut and ignoring the pricing realities in the market is analogous to the ostrich that puts its head in the sand. The customers are not ostriches—they shop the market.

THE RIGHT PRICE FOR THE RIGHT TARGET CUSTOMER

We carried a product in our paint department at The Home Depot called plaster of paris. It is a powdered compound that can be mixed with water to fill holes and cavities. Our sales volume on this item was quite low and the margin quite high. Our merchant felt that since this was a low volume item, a high gross margin was acceptable and smart.

It is true that plaster of paris was not a high volume item with traditional homebuilders. However, it was a high demand item with schools and the hobby/craft market. We turned our attention to these heavy users, checked out the real plaster of paris wholesale price, and then adjusted our pricing. Immediately this slow selling item that was generating little in sales—and therefore little in profits—became a high-volume item. We were soon enlarging our assortment with increased commercial sizes. Sales and the resulting gross margin dollars increased dramatically when we priced right.

The merchant needs to set pricing by understanding the target market as well as the customer's value perception and perceived alternatives. EDLP does not necessarily mean low margins. Smart retail pricing ignores costs and sees value through the customer's eyes. This may result in a low margin or a high margin, depending upon the customer's perception and alternatives.

The everyday price concept is that if the price is already right there is no need to run a temporary sale to create excitement and high sales volume. The objective is to have constant excitement and consistently high sales volume. Once the right price is found that maximizes sales and gross margin dollars, there is no reason to change up or down.

The right price will motivate the customer to buy today and, at the same time, create a trust relationship that will build a tendency to buy again from you in the future.

This has nothing to do with costs and everything to do with the customer's perception. Therefore, the right pricing strategy will lead to variable margins on products within a category, based upon the perceived relevant options and value perceptions of the customer. Traditional cost-plus pricing with preset margin goals set by past category averages is always the wrong policy.

VENDOR CONTROL OF PRICING

Another wrong way retailers price their products is to let their vendors set the retail pricing. In some cases, vendors intimidate retailers into maintaining a suggested price by threatening to prohibit the non-compliant retailer from obtaining the product. The vendors wish to be the channel captain and, therefore, set terms that keep their products distributed in the widest number of retail outlets. They realize they must have stable pricing that will keep even the least efficient retailer in the distribution channel viable. This tends to establish prices with relatively high margins, which then allows many of their dealers to offer discounts reserved for selected customers.

A retailer should not let a vendor set them up for failure by limiting the size of its market. The objectives of the big-box retailer are the opposite of the manufacturer. The big-box format requires pulling customers from a large catchment area. This requires consolidation of the market by taking market share and eliminating inefficient competitors. Offensive pricing strategies are an important tool to achieve this objective. The best defense is a great offense.

The vendor wishes to create *market fragmentation*, while the big-box retailer should be focused on *market consolidation*. Therefore, it is always wrong to set retail pricing in conjunction with a vendor. There is no reason ever to discuss retail price with a vendor. Complaining about, or even discussing, the retail pricing of a competitor with a vendor simply opens the door for the vendor to try to control the market price. This may be illegal. It should be illegal. The dominant big-box retailer should not create a price umbrella for other retailers by agreeing to maintain suggested vendor pricing.

EVERY PRICE MATTERS

The products that are most likely to be price maintained by the vendors are those with the most brand awareness and widest distribution. Even if most products in a store have been properly priced by the retailer with a competitive price gap, customers will see that the pricing is actually inconsistent in these well-known brands. That will lead them to question their trust assumption on the pricing for all the products in the store. Much of the smart pricing will then be discredited in the customers' minds. Consistency and credibility are critical in establishing a trust relationship with the customer.

Merchants may find that vendors of some very important brands require the merchant to maintain suggested retail prices. The correct response to that demand should be a simple and firm refusal. Such an arrangement restricts retailers' ability to set the right price, which must be set by understanding customer perception—not the directives of the vendor.

However, at the same time retail merchandisers should refrain from unilaterally selling branded products at unrealistically low prices, perhaps even below cost, simply to enhance their low-price image in the short run. This could lead to destroying the value of the brand to both the vendor and the retailer.

Instead, retailers should make it clear to their vendors that while they will not agree to maintain inflated retail prices, they will not capriciously destroy their brand with irrational pricing. They must shop the market and find the true net pricing of the relevant competitors and respond accordingly. They may decide to establish a price gap with competitors perceived as being high priced or to match the price of a wholesale distributor to the professional customer. The pricing decision must be at the retailer's discretion, not the vendor's.

Some vendors will accept this logic, but some will not. In the latter case, the retailer may have to agree to disagree and not stock their products. No brand is so important that the vendor's pricing policy should be allowed to destroy the store's own price image.

RETAILERS HAVE PRICING POWER

Leading brand suppliers in the paint business are notorious for establishing set retail pricing that they enforce on their dealers. These dominant brands may be willing to sell to big-box home centers only if the brand's suggested retail price is maintained. This kind of collusion can and should be avoided.

Over and over when confronting these dominate paint brands, my retail clients have found they can walk away from the leading name-brand paint label and offer an equal or even better quality paint under a private label. The attitude of most customers toward paint is one of *brand awareness* but *not brand insistence*.

Merchants can typically recite the name of every product brand in the marketplace. Street interviews with random customers would reveal that customers possess front-of-mind awareness for very few brands and insist upon even fewer. The power of the dominant brands is often overrated. This is especially true when the customer can be offered a better value.

Nobody really knows what is inside the paint can, so an educated sales force can greatly impact the customer's choice of product. When this happens, the big-box store can take market share and consolidate the paint market. The big-box retailer who sets specific quality standards, establishes a good marketing program, and trains its salespeople to sell its private-label paint will win the market share war.

The bottom line is that there is never a reason to turn retail pricing over to a supplier. Price discussions with vendors should focus on cost factors. They do need to be educated regarding your GMROI strategy so they can understand your pricing objectives. They should understand the goal of generating gross profit dollars with a fast-turning inventory. You must be the retail expert on setting the right price in your store and not simply accept the manufacturer's retail pricing edicts.

RIGHT RESPONSE TO COMPETITOR'S PRICING

Often a retailer will simply follow their major competitor in the market and match the competitor's price, hoping to avoid a price war. If you want the customer to believe there is no advantage to shopping at your store and that they should simply go to the closest store, a matching price is the right strategy. But this defensive position will not increase market share, nor will it reinforce a positive price perception of your brand in the customer's mind.

Don't give competitors more respect than they deserve. What smart pricing strategies have they demonstrated? What do they know about gross margin dollars or GMROI? The practice of following the pricing lead of a competitor is a case of the blind leading the blind. Retailers should not match the competition's pricing—they should *be* the competition.

Early in The Home Depot's history, we established a marketing tool we called the Price Patrol. The Price Patrol would shop the market so we could document pricing differences in the marketplace. Every Monday each merchant would receive a list of recently shopped items showing our price and the prices in the market. By Friday of that week, the merchant was required to have reviewed the list and taken appropriate pricing action up or down, based on the market reality. Some products were shopped monthly, some quarterly, some on an annual basis. The result was that every SKU was shopped on a repeated schedule so the merchants could maintain a comprehensive price file.

The interesting outcome of comprehensive retail price checking is that while it calls for reduction of some key price-elastic items, it generally reveals more inelastic items that represent opportunities for price increases. Competitors monitor the more volatile, high-volume items closely resulting in low margins as each retailer responds to competition. Meanwhile the slower selling items which tend to have inelastic demand are often priced with higher margins and are rarely reviewed. It is smart pricing policy to do comprehensive shops of the total SKU range which will provide opportunities to increase gross profit dollars by both driving elastic prices down and increasing many that are inelastic. Knowledge is power and good market data on pricing provides pricing power.

The Price Patrol would buy products in our competitors' stores. We would then do point-of-sale displays in our stores showing our price versus the competitor's, along with a copy of the competitor's register receipt. True price comparisons can positively impact a brand's pricing credibility.

The good news is that if you implement an aggressive, offensive pricing strategy, the competition will almost always assume a defensive posture and look for ways to avoid price competition. Most retailers are driven to protect their gross margin percentage ratios. They don't understand the concept of maximizing gross profit dollars and the advantages of growing GMROI.

It is important to intimidate the competition. They need to understand that it is a fool's game to mess with you. During my days with The Home Depot, we never avoided price competition. In fact, this was most likely to get our orange blood pumping!

Your competitors must understand that you are committed to price leadership. You must have current comprehensive pricing data, set the price gap, and not blink when challenged. Aggressive competitive pricing is an important tool to stymie competition and affirm your price leadership to your loyal customers.

CORRECT PRICING

When setting retail pricing, retailers need to use the right tools which are *benchmarking* and *elasticity analysis*.

• *Pricing by Benchmarking*

Benchmarking is a process that evaluates the customer's perception of their pricing alternatives. The first step is to define who the relevant competitor is. Then ask, "What does the customer perceive about this competitor and their pricing?" A relevant competitor is the most likely alternative supplier of the product in question. It is the benchmark a customer would use to compare pricing. This may be a brick-and-mortar store, a wholesale distributor, or an online retailer. It all depends on the target customer's point of view, which will vary by product category.

At The Home Depot we would typically do benchmarking by media market, defined as the relevant reach of the regional TV broadcasters. There were over fifty such markets in the U.S. We would define the relevant competitor by merchandise category in each of these markets. The relevant competitor for power tools might be the Internet while the relevant competitor for lumber might be a lumber wholesaler. The relevant competitor for batteries might be a warehouse club, while the relevant competitor for kitchen cabinets might be an IKEA store. For every product there is at least one relevant competitor. The resulting price point would generally apply to all the stores in that media market. It was, however, possible that for one of those stores to be in a unique competitive battle with a local competitor, so we had to build flexibility into our system. If an individual store had a unique issue with a competitor—something that impacted just that one store—we could adjust pricing accordingly. This simply required an agreement between the store manager and the product merchandiser. Our orange-blooded store managers were always alert to any price challenge in their immediate market. The only benchmark price that matters is the pricing perceived by the local customer.

If the relevant competitor is a specialty store, a large gap between your price and your competitor's may be necessary so the customer can clearly distinguish a substantial advantage to shopping with you. This might be an everyday low price that is 15 to 20 percent below the specialty store's. If the relevant competitor is a mass merchant, the customer might perceive the retail prices to be more reasonable and fair. Here a gap in the 5 to 10 percentage range might be sufficient. If the relevant competitor is a membership warehouse club, which the customer believes has the lowest wholesale prices available, a good policy would be to match the membership's retail price but without a membership fee. If the relevant competitor is a building material wholesaler, such a wholesaler has multiple price points for different customers. You should try to ascertain the discounted wholesale price charged to most of their professional customers and offer that price to the general public.

In other words, smart pricing should not be determined by your cost but by putting yourself in your customers' shoes, observing the pricing options from their point of view. The objective is to determine the right price to favorably impact the customer's purchase decision today and encourage them to return to your store in the future, rather than the relevant competitor's.

Smart pricing defines the gap or matching policy that determines your EDLP pricing posture with your most relevant competitors. Maintain that pricing ratio, whether the competitor's price goes up or down. Cost is not a factor; and it is not possible to fool the customer with phony sales or other diversions. Customers today have a world of pricing options at their fingertips and thorough knowledge of the right price for the product they are researching. Assume that your prices are totally transparent to your digitally savvy customers, because they are.

• Pricing by Considering Elasticity

By using benchmarking whenever possible and setting an EDLP price gap with your competitors, you show the customer you are relevant for their lives and are committed to saving them money. They will find your value claim is true when they shop in your stores and discover that you consistently price right and that your competitors are inconsistent with their *high/low* sale pricing, which is capricious and untrustworthy. This ultimately leads to a bonding relationship, where the customer fully trusts your brand. The battle for the customer's loyalty is won.

What if you have unique products not found elsewhere in the market-place and unavailable for benchmarking with competitors? In this case you employ the correct method of setting prices - price elasticity analysis. The goal is to find the sweet spot where you maximize your gross profit dollars while maintaining your customers' trust.

If you lower the price and the percentage change in the quantity sold is smaller than the percentage change in the price of the product, the item can be considered to have *inelastic demand* in regard to price. On the other hand, if you lower the price and the percentage change in the quantity sold is higher than the percentage change in the price, the item most likely has *elastic demand*.

Smart merchants, therefore, hypothesize customer reaction to a proposed price change, based on their knowledge and understanding of the customer. If they assume the price is elastic, they test their assumption by lowering the price; if they hypothesized it to be inelastic, they raise the price. The test will prove or disprove the hypothesis.

While this may seem a bit abstract, it works to keep customer trust while maximizing gross profit dollars because it is strictly based on customer perception and observation of their purchasing behavior. *Understand that elasticity and its implications are only relevant when you have unique products not available from your relevant competitors.*

Retailers often put an initial price on a new product using the naïve cost-plus established margins for the category and never again review that pricing unless the cost changes. This is because the product itself is unique and does not show up on price comparison shops. This leads to a static price that most likely will not maximize gross profit dollars because the price elasticity of that product has never been tested. The smart merchant will make a pricing hypothesis regarding the sweet spot for this product and then test the assumption to measure the customer's response.

RIGHT PRICING REQUIRES DISCIPLINE

By now it should be clear that cost should have nothing to do with retail pricing; smart pricing is based on knowing the customers and understanding that their perception must be our reality. The goal must always be to maximize gross profit dollars. Everyday low pricing is the best tool to achieve this goal, using benchmarking or elasticity analysis, depending upon the competitive alternatives. The pricing objective should be to keep faith with all target customers and, thereby, create loyal promoters of your brand.

We should not mistake inelastic demand to mean that some items are blind and, therefore, justify pricing above the market. Never allow your price to be higher than the customer's alternative choice. Only when the customer does not have an identical, alternative choice do you have price authority.

This is why innovation is so important. It keeps more of your products on the growth side of the product life cycle, where you have unique products and, therefore, pricing power. It is also the justification for a strong private-label program with products that have been produced to your own unique specifications.

You may, in responding to the competition, find yourself in a situation where the margin on a particular item is uncomfortably low. This may indicate that a competitor is buying better or is simply more aggressive in pricing. Whatever the reason, you must price right. It is not the customers' problem if you are not buying right. They don't know your cost and don't care.

Remember that we make zero gross profit dollars when the customer is standing in a competitor's store.

The price must be set based upon the customer's perception in order to ensure they will be standing in your store. The long-run impact of pricing right will be higher sales, which will ultimately lead to lower costs. Right pricing is an important tool in the mandate to maximize sales and gross profit dollars.

WINNING PRICE WARS

There is always a concern that aggressive pricing will lead to price wars. However, the truth is that timid pricing leads to price wars. Any competitor can take any single item and sell it for one percent less than your price. The temptation is then to lower that one item one percent below the competition. This can go on until you are paying the customer to take the product out of your store.

Such a price war is not sustainable. It also confuses your own employees and the customers because it does not make sense when you compare the pricing to other items in the product mix. Eventually someone blinks, and the war is called off, and prices return to normal. Neither party has really won, and each competitor has hurt their price image by creating irrational pricing that has their own employees and customers scratching their heads.

When we opened our first Home Depot stores in Houston, Texas, our competitor was Builders Square, a similar big-box home center we discussed in chapter one. We both featured Glidden Spred Satin brand paint. The promotional price in the market at the beginning was $9.99 per gallon. We dropped the price by a dollar. Then Builders Square dropped their price another dollar. This continued until we were offering Glidden Spred Satin paint at $2.00 a gallon with another $2.00 mail-in rebate. We were giving the paint away free!

Clearly this was not a long-term sustainable pricing strategy. A lot of paint was sold at a loss before a truce was called, and neither of our companies gained any perception of price advantage with the Houston customers. The biggest loser was Glidden Spred Satin, which became a damaged brand in the marketplace. The Spred Satin brand had lost its value as a quality product. Dropping one dollar at a time was a defensive tactic, not an offensive move.

The solution to this is to establish a *beat-beat-match* policy. Smart retailers always create a gap between their price and their competitor's price. If you see the competitor beat your price by a small percentage, you should reestablish a significant gap. If you do this twice in a row and it becomes obvious you are at the start of a price war on a single item, avoid taking the bait and continuing a downward spiral.

However, don't stop there. The right response is to compete on a broader scale that has more significant consequences in terms of markdowns and maintained margins. Commit to a pricing policy that means the customers will save, not just on a single product but across the board, on all their project needs. Challenge your competitors to compete on a larger scale, where much more is at stake. They will invariably back off. Anyone can play the penny game on an individual item. However, when attacked on multiple items across a category or department that amounts to big dollars, the competitor's management will not allow the company to take the margin hit. Game over!

Small reactions to competitors' pricing show your timidity and encourage future challenges. It is important—in fact, it is critical—if you find yourself in a price war to *go nuclear* to demonstrate pricing commitment and fortitude. This will cause short-term pain but long-run benefit. It will establish price leadership and actually prevent price wars by commanding respect from competitors.

This is *piranha pricing*. Don't follow your competitors down a single price-point rabbit hole. Rather, attack with a broad assortment of products—entire category assortments, and perhaps entire store assortments. While a single piranha may cause pain, its attack will not likely be fatal. However, a whole school of piranha will devour its victim. The examples of The Home Depot's pricing strategy in competition with Scotty's and later Costco in chapter four were examples of *piranha pricing* at work.

DEFINING EDLP

EDLP is the best policy for maximizing gross profit dollars while creating a trust relationship with your customer. This can be a winning strategy if you have the fortitude and discipline to honestly believe and implement it.

You must, of course, clearly understand what the term means. You want every purchase by the customer to reinforce the belief that they made the smart choice to shop at your store. EDLP simply means you will not offer limited-time discount sales—because you don't need to discount prices that are already discounted and the best alternative in the marketplace.

Of course, pricing will change over time, based on market trends and competitor initiatives, but your attitude should be that you consider those changes permanent until proven otherwise. The message to your customers is that you have the right price *every day on every item*. This is the trust message you must consistently stress as a core value of your brand.

The customers' perception of their shopping experience today potentially impacts a lifetime of purchases—not just their own but often those of their social group.

As a reminder, here are the elements of The Home Depot's original EDLP pricing promise, which we first listed in chapter four.

• You never pay high retail prices.

• There are no limited-time sales—it is always the right time to buy.

• No silly games or loyalty cards are required to get the best deal.

• Everybody buys at true professional wholesale prices.

• We shop the market, so you don't have to.

• Our competitors' ads are our ads. We will not only match our competitors' prices; we will beat them by at least 10 percent.

• You can trust us to increase your standard of living by driving down the costs of home improvement.

Right pricing will positively impact the GMROI index. It is important to understand the dynamics that make GMROI the best tool to measure pricing acuity. GMROI is impacted by gross margin dollars and inventory turnover. Both of these factors are driven by price. The right pricing policy is absolutely critical in order to gain and maintain the customer's trust. That trust is dependent solely on the customer's perception of your brand and its promise, which must include a right price element.

We will next turn to an in-depth review of the GMROI concept in the following chapter.

14

THE SMART PRICING INDICATOR
PRINCIPLE 4:
SUCCESS IS MEASURED BY GMROI
(GROSS MARGIN RETURN ON INVENTORY INVESTMENT).

Most retailers measure success by focusing on their profit and loss statement. This puts a spotlight on the gross margin percentage, since all expenses are deducted from that number. Therefore, it would seem that the higher the gross margin percentage, the more net profit can be achieved, assuming that expenses are held constant. However, this is only half the equation. It ignores the balance sheet, which has the inventory number—a significant element in the investment required to operate the business.

The better way to evaluate success is using the GMROI index number, which compares the gross margin dollars from the profit and loss statement with the inventory numbers found on the balance sheet. GMROI is a measurement of the actual gross margin dollars generated in a specific time period, divided by the average inventory at cost during that period. This becomes a great tool to compare the productivity of departments, categories, or even individual SKU productivity.

Inventory is the major element in the retail business that affects the investment in working capital. Each time a retailing operation turns its inventory, it spins off gross margin dollars that its management can take to the bank. It is not the gross margin percentage that is most important. It is how often a retailer can generate real returns on the working capital invested in inventory.

MARGIN VERSUS GMROI

Let's look at a hypothetical situation. Say you're evaluating the financial performance of a store that has both a hardware department and a lumber department. Both departments have an inventory that totals one million dollars at cost. The hardware department is making fifty percent gross margin. The lumber department is operating at a twenty-five percent gross margin. But the inventory turnover is quite different. Which is the most profitable department?

You cannot answer this simply by looking at the gross profit margin. You must also know the inventory investment and the rate of turnover of that inventory. We can see such a comparison in this chart.

Margin Does Not Define Profitability

Lumber – 25% Margin	Hardware – 50% margin
Assume a million-dollar investment in inventory with 12 inventory turns at a 25% margin	Assume a million-dollar investment in inventory with 2 inventory turns at a 50% margin
Results	Results
Sales - $15,996,000	Sales - $4,000,000 Gross
Gross Margin dollars $3,990,000	Gross Margin dollars $2,000,000
GMROI of 399	GMROI of 200

Objective is to maximize gross profit dollars not margin %

While in the example above the gross margin percentage of the lumber department was half that of the hardware department, it nevertheless generated twice the gross profit dollars. Therefore, it is not possible to judge the productivity and profitability of a business by looking solely at the gross margin percentage. The analysis is incomplete without knowing the relevant inventory turnover ratios.

The GMROI index tells us which department or category in a retail store is the most productive. Lumber, for example, is a commodity product with a small number of relatively high-volume items that should turn much faster than the hardware department, with its thousands of specialized nuts, bolts, and fittings. Hardware requires a broad assortment of products, resulting in lower inventory turns. Yet both departments could achieve similar GMROI results. Our goal must be to grow the GMROI in both of these departments. In the case of lumber, we will most likely increase GMROI by focusing on increased inventory turnover. In the case of hardware, increasing GMROI will most likely be achieved by focusing on increasing gross margins.

Low margin products tend to be the faster-selling, commodity-type products, while slow-selling products are less price sensitive and tend to have higher gross margins. The market seems to understand that there is a relationship between margin and inventory turnover since prices and margins tend to have a strong relationship to normal inventory turns. This relationship is best expressed in the GMROI index.

If the demand for a product is highly price sensitive, you may find that driving your pricing down leverages turnover by increasing sales. As turnover increases, the GMROI index will increase. If the demand for an item is somewhat inelastic, changing the price may not increase sales or inventory turn; but raising the gross margin percentage may increase gross margin dollars. Therefore, increasing the price will leverage gross margin dollars. In this case, as gross margin percentage increases, GMROI index will increase.

GMROI MEASURES MERCHANDISING COMPETENCE

The job of the merchant is to understand demand dynamics and set the price that will most likely increase GMROI. This requires the merchant to have an exceptionally good understanding of the market and of the customer, in order to predict the customer's reaction to a change in price, up or down.

The goal is always to maximize gross margin dollars. This is accomplished by finding that sweet spot for the right price. Once again, the success of business and pricing strategies is driven by a deep understanding of the customer's perception of your brand and their response to your pricing decisions.

MEASURING THE RIGHT VARIABLE

Some consultants and professors will encourage retailers to use gross margin return on retail square footage instead of gross margin return on inventory investment as a measure of productivity. This is the kiss of death for most stores in general, and home centers in particular.

In our previous example regarding the pricing of lumber versus hardware, the lumber products are obviously large and require extra space to stock and load. Measuring return of gross margin on the space required would tend to make the case that a store should decrease or eliminate the lumber department, in order to give more space to the hardware department, which is more compact. This would create a huge decline in the company's sales and profits.

First, you would lose much of the lumber sales, which drive related sales throughout the store. A strong lumber department creates derived demand for more hardware sales. You, obviously, also lose those gross margin dollars that the lumber department was providing. Expanding the hardware department would most likely drive the slow turns to an even lower number, with a negative impact on GMROI.

This would be a good example of using accurate data to make a detrimental decision. Having both a strong lumber department and a strong hardware department is necessary for a destination project store. It's a synergistic 1+1=3 equation. In other words, offering a project solution by supplying both lumber and the necessary hardware provides extra value to the customer. *The whole is greater than the sum of its parts.*

Make sure you are using the right metrics to measure your success. The formula to evaluate pricing acumen is GMROI.

Another example: The department that generates the most store traffic and sales in many home-center stores around the world is the garden and outdoor living department. This category of products has the unique ability to bring the customer back to the store multiple times throughout the year as the seasons change. Yet it is space intensive and cannot generally be justified on gross margin per square foot. However, a well-run garden department in a home center can generate an extremely high inventory turnover ratio and lead to a very favorable GMROI.

CONSTANTLY INCREASING GMROI

The merchants' job is to drive GMROI up; it should, therefore, be the major metric in setting their compensation package. The merchant can positively impact gross margin dollars and inventory turnover by designing the optimum model stock and by smart pricing. Smart pricing that increases GMROI can only be achieved if the decisions are clearly focused on customer perception and made by people who can understand the impact of a price change from the customer's standpoint.

Implementing a policy of smart pricing will, most likely, result in both markdowns and markups, as you put yourself in your customer's shoes and use *benchmarking* and *price elasticity analysis* (see chapter 13) to set rational pricing that maximizes gross profit dollars. Rational pricing demands good data and a complete market analysis of the pricing for every SKU in your product mix.

Maximizing gross profit dollars requires the merchant to go through a decision tree based on the customer's perception of prices combined with a hypothesis of their likely response.

Maximizing Gross Profit Dollars

```
                          ┌─────────────┐
                          │  Identify   │
                          │  Relevant   │
                  ┌──────►│ Competitor  │
         ┌──────────────┐ │   Set Gap   │   ┌──────────────────┐
         │ Competitive  │ └─────────────┘   │   Lower Price    │   ┌──┐
    ┌───►│ Benchmarked  │                    │ Test for price   │   │  │
    │    └──────────────┘   ┌──────────┐     │ that maximizes   │   │  │
┌─────────┐                 │ Elastic  │────►│  Gross Profit    │   │▼ │
│ Pricing │                 └──────────┘     │    Dollars       │   └──┘
└─────────┘  ┌──────────────┐                └──────────────────┘
    │        │  Exclusive   │
    └───────►│  Elasticity  │                 ┌──────────────────┐
             │  Analysis    │                 │  Increase Price  │   ┌──┐
             └──────────────┘  ┌──────────┐   │  Test for Price  │   │▲ │
                               │ Inelastic│──►│ that Maximizes   │   │  │
                               └──────────┘   │  Gross Profit    │   │  │
                                              │    Dollars       │   └──┘
                                              └──────────────────┘
```

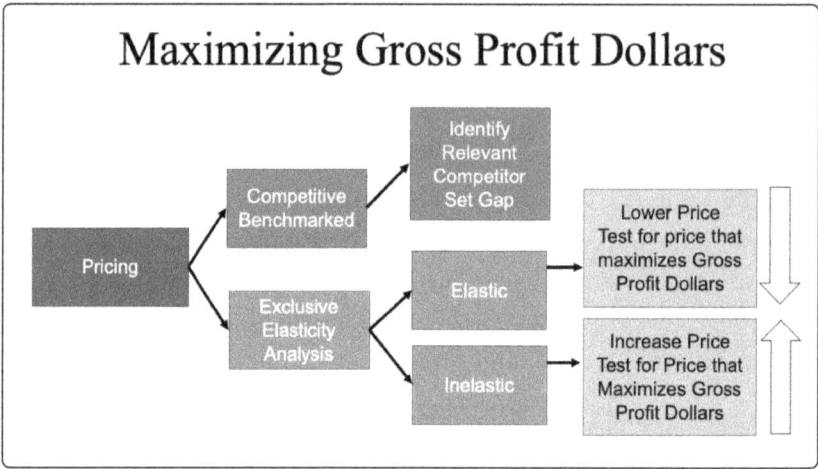

Perhaps you're asking, "What is the right or ideal GMROI number?" The answer is always the same: a higher number than last period.

Retailers are always competing against their own numbers by finding new ways to price right and, thereby, gain the customer's business today and trust for tomorrow. While it is impossible to increase gross margin percentage every quarter without destroying the business, it is very possible to increase GMROI every quarter, as we properly interpret and respond to the customer's price perception, while maintaining smart inventory management.

THE INVENTORY FACTOR

Another way the merchant impacts GMROI is by creating a more efficient *model stock,* which is composed of an SKU (item) matrix that sets the store assortment of items based on feature, benefit, and price point.

Most merchants are constantly looking to add more items to the product mix, on the mistaken notion that more SKUs will automatically generate more sales. This is an oversimplification that often proves false. The customers do not really want more items, they simply want the right item for their need. The easier you can make it for the customer to zero in on the right products for their project, whether in the store or on the internet, the more you become the customer's first choice to shop.

Instead of a product mix with redundancy and duplication, retailers need to make their stores *easy to stock, easy to sell, and easy to buy.* The same logic applies in making items on the website easy to locate, easy to distinguish, and easy to buy.

Overburdening the store with more and more SKUs makes it difficult to manage the display area without adding more manual labor to juggle the many items in a limited space. This also often results in being out of stock on the best-selling items, as valuable space is used for products with less customer demand.

An abundance of items with limited differences can make selling difficult for the salespeople. Too many SKUs with feature benefit redundancy can cause a customer to become frustrated and actually delay an intended purchase. This is true both off-line and online. Keeping the choices simple and logical will make the shopping experience more self-service, which is always the best service.

Over-assortment with redundant product ranges is a far too common practice and a major sin of most retailers. When the merchant tries to jam fifty pounds of stuff into a twenty-five pound bag, something has to give.

The customer loses because the store is:

- *Harder to stock:* Salespeople are busy moving merchandise and stocking shelves instead of assisting customers. The store management is more likely to hire people with strong backs instead of strong product knowledge and experience.

- **Harder to sell:** When there is too much redundancy in the product mix, the salespeople cannot understand all variations and, therefore, are of little help to the customer trying to make a decision. In fact, a confused salesperson will avoid helping a customer if they are not confident of their own product knowledge.

• **Harder to buy:** Having too many SKUs in the space available prevents the customer from quickly finding the product display, getting good point-of-sale information, and easily obtaining the product for purchase. In addition, it often forces needed inventory of the better sellers off the sales floor and into storage areas, where they are not readily available to customers. Even more likely is an out-of-stock situation, as display space and inventory dollars are tied up in slow-moving items.

Looking only at the average inventory turnover for the total store to determine appropriate inventory is misleading. A closer examination of subclasses and SKUs within the product mix will generally show an incredible number of items that are slow sellers and turning well below the department average, while the best sellers are spinning too fast to assure a consistent in-stock position. The average turnover number may seem to be within acceptable standards, but the customers may be frustrated and not well served if the store is out of the one item they need. The inventory level of every SKU needs to be set by the rate of sale and safety stock required for that specific item.

Merchants need to avoid racing to have more items than the competitor simply for bragging rights. This, unfortunately, is the direction merchants often receive from management. It is particularly grievous with regard to the internet and e-commerce assortments. There seems to be a race to out-SKU Amazon, without understanding the high cost of warehousing and logistics, in addition to the working capital tied up in the multitude of long-tailed products. Millions of SKUs produced by manufacturers may or may not be in demand at the mass-market level. Stocking some of these products in the store may be justified, while it may make sense to offer some additional items on the website. However, not everything made or offered by a manufacturer should be stocked in the store or even offered on the website. The rule must be to offer items that customers truly want to buy and then be able to deliver in a timely manner.

Smart merchants are curators who design model stock assortments, both off-line and online, to assure maximum choice of features and benefits for their customers with a minimum of needless redundancy and duplication. To this end, they must conduct systematic line reviews aimed at consolidating SKUs and vendors, in order to create a more efficient supply chain. (See chapter 6 for an explanation of the line review process.)

SKU DISCIPLINE CREATES COST SAVINGS

Line reviews deliver a dual benefit, in that reducing the SKU count forces vendors to compete for the limited shelf space. This often results in cost reductions. When a vendor does not have to compete for shelf space, the retailer will not be obtaining the lowest-cost price. Only when retail space becomes limited and, therefore, valuable will vendors vie for shelf space and offer their lowest-cost prices. Systematic line reviews will lower item costs while eliminating redundant inventory and, in some cases, unnecessary vendors. Both of these factors will positively impact GMROI. This same logic can be applied to increase the productivity of the many products sold online.

When you have redefined the appropriate model stock, you must control the depth of inventory in a store. The big danger here is that products may be reordered with the objective of filling the counter space to make the store *look good,* instead of having a balanced inventory that *works good* [sic].

Optimum inventory levels are dynamic and based on individual stores. The correct depth of inventory must be set by looking at each store's sales by item and setting a safety stock that is adjusted by a logarithm applied to the dynamics of lead times and that store's sales trends.

This whole process is best managed by computerized logarithms. Of course, provision should be made for human adjustment when outlying factors are involved that are not programmed into the logarithm. This requires proper education, as well as discipline to assure that the computerized orders are not overridden for the wrong reasons. It is also imperative that the inventory data maintained in the computer's perpetual inventory number be accurate and dependable. A credible reorder system demands the data generated be dependable to project rational reorders on a store-by-store basis.

ELIMINATING DEAD INVENTORY

Another inventory sin is to let dead or discontinued merchandise sit in the stores and distribution centers. This is often done to avoid making necessary markdowns that impact margin. However, such myopia fails to see the negative impact of dead merchandise on the GMROI of the stores and the expense of storing and handling non-selling products. Precious working capital needs to be invested in productive turning inventory, not inventory collecting dust in stockrooms and warehouses.

Even in the early years at The Home Depot, when our systems were less sophisticated, we were hyper-focused on moving slow or dead merchandise. We learned the value of scheduling monthly walks through our distribution centers to identify inventory problems. All pallets of merchandise were color coded by the month received. We would walk the warehouse and look for pallets that were not turning. These pallets would be dispersed to the stores with appropriate reduced prices. Nothing sells in the warehouse; overstocked products were forced to the stores. If the quantity was too large to put in the store, the parking lot became the selling area for these clearance-priced products.

Any time products stop moving, they cost money and limit GMROI productivity. It is the return on investment that attracts capital, which grows the company. Retailers must always focus on increasing the ROI for their own investors while working to destroy their competitors' ROI by capturing market share. Successful implementation will result in productivity ratios so apparent that the competition's boards ultimately lose confidence in both their management teams and their business models. This will lead to investors' redeploying their resources elsewhere—and forfeit of the market to the more productive retailer.

TURNING OUR FOCUS TO COSTS

So far the focus of this book has been on the importance of making sales the touchstone of every merchandising decision. Achieving higher sales improves inventory turns, which has a positive leveraged impact on GMROI, which is the ultimate measure of successful merchandising. Achieving high sales also sets the stage to negotiate lower costs. So, while sales must always be the first goal for merchants, they must use increased sales to negotiate lower costs. In effect the merchant has two hats—a *merchandiser hat* and a *buyer hat*. The next chapter will focus on the task of the merchant when wearing the *buyer hat*.

15

DRIVING DOWN COSTS
PRINCIPLE 5:
EVERYDAY LOW PRICE DEMANDS
EVERYDAY LOW COSTS.

If *everyday low price* is the goal of every smart retailer, *everyday low cost* is also a must. You must be certain you always have the ultimate cost advantage. This is facilitated by a culture that abhors waste, purchases directly from the prime sources, and uses the best technology to create an efficient logistic system.

SIMPLIFYING THE SUPPLY CHAIN

Many costs are involved in a supply chain, from the first cost of purchasing the product, to the logistics of getting it to the store, to the overhead of the store itself, to the marketing cost of promotion, to the delivery of the product to the customer's home or jobsite.

Every cost that can possibly be identified needs to be isolated, measured, and reduced as a percentage of total sales over time. A successful retailer must embrace a lean and mean attitude regarding costs. Obviously, in a growing company expenditures will increase every year. However, every cost should decrease as a percentage of gross sales every year. This forced efficiency ensures that you can drive down the prices for your customers and withstand any competitive challenge.

Just as you must focus on generating increased sales and higher gross profit dollars, you must demand the same pricing logic and efficiency from the vendors in your supply chain. They must understand that maximizing gross margin dollars often requires a decrease in the gross margin percentage. This may be a difficult hurdle for your vendors to comprehend. Buying right does require driving down margins in the supply chain. But this does not mean you negotiate costs down to a point where the vendor cannot make money. That would be counterproductive. You cannot plan on growth if your vendor is weak and unprofitable. Rather, you need to have the most efficient channel of distribution so your supply chain can profitably outperform your competitor's supply chain.

The objective for the entire supply chain should be to generate high gross profit dollars via high sales volume, as opposed to a high gross profit margin with lower sales volume.

PURCHASING UP THE SUPPLY CHAIN

The most important element in buying right is to remove intermediaries (often called middlemen) from the supply chain whenever possible. If you are going to stock an item in your store, it should be a product with sufficient demand to allow you to purchase directly from the most prime source.

This is where you can buy at *first cost* without any marketing or distribution costs loaded into the purchase price. You must define the specifications for your products that determine the production costs at the point of manufacturing to negotiate this first cost.

There are two equally important reasons for purchasing directly from prime source vendors. The first is obvious: to buy directly from the prime producer in order to purchase on a first-cost basis, which is the lowest cost at the point of production. This requires eliminating intermediaries, which may include wholesalers, distributors, importers, or trading companies. Admittedly, this assumes that you can perform the functions of these intermediaries with increased efficiency—and you must.

However, it is equally important to prevent intermediaries from using your purchasing power and marketing expertise to channel similar or identical products to your competitors. This vertical integration is achieved by controlling both the product's specifications at the point of production and the distribution process to the store and customer. You thereby achieve exclusivity, resulting in pricing power. Now you can market the products at that *sweet spot* where you maximize gross margin dollars.

The more your products are duplicated in the stores of other retailers, the more they become commodity items. You lose pricing power, resulting in low-margin sales. Don't make it easy for competitors to copy your success. You are stronger when your products are differentiated and clearly better than those of your competitors.

Eliminating intermediaries is a first step in protecting your sources and offering truly superior and unique products in the marketplace. Intermediaries exist to make your life easier. That is the problem. The easy way to buy is not the smart way. The intermediaries will promise to save you time and effort while assuring you of their loyalty and dedication to growing your sales and profits. They lie. Their interest is in selling more stuff, and they will use your buying power to subsidize business with your competitors.

THE DANGER OF OVERDEPENDENCE ON INTERMEDIARIES

The Home Depot established an early relationship with a Taiwanese trading company. Together, both companies became well-known, high-volume purchasers of products in the Asian market. This initially was expeditious for The Home Depot, as well as opportunistic for our importer. However, it led to three problems.

First, our volume gave this importer buying power to control the producers to their own advantage. (There can be many hidden allowances in the supply chain.) Further, with The Home Depot as their main client, they had great credibility with our competitors, who were able to benefit from our own research and buying power.

The third and biggest issue was that many manufacturers across Asia hesitated to present new items to us. In many cases they considered our trading company to be their competitor and did not want their data to fall into the hands of such a rival. We were limiting our access to direct manufacturers with products and pricing that could be beneficial to us.

It is easy to let such intermediaries run your business, but it is always detrimental in the long run. We ultimately took action to stop the growth of this supplier, and we shifted our attention toward purchasing directly from prime sources, without agents or trading companies.

Many third-party entities can be hidden in a supply chain. The chart below illustrates how a supply chain can become compromised. You need to peel back the overhead layers, much like peeling an onion, to finally arrive at a direct relationship with the prime producers.

The Strategic Challenge
Lower Costs and Offer Unique Products

D.C. Store	DOMESTIC MNFCTRER	DOMESTIC IMPORTER	DOMESTIC AGENT	FOREIGN AGENT	FOREIGN TRADING CO.	FOREIGN MNFCTRER
D.C. Store	DOMESTIC MNFCTRER	DOMESTIC IMPORTER	DOMESTIC AGENT	FOREIGN AGENT	FOREIGN TRADING CO.	FOREIGN MNFCTRER
D.C. Store		DOMESTIC IMPORTER	DOMESTIC AGENT	FOREIGN AGENT	FOREIGN TRADING CO.	FOREIGN MNFCTRER
D.C. Store			DOMESTIC AGENT	FOREIGN AGENT	FOREIGN TRADING CO.	FOREIGN MNFCTRER
D.C. Store				FOREIGN AGENT	FOREIGN TRADING CO.	FOREIGN MNFCTRER
D.C. Store					FOREIGN TRADING CO.	FOREIGN MNFCTRER
D.C. Store						FOREIGN MNFCTRER

Intermediaries do provide necessary functions within the supply chain, and those tasks and roles don't disappear when purchasing directly. Smart retailers must assume those functions and strive to perform them in the most efficient, world-class manner. Let's look at ways that can happen.

PRODUCT AND PACKAGING SPECIFICATIONS

When sourcing products, retailers need to search out the most competent manufacturers in the world. The next step is to become involved in developing the specifications for those products.

Retailers often position their private-label programs to offer proprietary products at a discount to the dominant, name-brand products. But downgrading specifications to hit a price point will often result in poor quality."

The first question most often asked of the foreign vendor is, "Can we buy this item cheaper?" The answer to that is always, "No problem." Of course the reduced price will result in reduced quality, which often results in products that ultimately disappoint the customer. In the worst case, creates a profoundly serious public relations snafu as the problem becomes public in the media.

China has the most modern equipment for producing consumer products in the world. They can make the best products or the worst products. It is all a matter of specifications and price. The right question to ask when sourcing in Asia is, "How can we make this better?" The answer may surprise you; sometimes for just pennies in improvements you can create dollars in increased value.

Many of your own brands can—and should—be perceived by the customer as top-quality, premium-branded products. This is simply a matter of positioning brands properly with clear brand statements and then maintaining quality to assure the customer will receive consistent performance.

Most manufacturers have some great ideas just waiting for someone to ask for innovation instead of another price reduction. Retailers should strive for an open-book relationship with foreign vendors that will allow them to create unique products, based upon their specifications, with transparent costs.

TEST AND VERIFY

Once a supplier has been identified and specifications set, there must be rigid tests to assure the specifications are actually met. People tend to blame China for the low-quality products often produced there. The blame, though, should be put on retailers. These retailers fail in two ways. First, they fail to establish quality specifications at the beginning of their purchasing negotiations, and, second, they neglect to test for compliance to the defined standards.

When I was with The Home Depot, we had an unpleasant surprise when testing our Chinese-sourced, hand-tufted, 100 percent wool rugs. The process uncovered the disturbing fact that the rugs had material in them besides wool. Their composition included sheep, goat, horse, yak, and even human hair!

When we confronted the vendor with the test results, we were told our rugs were 100 percent *Chinese wool*, which is different from wool produced elsewhere. Oh, really? Who knew *Chinese wool* was different from wool everywhere else in the world?

This lesson taught us to be much more skeptical and careful. Clearly, a competent quality-control program is essential and critical, both pre-purchase and post-purchase, to implement a viable private-label program. The retailer must establish and manage the testing of directly sourced products.

CARTONS AND PACKAGING MUST BE SPECIFIED

These standards must go beyond product design. The merchant must be intimately involved in the design of the shipping cartons and point-of-sale packaging. Product packaging guidelines need to address how to reduce the cubic size of the total package, which allows more individual products to be placed in each shipping container. This lowers the average landed cost of the product by spreading the transportation cost of the container over a wider number of units.

Then it is important to determine the ideal carton size and the number of individual products in the carton to allow your distribution centers and stores to efficiently deal with reorders. The item count in the carton for each individual SKU must be a function of its rate of sale in the average store. It must be set by the retailer, not the manufacturer.

A manufacturer may find it convenient to pack all the products in standard-sized cartons, regardless of the rate of sale at retail; or they may choose an arbitrary number of items, such as twenty-five or fifty per carton. The merchant must specify the size of the carton that best fits the store shelves and the quantity of items in a carton, which must be determined by the SKU rate-of-sale guidelines.

A good rule is that the merchant should specify the days of supply to be maintained in the average store and then set the case count to not exceed half of this number; when the inventory is 50 percent depleted, a new case can be ordered and safety stock brought back to the ideal days of supply level.

RIGHT PACKAGING INCREASES STORE PRODUCTIVITY

Sizing cartons with the proper item count prevents the need to open cases in the distribution centers. That creates labor savings there and efficiency at the store. It prevents unneeded inventory, which occurs when stores are shipped standard packages that greatly exceed their average rate of sale.

Appropriate use of right-sized packaging with proper labels also allows the shipping carton to be used to hold and merchandise products in the store. This can significantly reduce the use of peg hooks for merchandising.

Peg hooks are labor intensive for store associates to refill. They also do not use cubic space efficiently. Peg hooks hold a limited number of items, which necessitates multiple facings. You can see on the left side of the following chart that peg hooks do not make use of the total cubic space available on the counter. High-volume items require additional rows of peg hooks, which can require significant linear counter space. The only alternative to using an excessive number of peg hooks is to put a portion of this inventory in overhead storage or in stockrooms, necessitating extra labor to stock and restock.

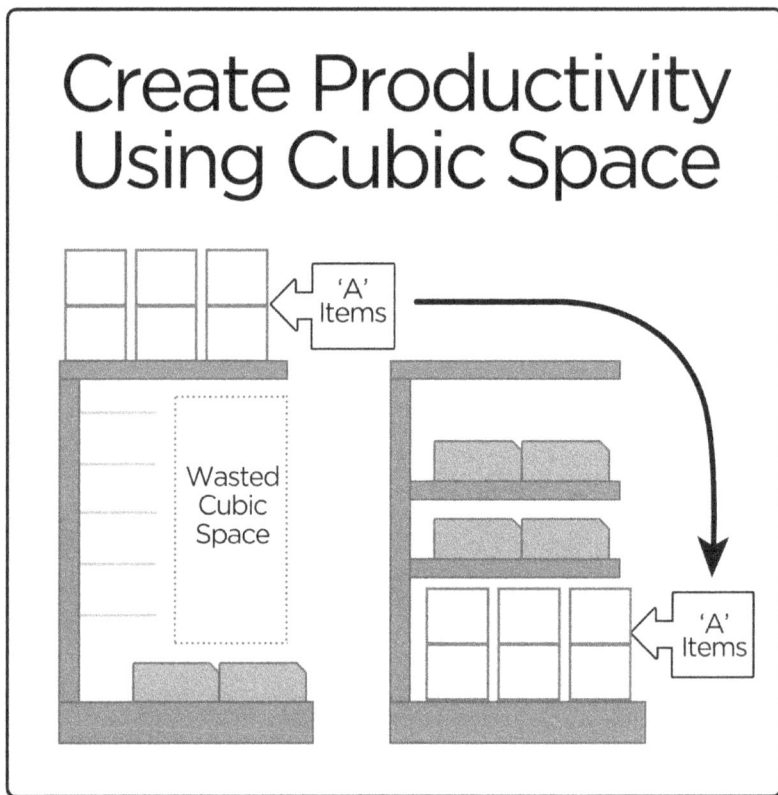

Create Productivity Using Cubic Space

'A' Items

Wasted Cubic Space

'A' Items

The right side of the chart shows the result of replacing peg hooks with cartons, which allows for better use of that cubic space. It reduces the facings of the individual SKUs, which saves linear space in the store. It also facilitates moving inventory that is in overheads or back rooms onto the sales floor, thereby putting more product at the customer level and eliminating a lot of manual labor in the process. The biggest labor saving factor is that the employees stock the shelves by moving full cartons, not individual items. The first person to touch an individual product is the customer who takes it to the cash register.

At The Home Depot we called this method of display "cut-case" merchandising. While today the vendors serving U.S. home centers have been conditioned to ship products in cartons that are easily opened and used to display the products, we originally supplied our salespeople with razor blade knives to cut the cases in order to display the products inside. Hence the term cut-case. (Yes, we maintained a good supply of bandages.)

Both The Home Depot and Lowe's have been instrumental in getting vendors to package in cut-case programs. In addition to increasing the productivity of the store's cubic space, these cartons now contain photos of the products inside and provide specific product information helpful to the customer. So they save space while increasing sales. This is a no-brainer in terms of increasing productivity in a big-box home-center store. Nevertheless, I have encountered many retailers who drag their feet, due to vendor pushback, even after management teams acknowledge the benefits of the proposed change.

In the early days of The Home Depot, we also had to push the vendors to comply with our packaging requirements. We knew the advantages of displaying our products with cut-case merchandising on pallet racking to optimize productivity, but the manufacturers were still packaging their products based on their traditional methods. It would have been far more efficient for the vendors to package the products in appropriately sized cartons that were serrated for easy display and didn't need to be cut at store level. In addition, these cartons could have proper labels to show the product visually and provide useful descriptions and specifications.

The problem was getting the manufacturers to change their method of packaging for our stores. To force the issue, when we opened our next new store, we purchased thousands of display cartons from Grainger supply company. Upon receipt of product from the manufacturers, we transferred the product from shipping cartons to these purchased display cartons. We set the entire store with cartons, eliminating most of the peg hooks.

We then invited the vendors to visit the store so we could show them how much more productive this type of packaging would be; putting more of their product on our counters made it more available to customers.

Many of the vendors initially raised multiple objections to changing the packaging requirements. There is always blind resistance to change. They complained, for example, that their other customers would not accept the revised packaging; changing their packaging just for our stores would raise their costs. It required changes on the production line and in their warehouses.

However, we were able to prove to the vendors that, rather than costing them more, the investment in new packaging would pay off in greatly increased sales, as demonstrated in our cut-case store. Some vendors saw the light, while others dragged their heels.

We ultimately gave the vendors an ultimatum. They needed to revise their packaging, and we gave them six months to do it. This was necessary to obtain widespread compliance and rapidly implement cut-case merchandising in our stores.

Another problem with pegged packaging is that it uses a lot of plastic, which has ecological downsides. Cut-case packaging can eliminate much of this expensive and unnecessary wrapping. Considering the environmental impact of packing materials—their disposal as well as the safety of the chemicals used in their manufacturing—is important today and will only become more crucial in the future.

PACKAGING FOR THE CUSTOMERS

Carton packaging with good labeling can increase sales by providing the customer with usable, relevant, product information and, perhaps, inspiration. This can include the product specifications and a photo or drawing of the product. In many cases the labels can be color coded to make key specifications more quickly identifiable. This information can immensely improve the customer's shopping experience.

Good packaging will have the combined benefits of increasing the unit capacity of shipping containers, thereby lowering freight cost, as well as lowering labor costs in the DCs and increasing sales in the stores.

When we began bringing products in from Asia, the vendors shipped the products in low-quality, brown cartons that looked cheap and imported. We learned that for a small cost we could have the vendors ship in white, cardboard cartons with full-color labels. This small expense at the production point created a much stronger value image at the point of sale.

Optimized packaging must be engineered based upon the relevant supply chain and customer needs. For example, there is a big difference between the criteria for good packaging at the physical store level and packaging requirements for e-commerce. Packaging for online products does not need the inspirational photos and copy that are so helpful in the store. But the package does need to survive the drop test, while keeping weight and cubic size minimal to lower freight costs when shipped via e-commerce. It could well be that the identical item requires different packaging depending upon how it will ultimately be distributed.

Packaging is a critical element of both the landed cost of the product and the ability to best serve the customer's needs. Product sourcing is not complete until the merchant has defined the shipping carton and the point-of-sale packaging required to make the store *easy to stock, easy to sell, and easy to buy.* The true cost is not the cost at the point of the production line but the cost after the product has been supplied to the ultimate consumer. All logistics and costs must be managed in order to obtain the lowest net cost, considering the entire supply chain.

EFFICIENT LOGISTICS

Buying right requires an understanding of the real landed cost, which includes the first cost plus the cost of getting the product from the manufacturer's shipping dock to the store's loading dock. Logistic cost can be a huge percentage of the total landed cost of the products. This is particularly true in the home-center business, where much of the product is high cube and low value.

Many variables impact logistic costs. They will vary by product and company. These costs can be grouped into transportation costs, warehousing costs, and the cost of working capital tied up in inventory. The goal is to remove all waste from the process thereby driving down landed costs.

The terms of purchase must always specify that ownership title changes from seller to buyer at the point of origin. This is termed buying free on board (FOB). It means taking total responsibility for logistics and cost from the domestic vendor's shipping dock or the foreign vendor's shipping port. This requires the retailer's own traffic department to negotiate the freight costs and select the carriers in order to control transportation costs and define service levels.

The value of the total freight volume of the entire company for all shipments, both foreign and domestic, when combined, provides huge buying power to facilitate negotiation of the lowest transportation costs. At the same time, this purchasing leverage can also be used to obtain the absolute best service in terms of timing and flexibility.

Huge discounts are available from shipping companies, plus there are great opportunities for consolidation and backhauls that should never be left in the hands of the retailer's fragmented product vendors. Great economies of scale are available to the retailer that takes control of the total logistic supply chain, consolidates freight volumes, and flexes its logistic muscles.

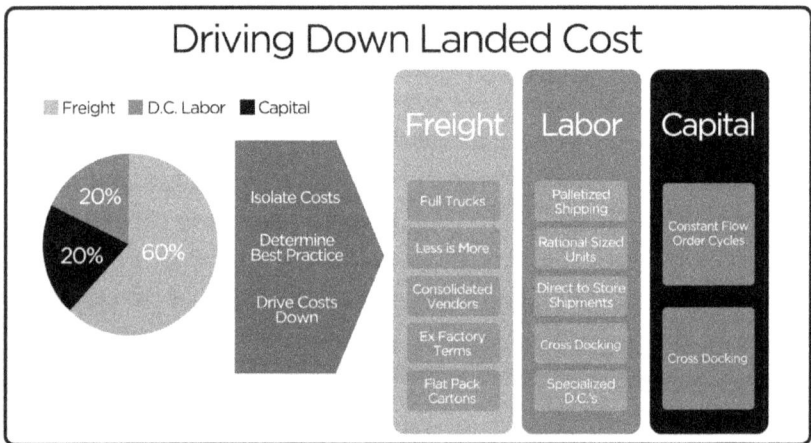

Driving Down Landed Cost

Freight ▨ D.C. Labor ▨ Capital ■

20%
20% 60%

Isolate Costs
Determine Best Practice
Drive Costs Down

Freight	Labor	Capital
Full Trucks	Palletized Shipping	
Less is More	Rational Sized Units	Constant Flow Order Cycles
Consolidated Vendors	Direct to Store Shipments	
Ex Factory Terms	Cross Docking	
Flat Pack Cartons	Specialized D.C.'s	Cross Docking

Percentages shown are typical but will vary by company.

Many retailers ask the vendors to ship prepaid to their stores or distribution centers. When this is done, the freight cost is buried in the product price. Clearly the vendors do not ship their product for free. The first step to control logistic costs is to isolate each function so it can be measured. Freight costs must be pulled away from the product cost to better manage landed costs. Furthermore, giving the vendor control of your freight allows this vendor to use your volume to subsidize the freight costs of their other customers, who are your competitors. It is surprising how many retailers are lax in their responsibility to exercise oversight of their transportation costs.

Once again, the easy way is often the wrong way. Committing to a competent in-house freight management department is a wise investment that pays back significantly in terms of cost, service, and strategic advantages.

TRANSPORTATION EVOLUTION

The Home Depot went through a series of process changes to gain control of the costs and service levels for freight shipments. Initially products were often purchased at a price that included delivery to the store. These shipments were often for less-than-truckload quantities, resulting in multiple trucks lined up behind the store for many hours, waiting to unload. These trucks could contain full capacity loads or only one or two pallets. The point is that all the trucks had to wait in line to be off-loaded. The vendors built the costs of these long waits into the product prices they charged us.

The next step was to receive by appointment only. This greatly reduced the lines by setting a receiving schedule that matched the capacity to unload promptly. This assurance of promptness allowed the vendors to prioritize our deliveries and drive down the landed cost of merchandise.

After this we set up core carriers across the country where less-than-truckload (LTL) shipments from multiple manufacturers in a region could be consolidated into core-carrier DCs, so trucks with consolidated, full loads would now do the long-haul runs into the major metro areas. Here the shipments would be cross-docked into fully loaded store delivery trucks going to the store on a preferred appointment basis. This allowed more products to be shipped on full trucks, which further lowered the landed cost of the products.

The final step was to purchase all products on ex-factory freight terms, with all costs and choice of carriers negotiated, controlled, and managed by The Home Depot. This control, combined with powerful IT systems, has created a very efficient supply chain, ensuring that virtually all store shipments arrive in full trucks. It has also given the stores control of specific delivery times, in order to avoid conflicting with customer service. Additionally, online products can be shipped at a significant discount from the normal prices charged by carriers for home delivery.

RIGHT LOGISTIC FACILITIES

Proper logistics for imported products must be designed to allow for a constant flow of products from foreign producers. It is important to have cross-dock facilities to consolidate or break out shipments as needed.

Cross-docking involves bringing full rail cars, shipping containers, or truckloads from a single manufacturer or source into a facility. The incoming product from an individual vendor is then combined with other incoming shipments from multiple vendors to facilitate shipping consolidated truckloads of mixed products to the ultimate destination. That could be a distribution center or, more likely, a store.

In the case of a retailer with distribution centers in multiple countries, the cross-docks need to be at each of the major foreign ports used. In the case of The Home Depot, where the distribution centers are all in North America, and primarily in the U.S., it makes more sense to have the cross-docking facilities at domestic ports.

These cross-dock facilities allow the retailer to combine orders from different distribution centers in different regions in order meet the minimum order quantities of a foreign factory. Having the ability to combine orders from multiple distribution centers by cross-docking avoids having to order full containers from a single vendor for each of the individual distribution centers. Being able to cross-dock in-coming full containers into mixed-container outbound shipments at the port creates a *constant flow* of imported product based upon rate of sale. This avoids the feast-and-famine cycles that result when full containers of single products must be ordered by each distribution center to gain shipment.

In most cases the lead time on imports will require dedicated distribution centers that can then feed these products to the stores as needed. However, these inventories need to be minimized by creating a logistic system focused on creating a *constant flow* of product, thereby minimizing the inventory levels required.

A critical element to achieve this *constant flow* of product is to place reorders for foreign vendors on a set schedule so production time is set aside in advance at the factory. This assures there will be no delay in production once the orders are received by the vendor. It will greatly reduce the lead time and, therefore, minimize the inventory levels that stores and distribution centers must maintain.

Isolating the distribution functions allows costs to be identified and driven down. Retailers will often build multipurpose distribution centers for import warehousing, domestic warehousing, and domestic cross-docking; they may even try to use these same facilities for shipping e-commerce orders. However, this kind of mixed use does not create cost efficiencies. It actually makes it difficult to isolate the true cost of each of these functions, which makes it infinitely harder to drive those costs down. These multipurpose distribution centers can become congested orifices when one of the functions backs up and destroys the total flow of all products. Service to the stores suffers and costs start to rise.

With inconsistent lead times, the stores get frustrated and start hoarding merchandise, which destroys their inventory turns. Erratic supply also results in periodic out-of-stock conditions, which causes customers to lose confidence and shop elsewhere. Merchandise needs to flow, not back up in ports or on receiving docks. Retailers need to invest in specialized facilities that are strategically located and cost engineered to provide the specific functions required at maximum efficiency.

The sourcing of products on a worldwide basis can drive down first cost and provide higher margins. Higher margins can greatly increase GMROI, but only if logistic functions are efficient. Constant flow of imported product is critical to avoid feast/famine inventory situations that would work against improved GMROI. The merchandising and logistic departments must work together, not as isolated silos, to assure an efficient process as you source internationally. The clear goal must be to lower landed costs while increasing the customer's confidence that the right product will be available when desired.

PRIVATE LABEL DEFINITIONS

The procurement and marketing of directly purchased products essentially becomes your private-label program. Since these products should be produced to your own specifications, they are unique. Therefore, you must establish a brand for marketing them.

The first impulse often is to put the store name on the products and use the store logo as the brand. However, the better way for most retailers to market private label is to establish category brands that have a specific promise to the customer, which adds value. Developing credible brands independent of the store brand gains pricing power, maximizing both sales and profits.

Store-brand labels often send the message that the product is generic and should be priced low. Low price often results in low quality. Costco's Kirkland and the Aldi grocery brands are unique examples in which the prices are below the name-brand alternative, but quality remains high. However, the point remains that the promise to the customer is a price discounted from those of alternative products.

Pricing products below the branded alternatives is certainly one successful method of increasing sales. However, it is not the only use—or even the optimum use—of private label. This is especially true for home-center retailers.

Some commodity items within a typical private-label program will be sold simply on the basis of low price. In such cases, the brand on the package is not critical. For example, the label on a roll of electrical tape can simply read "electrical tape." Branding this product does not tend to sell more units or create a higher-price opportunity.

Considerable opportunity exists, on the other hand, for retailers to sell a large percentage of their private-label products at a premium price if the product specifications are superior and the product is priced and marketed as a premium product. This requires defining the brand with a promise to the customer and exercising discipline to assure quality performance.

A successful private-label program should not be measured and judged only by its total sales penetration; instead, it should be evaluated primarily by its margin contribution. This is the real advantage of private label.

When private label is done right you should see gross margin contribution penetration that is much higher than the sales penetration itself. For example, assume private-label products constitute twenty percent of total sales. If so, it would be reasonable to expect the gross margin contribution of those products to represent perhaps thirty percent of the company's gross margin dollars. If the private-label program does not disproportionately increase gross profit percentages, gross profit dollars, and GMROI, something is wrong.

The most helpful way to think about the private-label program is to see it as a three-level approach. This was first outlined in the discussion of pricing objectives in chapter 5.

Opening-price-point or generic brands are commodity products sold strictly at the lowest price points. They have little differentiation from the competition. In a home center these might be items like cotton gloves or electrical tape. The product label might simply be descriptive: *cotton gloves* or *electrical tape*. The brand is not critical since demand for these products is driven by price alone. Generic labeling works fine.

Most home-improvement retailers do have a house brand for such OPP products. At The Home Depot the brand is HDX. At Lowe's the brand is Project Source. One caution: When a store brand is used across multiple categories, a bad customer experience with a product in one category can destroy the customer's perception of that brand in all the departments.

It is critical to control the specifications to assure an acceptable level of quality for house brands, as well as generic branded products. You may need to price such commodity products at the market price, but the product should, nevertheless, provide more value for the money than that of your competition. Do not confuse low price with low quality. Never sell a product unless you are comfortable with the quality.

Departmental or mainstream brands are products that make up a family. For example, at The Home Depot *Glacier Bay* is the private-label brand for products found in the plumbing department that have to do with water. This could be a faucet, a toilet, or a sink. *Glacier Bay* represents a quality product, but it is sold at a discount to the national name brands such as Kohler, Delta, and American Standard. *Commercial Electric* is The Home Depot's brand that serves the same function in electrical and lighting supplies.

Customers become familiar with these products over time simply by using them successfully. The dual objective is to give the customer a quality alternative with comparable features and benefits while being discounted from similar name-brand products. The customers receive a great value, while the store receives a higher gross margin, compared to sales of similar name-brand items. For this to work, the private label's retail price must be indexed at a specific discount to the branded retail, not the retailer's landed costs.

Equity or power brands are products that have superior features and can command premium pricing.

An example at The Home Depot is their *Husky* hand tools, which carry a lifetime guarantee, or their *Ridgid* power tools, which have features and benefits that compare favorably to name brands such as Bosch or DeWalt.

The success of these power brands requires that a marketing program be developed to establish the brand as a high-quality, name brand in the marketplace. In the case of The Home Depot, these tool brands have been heavily promoted in their Nascar racing program. Establishing such brands involves some marketing cost, but the investment can pay off in sales, increased gross margin, and customer loyalty when a multi-year horizon is established for marketing and sales. Great brands are not created overnight, but retailers are in a good position to create their own brands that can define the market and represent a standard of excellence.

Hand tools was one of the first product categories The Home Depot imported as a private-label program. Our first brand was called Ohio Forge. This was in our early days of developing a private-label program, and we did not distinguish between generic (OPP), departmental (mainstream) or equity (power) brands in terms of product or marketing. If it was a hand tool, we simply labeled it Ohio Forge.

However, tools that all carried the same Ohio Forge brand encompassed a wide range of feature benefits and quality levels. Our own salespeople became confused about which Ohio Forge tools were good and dependable and which were not. Customer complaints and returns on some items ultimately soured the salespeople on all Ohio Forge products. They would no longer recommend our private-label tools to customers. In fact, they steered the customers away from such products. We ultimately had to kill the brand.

This was a learning experience that created a more structured private-label program. Today Husky is The Home Depot's quality tool line that offers a lifetime warranty on all Husky hand tools. The Husky brand demands high quality specifications so the sales associates can comfortably recommend Husky tools.

QUALITY CANNOT BE COMPROMISED

While it is helpful to consider three distinct levels of private-label marketing based on pricing objectives, this should not lead to thinking there are three levels of quality. The price difference should be based primarily on features and benefits. It is important for the sales associates to be proud of all the private-label products and have confidence to recommend them.

Quality control must be based on specifications and monitored for consistency and compliance with the agreed-upon specifications. Every imported product purchased by The Home Depot had to go through quality control testing both before production, at the prototype stage, and then after, in post-production inspection. As previously mentioned, it is the retailer's responsibility to properly control the quality of the products carried. The private-label retailer has a further responsibility to verify that the production of the products is in keeping with accepted international standards regarding labor regulations and environmental criteria, which requires recurring on-site inspections.

Another benefit of a competent private-label program is that once expertise is shown in producing and marketing quality private-label products, domestic name-brand vendors may become more flexible in their pricing to maintain product placement within the model stock assortment. This can be especially helpful in today's e-commerce world, where name-brand products are easily shopped on the internet with resulting low margins. Competence to source successful private-label programs gains respect from domestic name-brand vendors.

This competence in sourcing and marketing private-label programs can, and should, give customers access to products both online and off-line with unique features and benefits, as well as real price advantages. This can move the customer's purchase from low-margin name brands to the higher margin, private-label products, while the customer wins in receiving superior features and better value.

It is a fact that political forces tend to encourage higher tariffs, in order to slow down the flow of imported products. However, as tariffs increase prices on domestically produced products increase accordingly. The customer loses twice. Brazil is a case in point. Import products are often double the prices elsewhere in the world, due to the high tariffs, which allows the domestic vendors to raise their prices even higher. When prices go up, the standard of living goes down.

DOMESTIC BRANDED PRODUCTS

It is always desirable to buy directly from the manufacturer at net costs based upon unique specifications. While this is often possible in Asia and other parts of the world, it tends to be difficult, if not impossible, with many of the domestic, name-brand vendors. Such cases require a completely different set of methods to *peel the onion* and drive down costs.

When working with domestic, name-brand vendors, be aware that they have already baked into their pricing the packaging, logistic, and marketing costs. They are not usually willing to quote a net-net price with these costs removed, nor are they generally open to providing unique products in the retailer's own brand. Therefore, a significantly different type of negotiation is required to buy right.

ACHIEVING DISCOUNTS

A review of The Home Depot's domestic negotiation process as described in chapter 6 provides some examples of how to *peel the onion* to obtain price concessions from domestic vendors. Here are four specific negotiating strategies:

1. Using line reviews to negotiate the pricing for individual items.

2. Negotiating corporate rebates based on increased volume with preferred vendors.

3. Requesting up-front promotional funds to support marketing efforts.

4. Obtaining additional discounts for new product lines and new stores.

Over time some retailers develop a list of additional discounts they request and even demand from their vendors. The justification can range from the reasonable to the outright foolish. This proliferation of requested discounts is a bad practice. It becomes a self-defeating game, with each party going through the motions of negotiating in order to arrive at an agreed upon price. The vendor has built an initial price offer, knowing that discounts will be demanded and given. The retailers know this, but they think they are smart enough to negotiate more than the fair share of discounts from any given vendor.

In essence, when it comes to retailer/vendor negotiations, additional discounts or allowances are only justified when they create a growth momentum of new sales and increased market share for both the retailer and the vendor.

DISCOUNT PROLIFERATION

The management of a major, big-box home-center chain sensed that they might not be obtaining the lowest costs possible from their vendors. They reviewed the discounts and allowances being requested by their merchandising group and, as a result, uncovered more than two-dozen unique requests for discounts and allowances in their system. It was obvious that with so many special discounts, the vendors were not always making their lowest-possible original price offer. The logical next step was to renegotiate lower net costs.

This is easier said than done. In fact, it is virtually impossible to truly reestablish a trust relationship that will allow open-book negotiations. There could be a whole string of allowances baked into the acquisition prices of any given vendor, and these suppliers always hesitate to net prices down, knowing a new request for discounts might follow.

Furthermore, they really don't want to disclose the allowances they have built into their cost, as they wish to maintain flexibility in how they leverage and administer these discounts and rebates.

There are no real secrets within an industry. The vendors talk with each other and know exactly the game they must play with each company and the hot buttons for specific buyers. They will adjust their offers accordingly. This is a game the retailer won't often win. The buyer most often is putting money in one pocket by taking it out of a different pocket, with no net gain.

The better vendor relationship is to have a trust relationship that opens the books to discuss specifications and costs of the products. This is difficult when the cost negotiations are based a zero-sum game of obtaining discounts that simply fall to the retailer's bottom line, without any real growth of additional business to the retailer or the vendor.

A certain level of transparency and shared objectives is required to develop the right pricing agreements. The best way to obtain cost reductions is to give the vendor a justification for lowering cost, such as a commitment to increased sales and market share. The goal of every vendor negotiation should be a win-win outcome, in order to maintain a strong, viable, and efficient supply chain.

It must be your goal to ensure that every element of your distribution channel is cost effective and able to deliver the best value to your customers. The strategic battle is a war between your supply chain versus your competitors' supply chains. This makes your vendors partners in taking market share. You both have a mutual obligation to drive down costs. There must be an understanding with your vendors that they gain market share and gross profit dollars as you mutually make your distribution channel more efficient and pass much of those savings on to the ultimate customer.

PREFERRED VENDOR TERMS

Many of The Home Depot vendors tended to see the line review process as a confrontational win-lose proposition. It was not unusual for a long-time vendor of The Home Depot to contact senior management with complaints about unfair treatment and reminders of their past good service and loyalty, in an effort to avoid reducing established margins.

Vendors often did face new, difficult pricing decisions as a result of the product line review. The vendor's sales group had to go back to their production and finance management and explain how accepting lower margins would create more sales and more gross profit dollars and how, in contrast, rejecting The Home Depot offer could mean cutting production and staffing. This was a hard sell for companies that were production oriented and used pricing formulas that had always worked in the past.

Some vendors did walk away from our business rather than accept our price proposals. However, those that accepted the challenge to become more efficient became stronger companies with increased market share. It was not unusual for a number two or three brand to accept and embrace The Home Depot's gross margin dollar challenge and emerge as the leading brand in the marketplace.

In chapter 6 it was explained how vendors could come to understand the advantages of a real partnership relationship that was possible when they were designated as a "preferred vendor," due to a mutual commitment to growth. This was based on confidence that this special relationship would provide a long-term stream of sales and profits. It was not just a matter of hammering down the vendors to get a better price but making them partners in growing the market and growing market share. Done right, this was a win-win-win outcome for the retailer, the vendor, and—most of all—the customers.

Everyday low price requires achieving *everyday low costs.* Achieving this competitive position requires buying direct and totally controlling the logistic functions, from the producer's factory to the customer's home. The key to success is to be assured of having the most efficient supply chain in the industry. Having achieved *everyday low cost* and established *everyday low price,* the next task is to tell the value story to the customers.

16

ITEM/PRICE VERSUS BRAND/IMAGE

PRINCIPLE 6:
ADVERTISING IS AN INVESTMENT, NOT AN EXPENSE.

"If you build a better mousetrap, the world will beat a path to your door." This is the common adaptation of words attributed to Ralph Waldo Emerson in *The Atlanta Constitution* in 1882. But that's not how things work.

If you invent a better mousetrap, you will need to identify your target market of people with a mouse problem, clearly understand their problem, identify the best way to make contact with them, educate them on how this new mousetrap will solve their problem, show them how the new product is superior to all others on the market, and make sure, in the process, that they clearly understand you have their best interest at heart.

Having accomplished all that, you will then need to go back to the drawing board and work on the next improvement to your new mousetrap. When you've completed that task, you'll need to start the communication process all over again.

The goal is not just to sell a mousetrap today but to become the trusted source for solving all mouse problems forever. This requires building trust and rapport with the customer through enlightened marketing.

Today the retailer must clearly identify and define its own *unique, sustainable, compelling, competitive advantage.* Next this advantage must be turned into a story that is true, emotionally engaging, and believable.

It must be communicated via new digital channels that the customer is actually using. In today's world the retailer must incorporate the magic of video to tell its important story.

And the message itself? It is no longer just a price story about a single sale item. It is now all about connecting with customers so they will trust the brand and, in fact, identify with the company it represents.

DIGITAL COMMUNICATION REVOLUTION

Marketing is an essential part of retailing, and nothing in retailing has changed more in the past decade than the world of advertising, public relations, and promotion.

The digital revolution has forever transformed the way customers get their information, communicate, and are entertained. E-commerce has had an *evolutionary* effect on retailing, but the digital impact on promotion has been *revolutionary.*

People now receive and send information through a profusion of rapidly changing digital avenues of communication. The world of digital communication spans the World Wide Web, which includes the millions of websites and individual pages that encompass the internet. It also includes communication devices such as smartphones, tablets, and smart watches. The options seem endless.

This puts pressure on retailers. First you need to realize that old communication methods are rapidly becoming obsolete. Next you have to find the specific media your target customers are using for information. Then you must embrace the new marketing channels and adapt your messages to them. In a dynamic technological environment, this is a never-ending learning process.

THE WAY WE WERE

Retailers have traditionally driven their promotional efforts with print media, specifically, run-of-press newspaper ads and multi-page sale catalogs inserted into newspapers or directly mailed to customers' homes. These methods were most effective with item/price advertising. The message demanded that the customer *Act Now!* to save on specific items for a *Limited Time Only!*

One downside of this type of advertising is its short lifespan. It requires consistent and, often, increasing exposure, with higher costs going forward. However, the larger problem with print advertising is that most customers no longer subscribe to newspapers. Print advertising is rapidly becoming passé. Video now rules over print. Nevertheless, some retailers are still using old media that few customers see to tell an old story that few customers care about.

Like Linus in the Peanuts comic strip, holding tightly to his security blanket, they hold on to print advertising because it is what they have always done, and their existing marketing methods and infrastructure revolve around newspaper ads and direct mail catalogs.

One of my home-center clients in Europe based its marketing program on a catalog that was faithfully printed every month, year after year. Eventually the management recognized that store traffic did not seem to be closely related to the release of the catalog. Without telling their sales associates, they decided not to send out the next monthly edition. To their surprise, no one at store level realized the catalog had been discontinued.

The store traffic was simply not driven by print advertising. Sales continued on track. Sales are driven by other variables, starting with seasonality and including many external factors, like the economy and competition, or internal factors, such as product assortment and in-store service. Together these can impact the customer's purchasing activity more than print advertising. Peer group word of mouth is perhaps the most important advertising, and that results primarily from a great shopping experience.

THE WAY WE NEED TO BE

The new reality is that the internet provides customers with knowledge of all pricing options, not just your sale inserts in the newspaper. Customers can now shop the entire marketplace for products they are interested in at this moment, in real time. Most customers will start their project journey on the internet before taking any other step.

On the flip side, retailers can now promote their merchandise and services 24/7 along a full continuum, from item/price for price comparison to brand/image messages, which can tell a convincing and emotionally engaging story.

Every retailer must be able to answer the question, "What are your competitive advantages?" If the retailer cannot answer quickly, in one succinct paragraph, there is a much bigger problem than picking items for a newspaper ad. If the retailer has no ammunition in terms of competitive advantages to aim at the target customer, perhaps the only tool left is to offer a temporary sale price. This sad dilemma goes way beyond the issue of pricing.

Building a marketing model that relies on this week's direct mail catalog or newspaper advertisement is no longer a viable long-run formula for success. Why? A main issue is that item/price advertising is not the primary motivator for most customers. It does not create in the customer's mind a trust relationship based upon a dependable value proposition.

Instead, you must make sure your customers are aware of your *unique, sustainable, compelling, competitive advantages*, whether those advantages are in pricing, service, assortment, quality, community relations, environmental stewardship, or any other hot button they may have. This will be an ongoing effort, using electronic media to reinforce brand messages over time.

All your promotional strategies should be formulated to take the customer on a journey from a general awareness of your brand to being a committed, loyal customer who is truly a fan of your brand.

THE MEDIA IS THE MESSAGE

Obviously, promotion is far more complicated today than in the past. It is important to understand, as you transition from print media to TV/radio and on to the internet, that your message can and should change with the media. What succeeds in a broadcast commercial may not work well on Facebook, Twitter, or Instagram. Every media has its own viewer following that needs a tailored message that is germane to each specific target market.

> *"People do not buy goods and services; they buy relations, stories, and magic."*
> — Seth Godin

Every retailer must rapidly respond to today's digital world with new flexibility in the choice of media and the creation of more impactful messages. This is an ongoing journey that involves a certain amount of experimentation. Whatever the media, communications should consistently focus on key messages, rather than on products and pricing. You need to communicate messages of trust and emotional affiliation that clearly differentiate your brand in order to build bonding relationships with your customers. Communication with customers has become a two-way dialogue.

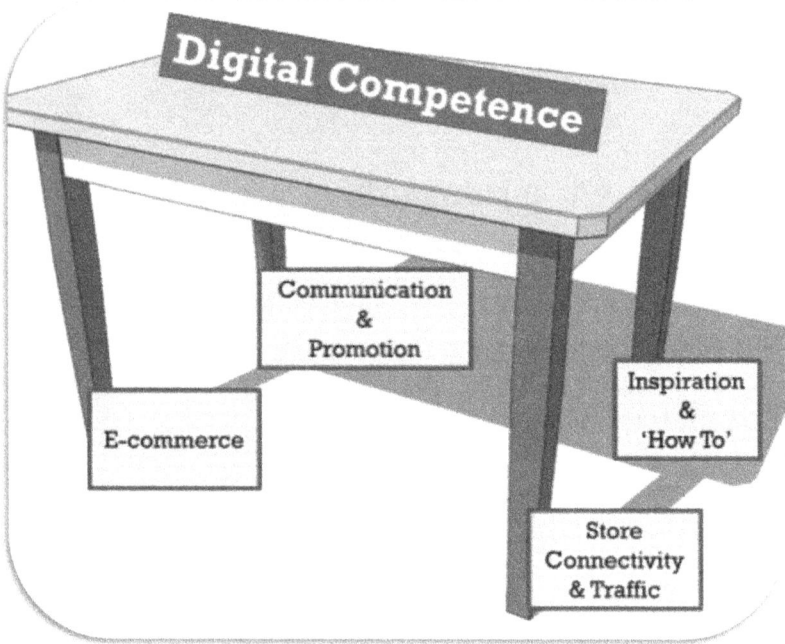

THE FOUR-LEGGED TABLE

Digital tools can be thought of as a four-legged table. One leg is *communication and promotion*. This can range from general information on your home page to very specific promotional messages.

The second leg encompasses *inspirational and how-to* items. This material is designed to instill in customers a desire to improve their lifestyle and give them confidence they can accomplish their projects (for which they need your merchandise).

The third leg is *e-commerce*. Here is your 24/7 way of helping customers buy what they want, when they want, and take possession of it however they want.

The fourth leg is *store connectivity and traffic*. This takes the customer from idea to action. It helps the customer find the right path toward project completion, which will often result in store visits. Once there, the in-store experience will be guided by a host of enhancements, such as phone-sourced product maps, interactive electronic information stations, and improved product information signing, which all add up to a better and faster shopping experience.

The most important enhancement will be interacting with great salespeople who are digitally competent and provided with advanced digital tools to take already knowledgeable customers to the next level of project competence and satisfaction. The salesperson is the most important and effective form of promotion.

The digital strategy must use these four legs to create an interconnected journey for the customers between your website and physical store. The customers will use your website, visit your store, and interact with your people, while navigating their way to a completed project. Their project success, then, will make them promoters of your brand.

THE EMOTIONAL ELEMENT

While item/price advertising works well in print, today's smart retailers implement integrated electronic communications that differentiate their brand in visual, exciting, engaging, and emotional ways. The goal is to move the customer from *like* to *love* when thinking of your company. Your messages need to stress your differentiation with a compelling message.

Electronic media is incredibly effective in creating brand/image awareness through emotional messages that go way beyond the single message of price, often playing to the customers' beliefs and core values.

Today people are more and more attuned to video. They are used to receiving information delivered by television but are rapidly moving to the internet. It is imperative that retailers rethink how to communicate effectively with their customers.

PROMOTION IS AN INVESTMENT, NOT AN EXPENSE

Given these momentous changes, retailers may need to dramatically alter their attitude toward the costs and objectives of promotional programs. In the past, advertising was often considered a necessary evil—an expense to be absorbed each week to entice the customers to the store on the weekend.

The better goal is to invest in impacting your customer's attitudes and building your brand by placing a lasting message in your customers' minds. This message goes beyond today's special price. Certainly, value is always an important message, but this must be reinforced by permanently positioning in the customer's mind a whole series of building blocks of the quality and service represented by your brand."

The message is no longer "come in today or miss a great price" but, rather, that your brand always offers the best solution. This is all about building trust, which is the primary element in a bonding relationship with the customer.

Once again, that means going beyond the simple message of price and exploring the customer's deeper attitudes and beliefs, in order to customize communication strategies.

Promotional Objectives

ADVERTISING – An Expense	ADVERTISING – An Investment
Goal is to change sales each week	Goal is to change minds forever
Focus is Item/Price	Focus is Image/Brand
Media is primarily Print	Media is primarily Electronic
Message is "Sale'"	Message is "trust"
$ALE!	**Trust**

THE CHALLENGE OF MEASURING

In the past the advertising industry had very sophisticated tools to measure the effectiveness of its old-school media. The problem for today's marketer is that convenient measuring tools may not exist to evaluate the productivity of rapidly changing communication channels.

Measuring the effectiveness of various alternative combinations of media in order to develop an appropriate advertising and marketing budget can be challenging. The key is to truly understand the customer's mindset, which requires some sophisticated data analytics

The customers' attitudes must be measured both before a promotional message is sent and then again at the completion of the campaign in order to understand the impact and effectiveness of media as well as message choices in creating a bond with them. It is not enough to measure sales this weekend; this must be an ongoing process to measure changes in perception. Most companies have a lot of work to do toward better understanding and tracking their customers' attitudes and beliefs.

Advertising and promotion require discipline to be cost effective. The goal must be to increase sales at a faster rate than you are increasing your marketing cost. It is easy to forget this rule when dealing with promotional efforts, so discipline is needed to assure true effectiveness of each promotional activity. Digital technology can be advantageous in terms of costs and impact, compared to more traditional advertising vehicles but still requires defining the objectives and then measuring the results at the customer level to ascertain the most effective promotional tools. Effectiveness must be defined and measured in terms of customer loyalty.

TRUE EVERYDAY LOW PRICES

A new focus on brand/image promotion allows you to efficiently create new paradigms in the customer's mind. For example, applying the *everyday low price* (EDLP) message to a total store product mix is a much more powerful and important message than advertising a limited-time special on a specific item available only this weekend.

Using electronic media to tell your story in a creative and emotional way and then performing as promised at the store level will create a relationship that moves the customer towards a trust relationship with your brand.

EDLP is a proven, effective tool that helps maximize both sales and gross margin contribution. However, it requires discipline to stay true to the concept. The easy way to hype sales this week is to simply run a limited-time sale in today's newspaper. However, this is the start of the slippery slope that ultimately destroys the company's price image. It sends the wrong message in the wrong media.

It is tempting to follow your competitors down that rabbit hole, but you need to stop and ask yourself why you would want to do that. They are probably simply doing what they have always done, without questioning why. Do not give your competitors more credit than they deserve.

THE BIG DADDY: BIG DATA

Clearly, you must have a close relationship with your customers, in order to know their hot buttons, so you can understand and appreciate their needs, desires, beliefs, and feelings. One powerful means of gathering this information is through the analysis of what's called big data.

Big data is the method of using data analytics to systematically gather large volumes of data from social media, websites, GPS-enabled devices, and public video. Specialized software can reveal new trends, ideas, and attitudes. The data can be combined with internal data from your own online and off-line operations. Then it can be evaluated in terms of buying patterns, customer motivation, or perhaps new target markets. Information like this can be invaluable for business strategy, especially in the realm of public relations and marketing messages.

It is also necessary to monitor social media to learn what peer groups are saying about your products, brand, or company. This must become a two-way dialogue with opinion leaders who are influential within their peer group communities. Sharp marketers digest this information internally to evaluate further strategic changes in business plans.

YOUR MARKETING PLAN

Retailers must have an annual plan to define which key messages are most relevant to their customers at which point in the year. These messages should be spelled out on a quarterly and monthly basis and then communicated repeatedly with each customer interaction. The strategy includes all the touch points you have with your customers: website, social media, external advertising, call center staff, salespeople, and point-of-sale signing. You must identify every place you have an opportunity to interact with your customers and then make sure they consistently receive the message that is most important and timely at that moment.

"Without promotion, something terrible happens: Nothing!"
— P.T. Barnum

THE PRICING QUESTION

Retailers who are still focusing their primary marketing efforts on print media to maintain store traffic for this weekend will face decreasing marginal returns. Limited-time sales are always self-defeating. Such sale pricing sends a bad message to the customer that there are good times to buy and bad times to buy. This works against the establishment of a trust relationship.

Percentage-off advertising is even worse. It sends a couple of even more negative messages. When a discount of 20 or 30 percent is offered, it implies that the retailer must have really high normal margins to be able to offer such discounts. It also compares the retailer's current sale price to its normal, everyday high price. If 20 percent off motivates the customers to buy today, will they want to shop next week, when they know pricing will be 20 percent more? What is the follow-up to this week's advertising? There must always be an encore, which becomes more and more expensive over time.

Retailers who play this game find themselves in a self-defeating cycle. Their promotional activity creates a lack of trust and loyalty. Without the repeating, limited-time sales, their business suffers because nobody trusts their regular prices. It is a game that tends to spiral into bigger and bigger discounts and increased promotional efforts, since the constantly advertised sale message loses its sense of urgency over time. How can this week always be the customer's last chance to save? Item/price limited-time advertising is like being on a spinning wheel that is gradually gaining speed. It is a vicious cycle, like taking dope. A little at first seems to feel good, but ultimately you are a slave to something you hate.

PERCENTAGE-OFF BACKFIRING

A classic case of percentage-off sales backfiring is the unfortunate history of the Praktiker home-center chain in Germany. At one time Praktiker had that country's largest number of home-center stores. Then it decided to run a promotion of 20 percent off everything in their store.

The first time this promotion was run, the sales volume was impressive. However, after the promotion ended, so did sales. Subsequent 20-percent-off promotions were scheduled, and these promotions became closer and closer together. As every new promotion was scheduled, however, the impact on sales volume was less and less. Further, to protect the margin, regular prices were raised, which led to further dismal sales following the promotions. Advertising costs increased as net margins fell.

The company had destroyed its price image. The result was a damaged brand. This led to bankruptcy and liquidation of the once viable Praktiker home-center chain.

ADDICTIVE ITEM/PRICE ADVERTISING

Do you remember when Black Friday was only the day after Thanksgiving? Now there are pre-Black Friday and post-Black Friday sales. These special prices can be seen from early November through the end of December. Some retailers offer "Black Friday pricing" close to sixteen percent of the year, with some running Spring Black Friday about ninety days later. There was a time when Black Friday was one day with incredible prices. Such door buster specials are no longer feasible.

This tradition began when retailers knew that the day after Thanksgiving, which falls on the fourth Thursday of November, was the start of the Christmas buying season. To assure that customers would make their first stop at a specific department store, each of the major department store retailers would offer prices that in many cases were below their cost and really were once-a-year opportunities for the lowest price. Since Christmas is the most important selling season for a department store, they were able to see their financial numbers go from red to black. Hence, the name Black Friday.

Now, of course, it's just another name for a sale—nothing really special, just another promotion that really means business as usual. There is no way that retailers can offer below-cost specials for weeks and months at a time as they did in the past for that one day. Plus, remember that generating foot traffic in the stores on a specific day has lost much of its importance now that people can sit at home and purchase 24/7. Black Friday has become a cliché.

Item/price advertising is addictive, requiring more and more effort to get less and less response. The customers become blasé. The marketing department requests more and more funding to sustain the unsustainable. Merchants must increase initial margins to help finance the expanded advertising efforts. Higher regular prices force more limited-time sales. The downward spiral intensifies.

Would anybody in their right mind, in past times, have shopped at Macy's, Kohl's, Harbor Freight, JCPenney, Michaels, or Office Depot without a pocket full of coupons? Does anybody trust their regular prices to be right? Wouldn't a person feel a little cheated if he or she were the only person in line to check out at Bed Bath & Beyond without a 20-percent-off coupon? And did anybody ever really believe those TV ads promising they could buy one suit at Jos. A. Bank men's clothier and get two more absolutely free? Of course not! These retailers have demonstrated a promotional pricing strategy that is not sustainable. They will promote more and more to a customer base that believes less and less.

THE POWER OF PRICE GUARANTEES

Retailers who rightly embrace EDLP pricing may find a competitor is running limited-time sales that beat their pricing. This is where a price guarantee policy comes into play. A limited-time promotion does not warrant a permanent change in your own pricing. The *price guarantee* allows store employees to save the customer, make the sale, and never have to tell the customer they are sorry they are not priced right this week.

The smarter move is to make sure the customers understand that a competitor's item/price advertisement is your advertisement as well. In fact, if they bring a competitor's ad to you, they can be assured of a better price. You need to empower salespeople to meet and beat any competitor's sale price cheerfully and quickly. Don't throw a series of red tape procedures or approval processes into the equation. You won't destroy your business by giving the customer the right price on quantities they would need for normal use.

At times it makes sense to limit quantities when asked to honor a price guarantee, especially if the individual is not a target customer and is demanding unreasonable quantities. But always find a way to say yes to your good, regular, target customers.

If your policy is to always beat any competitor's advertised price, if all your target customers understand this policy, and if their experience claiming the guarantee offer was pleasant, who would ever go to a competitor's store for an advertised special? If your competitor's ads do not drive customers into your own store, you are not making your price offer clear in your customer's mind. That's a marketing problem.

THE SHOPPING EXPERIENCE IS KEY

Today's customer's purchasing decisions are far more influenced by friends and relatives—by word of mouth and via social media—than by anything you can say in paid media.

It is an actual positive shopping experience, in the stores or on the website, that creates the positive buzz in the social community. The shopping experience is everything. The promise made outside your store (whether virtual or brick-and-mortar) must be realized inside the store. The moment of truth is always on the sales floor.

It always comes down to people, to the company culture as seen in your sales associates' responses. Their interaction validates or discredits all the effort made through external promotion and advertising.

You must have employees who truly believe in your brand's promises and will become your most important promoters. If they consistently demonstrate your message with credibility, the result will be word-of-mouth promotion by your customers to their families and friends. That literally is priceless.

The digital revolution has clearly changed how people communicate and provided better tools to both understand the customer's motivations and to tell competitive advantage stories more effectively. The end result should be that the customer develops a bonding relationship with your brand. This can result in longstanding loyalty.

17

WORK GOOD VERSUS LOOK GOOD
PRINCIPLE 7:
SELF-SERVICE IS THE BEST SERVICE.

The store design must enhance the customer's shopping experience by making it easy to access all the available choices and to quickly obtain merchandise. At the same time, operating costs must be kept low to assure price leadership in the market. Therefore, the goal must be to strive for the *best practice,* which drives costs down while simultaneously increasing customer satisfaction. The mantra must be to make the stores *easy to stock, easy to sell, and easy to buy.* This is the KISS method: *Keep It Simple, Stupid.*

THE FUNCTIONAL STORE

Many store displays are designed to create a Wow! impression that overpowers the customer with assortment, graphics, or other accoutrements. In the process, though, it becomes hard to stock, hard to sell, and hard to buy.

For example, a collection of products displayed on the sales floor in a vignette setting may catch the customer's eye. Such displays *look good* but often don't *work good [sic].*

Inventory to support the display might be found in separate areas that are out of sight and possibly spread throughout the store. Too often the merchandise is out of the customer's reach, in the overhead storage racking or in a storeroom. That makes it a very labor-intensive model.

There are also the twin dangers of, first, ignoring the cost of inventory sitting in these displays that may never be sold and, secondly, falling in love with a particular display that becomes old and stale. Displays may be built in such a permanent fashion that the effort and expense to change them and keep them current is prohibitive.

STORE VERSUS MUSEUM

One of our brainstorms at The Home Depot was to build a display of toilets that would show every color produced by our vendors. We designed a special, heavy-duty display rack that was twenty-four-feet high and held dozens of toilets. Seeing all those colorful toilets stacked vertically to the store ceiling was an eye catcher. However, we saw no reasonable return on investment.

First, the inventory cost of all those toilets was a big number. Then, we had to relate this investment to the number of colored toilets sold, which proved to be almost zero. Nearly all bathrooms in America have white or off-white toilets. We learned there is a big difference between running a productive retail store and being an impressive home-improvement museum.

Look good displays will normally require the customer to find a salesperson to make a purchase. That salesperson must find the merchandise, which can become like an Easter egg hunt. The result may be that there is no inventory, or that inventory cannot be found. There may be items on display with no back-up inventory. There may be items in the inventory but omitted from the display.

The store may look good, but the shopping experience can be time-consuming and frustrating. Keep in mind that while the sales associates are hunting for product, the labor expense clock is ticking. A store focused on looking good is often a labor-intensive store, which creates costs that, in turn, require higher store margins.

Of course you want the store to look good. You want the customer to have a Wow! experience. However, if you start with *works good,* you can often then move to *looks good.* But when the first priority is to *look good,* you are unlikely to arrive at a *works good* solution.

SELF-SERVICE IMPROVES FULL-SERVICE

How can stores make their point-of-sale displays work best? The more the stores can be self-service, the easier it will be for the customers to shop. It will also be easier for employees to sell, since the products will be logically displayed, properly signed, and readily available.

Ensuring that all these elements are in place requires discipline. A well merchandised store educates the customer as well as its salespeople. The entire shopping experience becomes more informative and functional when designed from the customer's point of view.

Retailers can easily fall into the trap of assuming that increasing the number of sales associates on the floor will answer all the customer's questions and fill in all the blanks for them, even if the store is missing a logical self-service layout and good signing. This is an example of throwing people at a problem instead of seeking the best solution to improve customer service.

There is often an inverse relationship between the quantity of salespeople and truly great service. When the focus is on maintaining a high quantity of salesclerks, there will most likely be a lack of helpful point-of-sale information and a dearth of quality sales associates with product knowledge and selling skills. Just filling the store with warm bodies is worse than having nobody to serve the customers. The customers quickly realize when they are dealing with unqualified people.

When the focus is on having high quality sales associates, the tendency will be to pay more but hire fewer salespeople. Of course, with good self-service displays, informative signing, and more productive salespeople, fewer people are needed. A well-merchandised self-service store will tend to move labor dollars from task-oriented manual laborers to customer-focused, expert sales associates.

MAKING IT EASY FOR THE CUSTOMERS

Your stores should be *easy to stock, easy to sell, and easy to buy.* This is the *best practice* that lowers cost while increasing customer satisfaction. There is a lesson to be learned from the pure internet retailers.

Online retailers know the key to getting the customer to buy is to make it easy. Why, then, should it be difficult to buy in your stores?

You need to provide the same information that can be found on the internet to the customers standing in your store. You must show your products in a format that offers product display, informational signing, access to inventory, and a shopping cart—in that order.

This provides the customers with a pathway to understanding and self-service. You will have created a presentation that is far superior to throwing uninformed salespeople onto the sales floor and hoping that somehow they will be able to provide the customers with knowledgeable and competent customer assistance.

Self Service is the Best Service

Hard to Stock, Hard to Sell, **Hard to Buy**

Easy to Stock, Easy to Sell, **Easy to Buy**

WORK GOOD MERCHANDISING

Most big-box home centers define the merchandise layout in eight-foot bays, as shown in the Easy to Buy photo. This is the length of the shelving between the vertical upright supports of the pallet racking. The key to an efficient layout is to define a *model stock* that should fit in each bay.

A *model stock* is a specific list of products by brand and model number that should be displayed and stocked in this space. This is a decision that should be made by the department merchandiser, based on a logical feature/ benefit product assortment and the expected rate of sale. The ideal arrangement includes a display model, a sign at eye level showing specifications, and pricing, and the inventory directly below. This is now a self-service display.

The reasonable rate of sale will be based on a computerized logarithm that involves lead time, seasonal trend, recent weeks' sales, and other factors that create a defined safety stock, assuring an inventory balanced between high- and low-selling items. This makes the product *easy to stock, easy to sell, and easy to buy*. Of course, it imposes a limit on the number of SKUs that can be jammed into a given bay. This is a benefit, as it forces model stock discipline upon the merchant.

When there is no assortment discipline, more and more SKUs are stuffed into the bay, to a point where there is no alternative but to have less inventory of each item available to the customer. Most of the safety stock then has to be placed in the overhead storage area or in a back room. This creates many problems. One is simply the labor cost of moving incoming merchandise off the sales floor and then back onto the sales floor later. Another problem is if the sales area is not restocked quickly enough in high-traffic periods, the customer perceives that the product is out of stock and sales are lost, even though there is inventory in the store. Customers can usually serve themselves if the product is readily available; if it is not, every customer requires a salesclerk to find the products he or she wishes to buy. The fact is if too many products are displayed in a limited selling area, the inventory of each individual item must be reduced to make space for all the different SKUs. During high traffic times the best-selling items will sell out quickly, disappointing other customers.

The problem of customer service is compounded when products are displayed without any inventory, in the mistaken opinion that somehow the store is more attractive, as we see in the photos on the left of a lawn mower display. This is incredibly labor intensive and often frustrates the customer. Many people have disagreed with me on this point, insisting that the customer wants to simulate using the product before buying it. But if this were true, fewer items would be sold on the internet.

I was told during a store visit in the country of Colombia that customers don't want to serve themselves; rich people in South America expect to be personally served by the salesclerks. My answer to that is that you can see a lot of Colombians in Miami rapidly filling their own shopping baskets at Costco with a smile on their face!

For whatever reason, there are many examples of labor intensive stores with poor service. In such cases, the store management tends to hire product movers focused on physical tasks, instead of knowledgeable salespeople focused on serving the customers with helpful advice. When merchants over-SKU the store, the focus must turn to manual labor and moving products, in which both the employees and the customers are abused.

THE SIN OF OVER ASSORTMENT

The argument could be that having more and more SKUs would create more and more sales volume. The counter-intuitive fact is that as additional brands and models are added to the store's inventory, with duplicated price points and similar feature benefits, this redundancy will ultimately decrease sales. Too much merchandise makes it harder for the sales associates to sell and more difficult for the customers to buy. The shopping experience becomes confusing and time-consuming, to a point where purchases are postponed.

Less is more. My clients have documented time and again that a rational product mix that sells up the continuum, without needless redundancy and duplication, increases sales dramatically. It cannot be overstated that allowing more space in the stores for top-selling items and reducing SKU count and space for slower-selling items increases sales, improves inventory turnover, and increases GMROI. An analysis of the product movement of virtually any category of merchandise within a store will show that a small number of SKUs represents a disproportionate amount of the sales in the assortment. You simply cannot allow an out of stock condition on these key items.

The 80/20 rule is generally true here: 20 percent of a store's SKUs are likely to represent 80 percent of its sales. It is, therefore, logical that 80 percent of your selling space should be devoted to that top 20 percent of the SKUs. However, if you continue to add more and more marginal-selling SKUs, the slower-selling items that make up only 20 percent of the total sales will ultimately consume 80 percent of the shelf space. This is completely upside down.

Retailers need to implement programs focused on the concept that *less is more.* This will prompt a review of actual stock movement, with the objective of consolidating the number of SKUs and perhaps consolidating the number of vendors in the process. It is a process of *majoring on the majors,* to make sure you are always in stock on the products your customers most desire.

Customers do not want more SKUs. They simply want the right product to solve their problem. They want to find it quickly, make the purchase, and leave.

You need to expedite this process by designing and enforcing a disciplined model stock that defines the optimum in store assortment. This will consist of a matrix of products that will solve all the target customer's needs, in terms of features, benefits, and price points, without needless duplication and redundancy. Add informative point-of-sale signing that explains these features and benefits, and much of the store becomes self-service. *Less is more,* and *self-service is the best service.* Smart merchandising develops a feature/benefit matrix by price point that will result in a product assortment that is curated to assure the customer can easily find the exact product for their needs.

Making the Big Box Work Good

Here is a checklist of merchandising methods and disciplines that will improve the customer's shopping experience.

Model Stock by Store Prototype: There must be clearly defined store prototypes, based upon store size. Each prototype must have its own specified model stock by category. The linear counter space or number of bays in each prototype needs to be designated by store size, and then an appropriate planogram needs to define the model-stock standard for each store size, indicating the SKUs and the number of facings of each SKU. The model stock will identify the items that must be stocked in the store. The actual depth of inventory on those items must be determined by a rate-of-sale logarithm based on that store's specific sales.

The various store sizes and formats should be kept to a minimum, to keep the business simple enough to be managed effectively. Merchants need to design and manage their model stocks to maximize the GMROI of their department. A proliferation of store prototypes makes this management more difficult. There is a danger that merchants may find managing too many different prototypes, each with its own unique model stock, leads them to forfeit control over the product mix to less qualified people outside of the merchandising group. This determination of the merchandise assortment might be defaulted to store personnel who are not knowledgeable in regard to important concepts such as selling up the continuum or GMROI management. The control of the model stock is a critical element in managing and improving GMROI, which is a merchant's primary responsibility.

It is commonly said that *retail is detail*. This must also be combined with *retail is simplicity.* It doesn't rhyme, but it is the right policy to keep focused on the right priorities.

What are the smart elements within the store layout that help to increase sales, improve inventory turnover, and maximize GMROI? Let's explore some specific display guidelines:

Self-Service: The best service is always self-service. This is accomplished by implementing a disciplined model stock that facilitates a point-of-purchase display, which first provides a sample of the product for the customer to see. (A toilet, a power saw, a light fixture, etc.)

The next element of self-service should be a sign, placed at eye level, that provides the customer with all the features and benefits that were considered by the merchant who designed the model stock. The information on this sign should mirror the data shown on the website for this same product, including specifications and price.

Directly under the product sample and sign should be the product inventory, in quantities that provide a safety stock to assure availability, based on the product movement metrics of that store. A nearby cart or shopping basket helps make the purchase easy for the customer.

Packaging: The retail packaging must be designed to promote self-selling. This requires good art as well as product specifications that would be helpful to the customer.

It must be easy for the salesperson to quickly stock the counter with self-selling (cut-case) cartons so the first person touching the product is the customer taking it to the register to buy. Good packaging increases sales, while lowering operating cost.

Impulse Sales: Having a plan for creating impulse sales is incredibly important to increasing the average sales ticket. Impulse sales are purchases made by the customer over and above the purchase they planned to make when entering the store.

You need to have a process to obtain and feed special purchases to the store. These products need to be in self-merchandising displays, whenever possible, to facilitate in-store merchandising.

Dedicated spaces in the highest traffic areas of store need to be programmed by season and month. This impulse sales initiative requires prepackaged quarter-pallet displays and/or tray-packed product cartons that facilitate mass stacking at registers, end caps, and other impulse locations, for a minimum of labor and a maximum of customer impact. .

Design Stations and Show-rooming: While the store needs to be as self-service as possible, important areas of the store require personal service, such as design services, how-to knowledge, or project information. This requires comfortable meeting areas, with seating and tables, to allow consultation and design interaction in a relatively intimate setting. These design areas need to showcase products you have in stock as well as products you offer on your website that are not stocked in the store.

Cross-Merchandising: You need to facilitate cross-merchandising throughout the store by defining the SKUs that help customers complete their projects. Such products may have their normal home in a particular department but also need to be displayed adjacent to related products in another department. For example, gloves may be sold in the tool department but also need to be available in the gardening area. There are obviously multiple locations in a home-improvement store where it would be logical to cross-merchandise screwdrivers or measuring tapes. These items might be overlooked when purchasing the main products for a project, forcing the customers to shop again. This might result in losing the related sale, as customers might pick up this needed product in a more convenient store. You are doing the customer a favor by making sure they have purchased all the products needed for their project during their first visit to your store.

Manufacturers should be required to package products specifically for cross-merchandising purposes. This may be in cut-cases, on pre-hung vertical hanging strips, or in self-merchandising floor displays. Anything you can do to help the store more easily cross-merchandise products will lower costs and increase sales.

A clearly defined process to assure that cross-merchandising is accomplished is an obvious benefit for the customer and a win for the retailer. Yet it is an area where discipline is lacking in many stores. When this happens the customers are not well served.

Clearance of Discontinued and Dead Items: Each store needs a dedicated clearance display space and a system for identifying slow-selling and discontinued items. This will require an aggressive markdown and display program that can quickly liquidate dead items from the store's inventory.

Letting dead merchandise sit ties up working capital and uses valuable floor space. Moving it around or storing it eats up employee hours. Merchants must be given specified, limited time periods to eliminate such products, using progressive markdowns, after which the value of any remaining product is marked to zero and the items are eliminated from inventory.

Hands-on Merchandising Involvement: Promotions, new product introductions, and special buys often are created centrally and then flow down to the store. This can create implementation issues, as the store team is forced to respond to these programs. New products and programs do need to flow to the stores. However, sometimes this flow can be untimely and even ill conceived. Headquarters staff may think they understand the store issues, but they often lack empathy for what is really happening in the stores.

Empathy means you feel the pain; that can only happen through interaction with store personnel and customers by working in the store. New programs must flow into the stores with a minimum of pain and on a scheduled calendar, which requires an understanding of the current store situation and the impact of the desired change.

Assuring Display Compliance: A system must be in place to assure that all store product bays follow approved planograms, that cross-merchandising is complete, and that all impulse merchandise scheduled for mass-stack areas is in place on a timely basis. This will assure a great shopping experience for the customer. Compliance with approved plans also greatly eases the process of updating model stocks and then implementing future changes, to keep improving that experience.

Embrace Change: Change is imperative and inevitable. Processes must be established that facilitate change and embrace new ideas and new programs. This involves openness to change and procedures that ensure speed to market.

I have worked with home centers around the world. Merchandising and operations of the various store models differ significantly based upon geography.

The European model is far more focused on *looking good*, with a flair for fashion, color, and design. U.S. stores tend to focus on *working good*, with a predilection for efficiency. The Japanese format is very focused on *looking the same,* with virtually the same assortment and layout as their competitors.

The interesting thing is that in each of these markets, retailers tend to follow the leader in their market. Too often this is analogous to the blind leading the blind. Following the leader is not a winning strategy.

The winning strategy is to be clearly different from and superior to the competition. This means going back to the principles and building the merchandising strategy with a hyper-focus on the customer's needs and desires. This will lead to innovation, which will result in differentiation. This is far superior to following the competition to mediocre sameness.

18

EMBRACING DIGITAL SOLUTIONS
PRINCIPLE 8:
RETAILING MUST TRANSITION FROM PRODUCT ORIENTATION TO A SERVICE AGENDA.

The previous chapter looked at how crucial a good shopping experience is in a brick-and-mortar store and how retailers must always work to improve it. Now we need to explore the online store and how the physical and the virtual stores compare, compete with, and complement each other.

The new world of e-commerce has not made physical stores obsolete. Quite the opposite. The big-box home center provides a solid base on which to build a better online and physical store shopping experience— if you marry your product mix with customer service, using world-class technology to provide customized digital solutions. Your website becomes the front door of the store, and *interconnected retailing* processes offer customers a *total-solution portal* for goods and services.

The digital revolution in retailing is about a lot more than simply allowing the customer to shop online at home. It also goes way beyond pricing. It is about making all the company's resources available to the customer and personalizing that experience. It's about establishing your brand as the trusted solution provider for all the customer's wants, needs, and project requirements.

The customers will search out and bond with the company they can trust to solve their problems and make their lives easier while providing the best value. Trust is the actionable word.

The home-improvement store of the future must be the low-cost source for the best-selling products and a showroom for expanded choice via

The customer sees only one brand for any retailer. The experience online defines the brand image off-line and vice versa.

e-commerce offerings. This will include customized product choices and configured project solutions. Showrooming must be embraced to enhance the in-store shopping experience, in order for customers to be able to touch and feel *more options* in their actual colors and textures. This customer benefit is impossible to accomplish on a computer screen or small phone display outside the store. It is particularly helpful when combined with in-store, project experts who can provide decor and project advice.

Some current in-stock items that are slow-selling or difficult to handle at store level can be removed from store stock and become online items. This frees store space and working capital for enlarged showrooms to better educate the customer on their total choice of options for their projects.

The digitally empowered store can drive new project sales and must also be a transit point for the customer to receive and return their online purchases. It should also serve as the local warehouse for home and jobsite delivery options. Expanded services will be able to take a customer from a home-improvement idea to completion, with all products and related services provided in a timely manner.

THE VIABILITY OF PHYSICAL STORES

Some people still believe the brick-and-mortar store will be replaced by the internet. This is a recurring theme in trade journals and mass media, but it is wrong. There are always people who want to chase the newest shiny thing. In doing so they sometimes lose contact with reality and draw wrong conclusions.

E-commerce has had huge percentage growth, partially because it has been computed on a relatively small base, compared to the percentage growth for all retail. Every chart on retail trends shows constantly increasing online sales every year and market share growth in virtually every market worldwide. The logical conclusion, based on these charts, is that this trend will increase to infinity and that, ultimately, there will be no physical stores.

However, if you were to chart the percentage change in the growth of e-commerce in each of these years, the chart would generally show a decreasing trend. This is a result of the *law of large numbers*, in which percentage growth slows as the base increases. It is also a measurement of market saturation and maturity. This down-sloping percentage growth trend will ultimately work to flatten the sales curve. The result will be that e-commerce will prove to be a stable percentage of the retail business but certainly not the majority, in most retail categories.

The COVID-19 pandemic greatly increased the penetration of online sales for most retailers. The number of customers using e-commerce increased, as did frequency and purchase volume. This increased the existing growth trend. The increased sales caused retailers to accelerate their investments in direct fulfillment. However, I suggest that all of this would have happened over time and that the pandemic simply accelerated the trend and helped bring maturity to the market, without significantly changing the end result. Most retail products will still be sold at physical stores but with enhanced customer service, using digital tools and omnichannel merchandising. Customers have increasingly used the internet to initiate their orders but have also increased their use of the physical store for fulfillment.

The omni-channel retailer will be the norm and the question as to percentage of business done via e-commerce versus the physical store will simply become irrelevant as these functions become totally interconnected. There are not digital customers and physical customers - there are only customers - and all the retailers' resources must be easily available to them in an integrated and seamless shopping experience.

The important point is that the goal must be to simultaneously grow *both* online and off-line sales volumes. They are symbiotic when fully integrated and customer-centric. Investments are required to assure in-store and online tasks can be integrated and performed with speed and accuracy.

Business must be driven by a focus on *working good* as opposed to simply *looking good*. In other words, there must be increased attention and investment on the fulfillment part of the transaction so that a better job is done in delivering what has been promised and sold. Best practices must be determined to drive up customer service while driving down costs. Whether the focus is on the brick-and-mortar store or the online business, they both must *work good*.

GOOD PHYSICAL STORES CONTINUE TO GROW

Consider that the e-commerce business in the United States showed a 22.40 percent growth from $370 billion in 2016 to $453 billion in 2017. *That is a net increase of $83 billion.* Now consider the growth of the entire retail business in the U.S. during this same period. It only grew 4.39 percent, from $4.076 trillion to $4.255 trillion dollars. *This is an increase of $180 billion.*

Clearly physical retail is not dead or dying. It is alive and growing. It is easy to get confused by percentages and not focus on the facts critical to making good decisions.

Assume a typical big-box home-improvement store has annual sales of U.S. $30 million. Further assume that 5 percent of its sales are on the internet, which has been typical [pre-pandemic]. This represents $1.5 million dollars of online sales per year. Now say a 20 percent increase is budgeted for online sales this year, which will create additional sales of $300,000. The question is, What is the percentage increase required in the brick-and-mortar store to have the same dollar increase in sales?

The math is easy. The answer is only one percent. How difficult would it be to increase physical store sales by one percent? Wouldn't it be feasible to obtain a physical store growth in excess of one percent? This illustrates how important it is to keep focused on the off-line business as the smaller online volume grows. It is a hand-and-glove relationship, where both pieces of the puzzle must grow and be viable.

The logic is simple: Investments must be made in the physical stores to assure growth while simultaneous investments are made in growing the e-commerce business. Don't get confused by percentage numbers. Understand where the customers are purchasing and why they are choosing the stores in some cases and the website in other cases. Online and off-line are simply two arms of the same business.

Furthermore, these two arms must be coordinated by a common vision and mission for a well-defined brand. This will result in a truly *interconnected retailing* reality that improves the customer's total shopping experience.

THE REALITY OF TRUE COSTS

There was a mistaken belief in the past that the pure e-commerce retailer was a virtual store that could avoid the overhead expenses of a physical store and was, therefore, able to offer convenient services and better prices. The retail community is becoming aware that this is a false narrative and a faulty assumption upon which to base a profitable and viable business.

In reality, direct customer shipping requires significant capital investments in software and facilities. These costs are then compounded by those of the working capital tied up in inventory. Remember, one advantage of e-commerce is being able to offer the *long tail* of unique or hard-to-find products. However, those products are, by definition, slow-selling products that tie up money in inventory. The online retailer must then deal with the high freight expenses of shipping single products to a customer. Individual shipments to customers' homes are far more expensive than full truck shipments to physical store locations. Once products are brought into the physical store in truckloads, customers most often transport the products to their own home or jobsite at no cost to the store.

Another burden of the direct online retailer is the significant logistic cost of direct shipped products that are returned by the customer. Returns from online sales average two to three times the rate of return from purchases in physical stores, and they are more costly to dispatch. The growing dilemma is that competition is forcing more prepaid shipping to and from the customers, so they have little reason to be selective in their original purchases.

As more and more e-commerce companies enter the market, promotional expenses are skyrocketing. Competition for eyeballs on the internet—among an increasing number of players—has allowed Facebook and Google and other platforms oligopolistic pricing power over advertising. Yet without advertising the online retailer becomes invisible and vulnerable.

In reality, online retailing requires significant investments in capital facilities and equipment in addition to working capital. Add to this the logistic and marketing expenses, and it becomes clear that for many online retailers, the resulting cost pressures amount to a challenge to their very existence.

In addition, the operational overhead of online retailing is certainly not virtual. There still is a need to staff call centers for sales, customer service, and other administrative tasks. While robots, artificial intelligence, and other technologies can help drive down these logistic and customer service costs, the pure-play online retailer will continue to be at an operational disadvantage to the physical store on the high-volume, most often purchased products.

A well-merchandised big-box home center with competent logistics can be a more efficient business model to drive down costs and pass on value to the customer than an e-commerce provider marketing similar products exclusively on the internet.

Yes, there is both a more-choice benefit and a convenience factor to e-commerce, which the physical store must now offer as an omnichannel retailer. These service enhancements come at significant cost. If all investment and interest is focused online and physical store sales decrease, the likelihood is that the business will be less profitable, not more, due to the increased costs of e-commerce. It is, therefore, imperative that a retailer's growing online business be balanced with continued sales growth in the physical store, to assure both sales and profit increases.

The Evolution of Interconnected Retailing

The Home Depot's e-commerce experience was not without significant problems in the beginning. The initial focus was expediency—getting a program up and running from point zero.

To accomplish this, a team of external people with e-commerce experience was brought into the company and given *carte blanche* to create a new business. They did not have home-center product expertise, nor did they understand the founding culture and principles with which the physical stores had prospered. The team's experience was in general merchandise, so their model looked a lot more like Amazon than The Home Depot.

This created two very separate companies operating under The Home Depot brand: one digital and one physical. These two groups were headed in different directions with different missions, different objectives, and different messages to the customers. There was a wide gap between the product and pricing strategies of the e-commerce group and the brick-and-mortar group. Each of these two groups had its own merchandising, marketing, logistics, IT, and finance operations. That meant they operated in their own silos, without integrating their activities or strategies.

This was not tenable. It confused the employees, the vendors, and, more importantly, the customers. The first step to solving the problem was to combine the two merchandising groups into one group and integrate the mission. Step two merged all the other support groups into fully integrated support units. Only then could the company set its sights on a "One Home Depot" mission.

The result of this journey is that The Home Depot is one of the most successful omnichannel retailers. They have achieved a top position in the U.S. for internet sales while showing strong continued comparable store growth in their physical stores.

It's not uncommon for companies to go through a similar evolution. Wrong-headed e-commerce programs that direct all innovation and investment to e-commerce while taking the physical store sales volume for granted can result in stagnant or declining store sales while the e-commerce programs grow. This is a death cycle, as higher margin business is transferred to lower margin sales. This can and must be avoided by instituting a more enlightened *interconnected retail* program, which allows for the simultaneous growth of both online and off-line revenues, in order to significantly increase total revenue instead of simply trading online sales for off-line sales.

THE RACE FOR MORE SKUS

The goal must be higher profitable sales. However, there is always a danger that the online operation will get hyper-focused on creating sales at any cost to justify their ever increasing resource requirements. To this end they may find themselves chasing Amazon instead of embracing the brand promises and mission of their own core physical store base. This is like the cowboy who jumps on his horse and tries to ride off in all directions at once.

The race to increase SKU count online can lead to spreading your supply lines too thin and ultimately disappointing your customers. You may be featuring products that are not within your core competency and to which you have not secured guaranteed in-stock finished goods inventories. You may not have a landed cost advantage, causing your prices to be uncompetitive and damaging your price image. Many of the products may not fit the company's brand image of competence, resulting in confusion for the customers.

The goal should never be to become another Amazon. The goal should be to differentiate your brand from Amazon by creating an *interconnected retailing* experience, using the unique resource that Amazon does not have— *your stores.*

They are already in place and close to your customers. They already have the most popular items in stock. There are already resources in place that can handle more business by channeling *more choices,* using improved logistics and new technologies. The store can step up to become a more complete solution provider to those who are already valued customers. They can aggregate additional customers who demand service, which is enhanced by implementing new technology. The big-box store has the capital and infrastructure to invest in this kind of innovation.

> *The Amazon is an impressive river, but then, so are the Nile, Mississippi, Yangtze, Ganges, Danube, Volga, Mekong, and Congo. There is not one right way to the customer's wallet.*

The stores need to be seen not as the end of the distribution channel but, rather, as one step in the supply chain to the customer's home. This will change some of the space utilization and the functions in the store as it becomes both a pickup and a shipping location, to complete the journey from the producer to the customer. Some people say the digital revolution will result in smaller stores. I believe the opposite is an equally valid argument. It is generally a truism that the big store always wins. This is due to its greater size and flexibility to offer the customer more. Certainly, *flexibility* will be the key to responding to the many changes we can expect as the digital world expands and the customer's expectations increase.

THE UTILITY OF THE PHYSICAL STORE

To better understand the relative strengths and weaknesses of online versus physical store operations, one must realize that any retailer has to absorb the cost of the logistics, financing, and marketing functions required to procure and deliver products to the customer. It is important to consider all the expenses the retailer assumes in taking a product from the factory door to the customer's home, which is the true landed cost. Both physical stores and pure online sellers incur all these costs, but they can vary greatly between the two models.

The e-commerce business can best deal with products that are low cube (compact in size) and high value, such as a Mont Blanc pen that may sell for hundreds or even thousands of dollars. This can be a profitable online transaction due to its high retail price and the fact that it is small and lightweight. The online retailer has the advantage here, since the shipping cost is a small percentage of the total retail price.

There are, of course, many products that, due to value, size, or uniqueness, make them good candidates for pure e-commerce retailers to market. However, high-value, low-cube products tend to be the exception and not the rule among high-volume, mass-produced consumer products. On the other end of the spectrum, products that are high cube and low priced have relatively high logistic costs and can generally be sold much more efficiently in actual stores. Advantage: the big-box home center.

Consider a single bag of cement or a carton of ceramic tile. The freight expense of shipping such items would be an extremely high percentage of the total selling price—in fact, it could easily exceed the cost of the product. Physical stores purchase such products in full pallet and full truckload shipments that drive down freight costs, which they then own at the lowest landed cost.

Home-center products are often high cube and low value. The result is that the online penetration in the home-center industry tends to be much lower than, for example, the electronics or fashion businesses.

TIME UTILITY FOR THE CUSTOMER

Another advantage of the local store is the ready availability of products customers might need immediately. This could be a pipefitting, a plastic tarp, or cleaning supplies crucial to an ongoing project. In these cases the customer will generally prefer to go to the nearest home center, as opposed to shopping online and waiting for home delivery.

The online world is working hard to establish same-day shipping, which is good. But most American homeowners live fewer than twenty minutes from a big-box store such as The Home Depot, Lowe's, Walmart, Target, or other in-stock physical stores. If an emergency need arises, it can usually be sourced faster at the local store.

Many home-improvement items have a rather low unit retail price. In the case of items like a screw or screwdriver, the cost of home delivery to an e-commerce customer would exceed the value of the product. Again, the nearby store has a distinct advantage to the customer in both time and money. This will become a bigger factor as the true logistic costs are rationalized more and more into the cost of home-delivered products.

MAKING E-COMMERCE WORK WELL

Please don't conclude that you should de-emphasize digital opportunities. The truth is quite the opposite. You must embrace technology in order to provide better services to your customers and meet their increased expectations. However, it is critical to do this in a smart and rational manner.

Interconnected retailing refers to combining digital technology and the supply chain of e-commerce with the physical brick-and-mortar store in a powerful and successful model that enhances brand and customer loyalty. Think of the internet as the new front door of the store. Invite potential customers to enter that door and discover that it ultimately leads to a great in-store experience.

The retailer's brand image on the internet must reinforce, support and enhance the brick-and-mortar brand and image. It is counterproductive for a company to have two isolated merchandising groups that are heading in two different directions and presenting different pricing programs and brand images to the public. The danger, in addition to causing brand confusion, is that all the company's energy, time, and capital might be redirected exclusively to the online side of the business, while the core store business atrophies. Why is this such an issue? The unspoken problem is that many omnichannel retailers have discovered that the physical stores must subsidize the new, less profitable online business.

The retail industry has experienced profit pressure as more and more retailers have embraced omnichannel retailing. We have already outlined many of the costs directly associated with the online business. However, the point that is often overlooked is the increased labor costs built into omnichannel retailing. The rise in e-commerce has resulted in a transition of labor from the retail store to the direct-fulfillment warehouse.

Labor costs per hour in a fulfillment warehouse have typically been 50 percent higher than the hourly rate at the retail store. The industry as a whole has increased its cost per hour at the same time it has increased the total headcount; the number of people in warehouse fulfillment has exceeded the reduction in the number of people on the retail sales floor. Many functions, such as pulling stock to put an order together and transporting these products to the customer's home, were done in the past at no cost by the customer. Now they are costly services provided by the retailer.

This has been a learning process for retailers and will result in significant changes in their assumptions and strategies as they adapt to the new realities of the marketplace. The customer is requesting more service, but those new services are often costly; this needs to be considered in developing smart omnichannel programs going forward.

CLARIFYING PRIORITIES

The online business in today's most competent home centers has, until recently, constituted less than ten percent of the total sales volume, leaving at least ninety percent of the business coming out of the store itself. (This number more than doubled during the pandemic of 2020, but that is not the norm.)

Visualize a dog. Consider the brick-and-mortar business as the body of the dog, while e-commerce is its tail. The tail has a function, but it should not wag the dog. The concern must be for the dog's total welfare.

My considered opinion is that the majority of sales in home improvement retailers will be fulfilled at the store level. This recognizes that many purchases will originate digitally in the physical store and be fulfilled in the home or jobsite. Conversely, many sales will originate digitally at the home and jobsite but be fulfilled in the physical store. It will become virtually impossible to distinguish where off-line ends and online begins in the purchase of any given project.

The digitally competent omni-channel website has huge advantages over the pure digital website or non-digital physical store when it comes to the mass marketing of the most needed and wanted products. While the omni-channel home center will find many products previously sold in-store transitioned to on-line purchases, it will find that the total sales in the store can nevertheless increase as digital tools allow the store to make bigger and better project sales. This is facilitated by investments in technology and logistics to provide increased product assortment and services to the homeowner and the professional customer. Thus, the number of target markets can be increased and the share of wallet from those customers expanded. The whole scenario of digital investment in omni-channel retailing is justified when both online and off-line sales grow simultaneously - and they must.

OFFERING MORE CHOICES WHILE MANAGING INVENTORIES

There is a real opportunity for the physical store to enhance the shopping experience for the customer with the choices offered by an online program that is fully integrated into the core business model. Combining the special order and e-commerce programs will result in a *more-choice* program for the customer. This will provide new tools for the sales associates to make bigger and better project sales. The ability to quickly procure a wide range of products through a *more-choice* e-commerce arm will allow the merchant to focus in-store inventories on those products that represent the highest unit and dollar volume products.

A big-box home center can choose from millions of possible products to stock in their brick-and-mortar store. However, most select 30,000–50,000 items as model stock, based on inventorying the merchandise that will provide the most sales, the highest stock turnover, and resulting increases in GMROI.

The cost of working capital is directly related to the physical rate of inventory turnover. Selecting high-turning items for the store's model stock makes efficient use of working capital. Not only does buying in quantity provide a cost advantage, but dealing in high-volume products that sell rapidly offers a return on investment benefit.

SELLING UP THE CONTINUUM

The first priority in determining a model stock is to stop doing the wrong thing. There is an opportunity to redefine the product mix both in the store and on the website to offer the customer more choices, while rationalizing inventories and making the selection process easier. The other advantage of a more thoughtfully curated stock assortment is a more responsive supply chain with better availability of requested products.

It is easy to fall into the trap of doubling down on commodity items that sell in quantity. However, this shifts the focus to items in the declining portion of the product life cycle. This results in attempting to drive the business with lower priced items that sell in quantity. The result is duplication of similar low-end products, as well as wasted inventory dollars and display space.

A more eclectic and profitable model stock appeals to a broader portion of the total market. Most stores and websites are over SKU-ed with redundant products that will maximize sales or return on investment. The merchant's job is to curate a mix of products and services that can totally satisfy the target markets, without making the task so convoluted that the decision process is difficult and the fulfillment process disappointing.

WHAT DOES THE CUSTOMER WANT?

When we bought our first house in Atlanta, my wife wanted to change the cabinet hardware in our kitchen. The Home Depot's cabinet hardware display at that time consisted of thirty-two linear feet of cabinet hardware on multiple levels of shelving, which meant that there were hundreds of cabinet pulls and knobs from which to choose. However, my wife couldn't find anything she liked. Since I was in charge of product purchasing at The Home Depot, this concerned me.

I had a habit on personal trips of stopping at competing businesses. My family was used to being dragged through every home center we saw on the road. On one trip to visit our daughter in college, we went into a Hechinger home center in North Carolina. When I was ready to leave the store, I found my wife at the cash register with a basket full of cabinet hardware from the same vendor that sold us the category at The Home Depot.

The next day I called the vendor and asked, "What is different about the Hechinger cabinet hardware assortment?"

The answer was that The Home Depot's merchant used a computer readout to determine that the most popular cabinet hardware finish at that time was antique brass. Therefore, the assortment in The Home Depot was heavily skewed toward antique brass, which led to duplication of similar products. The inventory focused on one segment of the cabinet hardware market, which did not include my wife.

On the other hand, the Hechinger buyer understood that there were many other metal finishes, even though antique brass was the best seller. Chrome, polished brass, satin nickel, oil-rubbed bronze, and white might appeal to a broader customer mix. Some customers might even be interested in more exotic and costlier styles, such as porcelain or cut crystal hardware. Hechinger was better at selling *up the continuum* in the category of cabinet hardware.

Offering a product line that sells *up the continuum,* with unique choices, will expand the product choices to a larger group of customers. In the process, it is likely that gross margin percentages and gross margin dollars will increase with a more eclectic assortment of higher-value products. The result will be to increase sales and gross margin dollars, while increasing market share.

It is important for the merchant to have good, objective data, but these facts must be combined with an intimate knowledge of the product category and customer preferences, in order to make the best merchandising decisions regarding product assortment and pricing.

This concept of selling *up the continuum* needs to be applied both in the store and on the website. In both situations, it is dysfunctional to allow redundancy and duplication; it is beneficial to offer more unique choices.

GOOD, BETTER, AND BEST

It helps to picture product demand using the image of an hourglass. The lower section of the hourglass represents the commodity portion of demand, where unit sales are high. This portion of the market is driven by price. The upper section of the hourglass represents the higher-end products that are more unique, more exclusive, and often more expensive. This portion of the market is driven by style and quality.

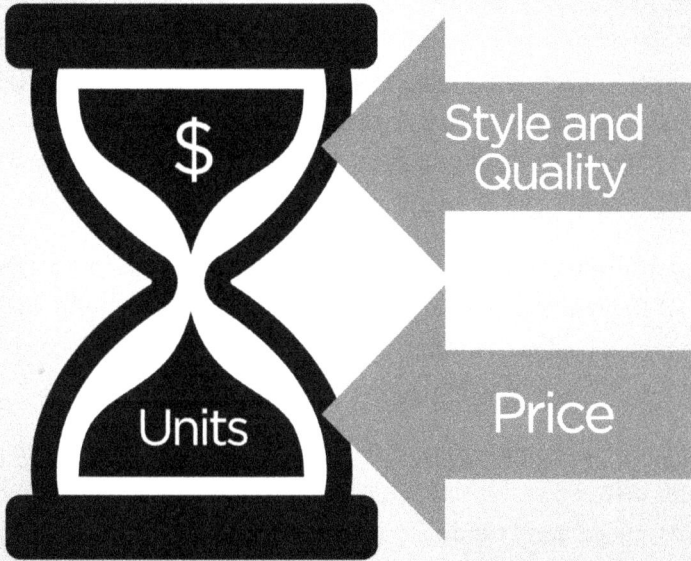

Multiple Target Markets

While the unit sales may be higher in the price segment of the market, often the dollar sales and gross margin dollars can best be maximized where style and quality are more important to the customer. This is not an either/or decision. The ideal is to create a product mix that starts at the opening price point-products and sells *up the continuum* to the style and quality products.

These better and best products, driven by style and quality, may be in stock at the store or part of the online assortment. These *more-choice* items assure being the complete project store with more solutions for the customer. Selling *up the continuum* is a winning strategy and can be an important *unique, sustainable, compelling, competitive advantage* that appeals to a wide range of customers.

INCREASING CHOICES EFFICIENTLY

The key issue going forward will be how to enhance the store experience without destroying the cost efficiencies of the big box. The answer must be found in enlarging the market by offering expanded products and service solutions to the customer and then obtaining a bigger share of that market. It is about evolving from a product-oriented business to a service-oriented business. This, in turn, requires embracing digital technology, to be able to manage a more complex business with speed and without errors.

The digital revolution in retail does not mean brick-and-mortar stores should set themselves up to be Amazon clones. Not everything that can be done should be done. Amazon is great at selling items, while the home center must be better at selling projects.

Technology provides tools to facilitate these projects from design to procurement, delivery, and installation. Project dominance will strengthen the store's image and brand as a solution provider, which is *a unique, sustainable, compelling, competitive advantage.* The home center's brand must become the portal to all home-improvement projects. This will increasingly evolve from focusing on products to offering more and better services for a wide range of customer-oriented project solutions.

DELIVERING ON PROMISES

The brick-and-mortar stores now need to bring their special order programs up to e-commerce standards that make it easy for the customer to order and receive quick fulfillment.

How is this done efficiently? First, define the products to be offered. This should not be a race to obtain all the items in the universe. Do not get into a contest for bragging rights about the number of SKUs offered. Stock the products really demanded by the customers. Secondly, make the inventory commitment to be able to deliver to the customer in a timely manner. This increasingly means most items need to ship on the day of order if that is the customer's wish.

Too many retailers are in a race to add SKUs to their website, with no strategy other than to have more SKUs than the competition. This is like driving on a road with no speed limits or guardrails. It does not end well. If there are no defined parameters, a website could theoretically continue to increase its SKUs to infinity. Clearly, some guidelines must be put in place.

Sooner or later, parameters must be defined and established that are consistent with the company's mission and brand. Any product offered must be the right product, the right quality, the right cost, and it must be available at the right time. Spreading the product offering to an infinite number of SKUs will result in a supply chain that cannot meet these criteria. In fact, there tends to be an inverse relationship between the quantity of SKUs and competence in sourcing, distributing, and selling the products. This same inverse relationship is also likely to be felt in the ROI.

If the product is configured and custom made for a customer, as in the case of a custom window, it is reasonable to expect a lead time before shipment and delivery of this unique product. However, if the product is mass produced, it is either in stock within the supply chain or it is not.

If a mass-produced product is offered on the website, it must be immediately available in finished goods inventory. When the customers pay their money at time of purchase, they have a right to expect their order to be shipped immediately.

It is important to identify those online products that make economic sense to stock in your own direct-fulfillment centers, versus products that work better when stocked and shipped by vendors from their own finished goods inventory. In any case, the commitment must be to have the products in stock and ready for immediate shipment.

SMART MORE-CHOICE LOGISTICS

There is a cost for online fulfillment, regardless of whether you provide the logistic support yourself or whether you rely on third-party vendors. Logistic alternatives must be defined and selected. The merchant must consider these alternatives to determine the optimum supply chain for customer service and profitability.

- *Store Stock:* Identify the high-volume items customers most often need, buy them at the lowest landed cost, and make them readily available in the stores.

- *Direct Fulfillment Centers [DFCs]:* Identify items that may not have high enough demand to be stocked in the stores but can be economically distributed from your own facilities with reasonable turnover and that are accretive to the GMROI. This could also include products that are bulky or difficult for the stores to handle and, therefore, easier to centrally stock and deliver directly to the customer. A third category is private-label products that have been imported and are not available from domestic vendors.

- *Vendor DC:* Determine with the vendors which items they produce that you do not wish to stock in your own DFCs, but that the vendor is willing to maintain in finished goods inventory. These are products the vendors will ship directly to the customer or to the store, if they choose. The deal must be that you will provide exposure for these products on your e-commerce website, and they, in turn, will provide immediate fulfillment. This is the primary distribution channel for the vast majority of items offered on The Home Depot's website. You must understand that the vendors are being asked to perform a wholesaling function of breaking bulk and shipping individual items and, therefore, costs will be higher than if the same product was being ordered in full production runs.

- *Products Not Offered:* There may be products in a vendor's offerings that do not justify stocking, due to low demand, and that even the vendor does not wish to carry in finished goods inventory. These products should not be offered on your website. The juice is simply not worth the squeeze.

Please understand that regardless of the methods used to provide these products directly to the customer, there is a cost—a big cost—to processing these individual orders that make up this *long tail of e-commerce*.

These costs include:

• Specialized DC facilities

• DC equipment, including racking, automated conveyor belts, and robots

• Systems development and maintenance

• DC labor

• Working capital to support the long tail inventory

• Outbound freight on individual orders

• Return freight from customers

• Call center management and staff

THE FOOLISH RACE FOR SKUS

The fatal flaw of so many omnichannel retailers is that they find themselves in a race for SKUs, without considering customer demand or the total costs involved. They assume that since everyone else is doing it, they should forge ahead—even though they have not defined a profitable business model. This is incredibly naive. They often lose money by the time they absorb all the costs of stocking and shipping individual products, and then they get hit with additional costs when the returns start arriving. Having been caught napping when it comes to using technology to enhance the store experience, there is now a mad dash to create sales on the internet, without really considering which specific products and services will be embraced by their customers and truly be synergistic for the company.

Somehow, they accept on blind faith that while they are losing money now, this whole system will become profitable when they hit a critical mass that is not yet defined. This leads them to throw more and more items onto their website, without considering whether they can competently deliver the product or make money once they do.

This is when leadership needs to say, "Whoa!" All the company's resources must be brought together to redefine the products and services necessary to establish and defend the company's *unique, sustainable, compelling, competitive advantages* in its market segments.

A LOOK INTO THE FUTURE

What is the store of the future? It has to be different from today's format. The internet will have an impact on certain products and categories of merchandise that will result in changes in the brick-and-mortar operation. The customers' expectations are rapidly rising as they learn that they are in charge.

The big-box store that keeps its focus on *working good* will continue to validate that the physical store is still the most efficient retail format to sell the highest product volume to the most people at the lowest prices. This fanatical focus on *working good* needs to represent "true north," defining merchandising guidelines that make the stores—*easy to stock, easy to sell, and easy to buy.* The website serves as both the front door of the store and the *more-choice* tool to improve and accentuate product and service options for the customers.

Unorthodox companies will enter the marketplace, both online and offline, offering new products and better services. Manufactures will tend to become retailers and vice versa. The world is changing, and the stores must aggregate new target markets and improve the loyalty of existing customers. The issue will be, who does the customer trust?

It is not reasonable to continue doing business as usual and expect sales to increase. In fact, commitment to the status quo will surely result in decreased sales and profits. An impetus on designing and operating better stores and websites is imperative. These assets must be integrated into an *interconnected retailing* model that is customer-centric and driven by merchants with a clear, unified vision and mission. Embracing change and operating in a learning mode must be ingrained into the corporate culture.

19

COMPLETING THE SOLUTION PORTAL

PRINCIPLE 8:
RETAILING MUST TRANSITION FROM PRODUCT ORIENTATION TO A SERVICE AGENDA.

This chapter will continue to expand on Principle 8. Chapter 18 discussed the use of technology to enable the transition from a relatively simple product-oriented business to the much more complex service orientation. The next step will be to explore specific services that are critical for the big-box home center to be the solution provider for their customer's home-improvement projects.

Most developed markets for big-box home centers are nearly saturated. Therefore, company growth must come from comparable store sales increases, not the launch of a new location. Existing stores must focus on increasing year-over-year sales.

Your goal as a retailer must be to get more share of the wallet from your existing customers and to amass a larger customer base. This requires implementing strategies to improve store traffic while increasing the average ticket. The key to achieving this as a big-box home center is to be seen as the best solution provider for repair, maintenance, and remodeling projects for both homeowners and professional customers.

Through a combination of improved personal service and greatly expanded product choice, your brand can become synonymous with project competence.

PROJECT PROFICIENCY

The best strategy for growth is to offer a continuum of service, from the first design elements to the final, fully completed installation. The goal must be to offer a complete journey from the initial idea to the completion of the dream. This may be accomplished in house or perhaps by forming strategic links with third-party service providers, thereby reinforcing your brand as a solution provider. The important point is that while the customer has numerous alternatives, it is critical that the portal, be it the website or the store itself, must be the trusted, front-of-mind starting point for any project.

A huge reservoir of potential project sales is available to home centers that transition to service orientation. Customers have an abundance of stores and websites to turn to for products, but they don't have an abundance of trustworthy, competent service providers that can take a project from idea to completion. There are actually many alternative service providers, but the key word is *trustworthy*. The service industry today is highly fragmented and often full of horror stories. This can make many homeowners apprehensive about embarking on a project. There is an opportunity to consolidate this service market and to assume the dominant position as the trusted solution provider.

GOOD SERVICE REQUIRES THE RIGHT PROCESS

There is a challenge, though. It is much more difficult to provide competent service than to simply sell products. However, the effort required to provide service with competence is what gives you a *sustainability* advantage.

Competent project service involves defining the specific steps required to assure a successful journey from design to project completion. The problem in many big-box stores is that there is a synapse between each of the fulfillment steps, which is where the customer's project can, unfortunately, be dropped. Most big-box stores today tend to be well organized for offering products to the masses but often fail at offering good service to the individual. The goal is to be the provider of solutions, not the source of frustration.

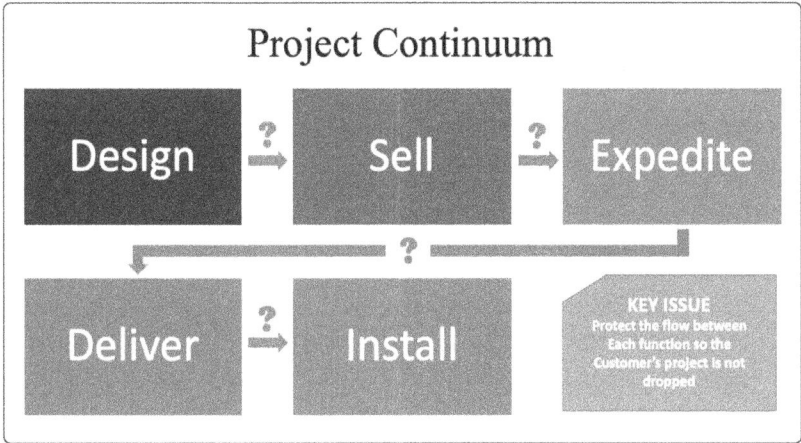

Project Continuum

Design ➡️ ? Sell ➡️ ? Expedite

Deliver ➡️ ? Install

KEY ISSUE
Protect the flow between Each function so the Customer's project is not dropped

Any given project may require the retailer to take successive steps, from designing to selling, expediting, delivering, and installing. Multiply that by numerous customers, and the level of complexity clearly requires technology. You need systems and processes that let you track every project in real time, from idea to completion—quickly and accurately. The challenge gives you an opportunity to excel and show your competitive advantage—or reveal your weaknesses.

As shown in the Project Continuum chart, a project must start with the design process. A customer may have a general idea for a new kitchen or bathroom, but that idea needs to be defined and turned into specifications. It needs to morph from an idea into a physical plan that can be visualized. This transition requires knowledgeable, talented people.

These designers must have the right tools to design and present the project plans. This may require configuration software. It certainly requires an in-store selling center where customers can meet designers in a setting that includes product samples and point-of-sale visual aids to help them visualize the project in their homes. A wide range of products on the company's website provides an electronic catalogue to showcase unique items that will customize the project to the customer's personality and style. The website can also provide inspiration by showing design ideas. Clearly, the sales associates must know how to use these tools, in order to give customers confidence that their project is in good hands.

Of course, costs are involved to hire the right people, train the right people, and keep the right people. However, this is the key to establishing a trust relationship with the customer. This, in turn, helps sell total projects that will provide the revenue to more than pay for this investment.

Offering great project service requires an investment in people, which can become a real and lasting competitive advantage. While every CEO says he or she wants to build a business with great people, the reality often falls short of this announced goal. This is why good service is so lacking in many retail establishments. (The criteria for hiring great people will be further explained in chapter 20.)

SELLING THE BIG-TICKET CUSTOMER

In the United States, home-improvement projects valued at more than ten thousand dollars constitute almost half of the gross dollar sales of home-improvement products. Yet such projects are undertaken by less than 6 percent of the homeowners.

This high-value group of project-oriented homeowners demands unique products and specialized services. They want to be confident the retailer can:

• Design the project and create the specifications.

• Offer the necessary products from both in-stock and online choices.

• Assemble the project elements and deliver them to the jobsite complete, on time, and undamaged.

• Install the project with competence.

Quite often, these important customers shop at specialty stores, as opposed to the big-box home centers. There is a trust element embodied in the smaller store that offers personalized service. Big projects are the lifeblood of the specialty retailer, who can provide all these services and instill confidence in the customer that the job is in good hands. To give you an idea of the importance of the specialty store, consider the membership of the National Kitchen and Bath Association (NKBA). The more than 14,000 independent members of this specialty trade organization are focused on this one area of home improvement.

The owner of a specialty kitchen and bath store in Houston, Texas, explained to me that she intentionally located her office at the front of the store, where she could watch customers drive into the parking lot. She would quickly evaluate the price of the car the person was driving knowing that would most likely represent the budget for the kitchen project she would design. Specialty retailers do not need large parking lots; they just need a few customers driving the right cars.

There is no reason why this huge upscale market should not be tapped by the big-box home center with the right commitment to and investment in systems and people. Technology can provide the breakthrough advantage to enable great service. Most large retailers have the resources available to access the latest and best systems to manage complex processes. It is via technology that we gain speed and accuracy. However, cutting edge technology must be married to competent people with design talent to create successful project sales.

Offering complex project services does have a cost. Some retailers are tempted either to not offer these services or to skimp on the quality of the service to avoid additional overhead expense. However, in an effort to keep the business simple, they may lose the customers who can generate the largest project sales. This lack of vision is clearly a severe case of *merchandising myopia.*

If services are done right, the size of the projects can result in an amazing increase in sales. The significant gross margin dollars generated can cover the new infrastructure costs while bringing new revenue to the bottom line as well. It is a chicken-and-egg story, where the investment in people and systems must be put in place to create the future flow of big-ticket sales.

Furthermore, complex and difficult projects are a great way to differentiate your brand in a sustainable way that creates customer trust. Lifetime customer loyalty can be achieved via project competence.

SERVICING THE DO-IT-FOR-ME CUSTOMER

It is not too hard to convince retailers that their products must meet high quality standards. But it can be much more difficult to create the same high quality standards for service. Too often retail management sees service as an expense instead of an investment.

For one thing, great service involves time and accuracy issues that require great people, sophisticated systems, and clearly defined processes. Another prerequisite for great service is for the different departmental "silos" in the business to come together with a focused strategy. After all, a successful project requires the right products from the merchandising department, as well as the right people, who must be hired by store operations. Further, human resources must develop the right training and retention programs. Flexible credit programs are needed from finance. Logistic support is critical for competent delivery. Marketing needs to tell the story, while store planning and visual merchandising must set the stage within the store.

Putting all this in place requires a commitment from senior management to funding the critical infrastructure and talent required to assure the customer's successful project journey. Unfortunately, a lack of engagement and leadership at the executive level will doom a project of this magnitude to failure. This would be a shame, since most homeowners have a backlog of projects that they would like to accomplish but that sit on the back burner due to a lack of time and hesitancy to start. Buying a $20,000 car in a few hours is relatively easy, as is making online arrangements for a $20,000 vacation. But planning a $20,000 kitchen remodel? Not so appealing, if it leads to an incredible expenditure of time, frustration, and unhappy surprises.

If big-box home centers are going to reach this huge market, they must be able to provide the customer with a clear, timely, and trusted path to completion. The customer must be guided though each stage of the designing, selling, procuring, delivering, and installing steps of the project—without being dropped through one of those synapses previously mentioned. Large projects that are currently delayed represent a huge reservoir of untapped revenue.

COMPLETING THE PROJECT JOURNEY

The home center industry has had a great run of over fifty years focusing on the do-it-yourself (DIY) customer. However, the retail business is now evolving from being a product-oriented DIY business to a do-it-for-me (DIFM) service orientation.

Homeowners who were working around their homes twenty-five years ago when they were forty are now sixty-five. The average age of the population in every developed market is rapidly rising. These customers often have significant disposable income and still have multiple projects they either need or want to have done, but they are far less inclined to do those projects themselves.

Growth of the home center business will depend on a new business model that provides the homeowner with comprehensive project services and, at the same time, grows a partnership relationship with the professional tradesmen who will do most of the manual labor. This is complicated by the fact that labor today is both harder to obtain and more expensive.

Project sales can be considered a three-legged stool. Each leg of this do-it-for-me stool represents both a unique customer and a specific tradesperson and, therefore, requires a differentiated marketing strategy.

Do-It-For-Me Customer

DIFM Customer

Independent Pros   On-line Reference Pros

In-house Pro Service

Let's look at each of these three legs in detail:

LEG 1: INDEPENDENT PROFESSIONALS

This leg requires aggregating a growing and loyal professional customer base. It necessitates focusing on the independent repair, maintenance, and remodeling professional. The Home Depot is leading the way to professional customer growth, with over 45 percent of its business reportedly done with professionals who represent only 4 percent of the store's actual customers.

The five most important customer issues for gaining professional customer loyalty are listed below in order of importance:

• Saving the professional customer time.

• Building personal relationships.

- Providing high-quality products and services.

- Establishing flexible credit programs.

- Pricing at the true wholesale level.

The key is to level the field with right pricing, but superior performance on the other four service variables will determine the loyalty of the professional customer.

LEG 2: IN-HOUSE PROFESSIONAL SERVICE

The most important factor that determines who the customers will invite into their homes for service is the element of trust. In this regard, the home center has the inside track to get first opportunity on a job, since the customer most likely is already a DIY customer and already has a certain element of confidence in their favorite home center. This is why it is so important to handle everyday transactions with great customer service. The customer who experiences hassle free returns will tend to trust the store brand when it comes to the big projects.

The home center should be able to provide fully guaranteed, installed, sales programs to the customer, through which the store takes full responsibility for total customer satisfaction. This peace of mind message is demonstrated by The Home Depot's Home Services program, in which trust is its primary promotional message.

The home center must search out the best installers in the market and offer premium service to the customer; it may cost more, but it provides a peace-of-mind guarantee that nothing will go wrong. The store's brand is at risk if the project is not up to par.

This requires a whole new infrastructure, involving people, processes, and work progress technology. It involves hiring the best tradesmen, training them in customer service, establishing a relationship of mutual commitment to profitable growth, and implementing work progress systems to assure compliance. This is easy to say but hard to accomplish.

The very fact that it is hard to accomplish gives the home center that successfully implements such a program a truly *unique, sustainable, compelling, competitive advantage.*

"Sustainable" is the key word since it will be the most difficult element for the competition to duplicate. The marketing of a guaranteed in-house installation program must be trust based, as opposed to price based. This requires the dual message that you are proud of having the lowest prices on products but equally proud of your service programs, which can justify a premium price.

LEG 3: ONLINE REFERENCE PROS

A wide range of home-improvement services includes—and goes beyond—installing products purchased from the home center. For example, services might include mowing lawns or hauling trash; these are not product-oriented projects but, nevertheless, are services the homeowner needs. Since the store and website must be the portal for all home products and services, a referral program is needed to unite service providers with homeowners.

This is a broker function best performed electronically in real time on the internet. Having this service is an important step in becoming the customer's first-of-mind option for all home-improvement needs. The home center portal must be the best, easiest, and most trusted entry point to start any home-improvement project or service.

ASSURING COMPETENCE, BUILDING TRUST

It has already been mentioned that the customers are looking for a solution for their project from a provider they can trust. This tees up the home center, which is the good news. The bad—or at least sobering—news is that the home center must deliver competent service or risk destroying its brand in the process.

Presenting a *trust-me* message on project implementation involves both opportunity and danger. Trust is the winning message, but it brings with it a huge obligation to perform at an extremely high customer service level on all projects all the time.

Fulfilling the trust imperative was a ten-year journey for The Home Depot. We found that providing competent in-home service was incredibly difficult. We learned by trial and error that we needed specialized workflow management systems. We needed to select and train a highly motivated group of local tradespeople. We needed to have a whole new level of urgency when it came to customer care.

At times we tore up customers' kitchens, only to find we did not have the right products to complete the new kitchens. This led to putting whole families up in hotels for months at a time. Local television news stations were doing stories on our project disasters and even attempting to do live broadcasts in front of our stores. This was a public relations nightmare and an incredibly painful period of learning how to be truly service oriented.

LESSONS LEARNED

Our decade of learning made us realize that the key to success in services was to clearly define the processes and then establish disciplines to assure compliance. As with walking a balance beam, you can fall off in two directions. A fall to one side is caused by putting too few quality control measures in place, leading to customer problems that damage the store's brand.

On the other side, overcompensation can lead to putting so much infrastructure and people into the job-management process that it is impossible to make a profit. In either case, falling off the beam can seriously damage or even kill the service program.

The key is to define the minimum infrastructure to assure complete customer satisfaction. This requires standardized programs that are clearly defined and disciplined business processes that are understood by the personnel in all five stages of the project continuum (design, sell, expedite, deliver, install). Combining these programs with project management software will assure that the customer's job is completed as promised, on time, with total satisfaction.

The good news is that it will not be easy for competitors to duplicate a competent, trustworthy program. It is, therefore, critical that very specific processes and procedures be put in place to provide adequate assurance of customer satisfaction. A high degree of compliance with these processes is required to make sure the program stays on the balance beam of great service and realistic costs.

Every installed sales program must generate a margin on labor that, in turn, can support the infrastructure required to assure project competence.

Finally, every job must be tracked with a *voice-of-customer* measure of satisfaction to assure consistent performance. Every member of the project service chain, from design to installation, needs to know and work to constantly improve their customer satisfaction score.

PRICING SERVICES

Service is sold on a trust basis, which is far more important than price. This applies to any service, whether it is design, delivery, or installation. When offering a service, your policy and brand statement should not be that you have the lowest price or a low price guarantee. The message should be that this is the absolute best service available.

If you were about to have brain surgery, you would not search for the lowest priced doctor but for one you can trust. The lady who is opening her home to strangers is looking for a project provider she can trust inside her home. And she must be assured that when all is said and done, the job itself will be a compliment to her good judgment. The contractor who is depending upon a delivery to meet his construction schedule is not worried about price nearly so much as the ticking of his clock.

If it can't be done well, do not do it at all. Quality service is critical to reinforcing a strong brand image of trust. However, unlike many product choices, labor is not standardized. Good services have a cost. The only way to ensure the best service is to charge a premium price and make sure your sales associates—and your customers—understand that the services offered are clearly above the industry standards and, therefore, justify a top-line fee.

If any service program is to be viable and grow, you have no choice but to perform on a consistent, proven basis. If your sales force does not believe the customer will be completely satisfied with a service, they won't recommend it. It's that simple.

You must teach your salespeople to be proud that you have the lowest prices for products and equally proud that you charge a premium for services. Both of these statements should give the customer peace of mind.

THE CHANGING MARKETPLACE

The traditional home-center business began as a convenient store for the DIY customer in the 1960s and was pretty much unchanged until 1980. This changed with the opening of The Home Depot warehouse stores, which were based on product dominance and reached out to both the homeowner and the pro. This new format dominated the 1980s and worked well into the 1990s. However, as the number of big-box stores increased, the result was cannibalization of sales in existing stores, resulting in lower sales per store and falling productivity.

The 2000 era saw the warehouse home center respond to this challenge and evolve to the service home center, which is project based and driven by technology. This third evolution opened the door to a larger customer base and the ability to make more project sales. Big-ticket projects are the main driver of increased comparable store sales in today's home centers.

Home Center Evolution
From Product to Service orientation

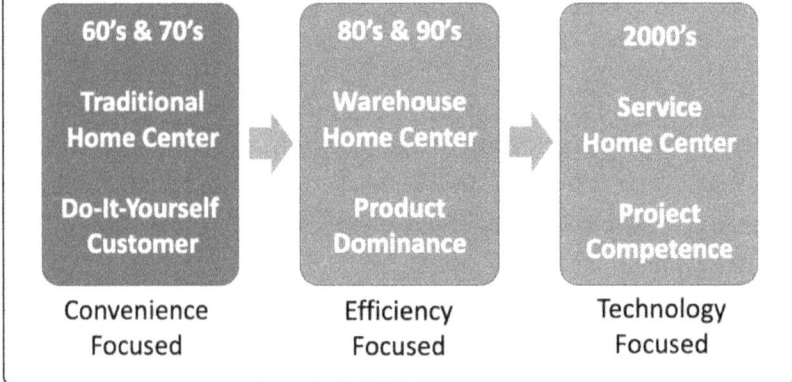

60's & 70's	80's & 90's	2000's
Traditional Home Center	**Warehouse Home Center**	**Service Home Center**
Do-It-Yourself Customer	**Product Dominance**	**Project Competence**
Convenience Focused	Efficiency Focused	Technology Focused

This evolution must take place in the retail business, where the traditional product orientation gives way to a service-oriented model. Achieving this requires advanced technology and a new definition of the business.

The core home-center business will continue to be driven by the do-it-yourself customer, while future growth must come from increased services, which will be seen in offering 1) a wide range of in-home projects, 2) increased services to the professional customer, and 3) an expanded *more-choice* product mix via e-commerce.

Every retailer must consider how to be the total solution provider. The example from the home center industry starts with project design and concludes with its installation. While this specific pathway may not be relevant to other types of retailing, the truth that retailers must transition from product orientation to service orientation is valid, regardless of how that service is defined.

The following chapter will turn to a discussion about people, since all the processes developed and all the technology in the world will be worthless without the people who know how to execute.

PEOPLE MATTER
PRINCIPLE 9:
HIRE THE RIGHT PEOPLE, TRAIN THE RIGHT PEOPLE, KEEP THE RIGHT PEOPLE.

Great people create great companies. The reverse is also true. Great companies develop great people. Ordinary people can perform at an extraordinary level, given the right circumstances. The main point of this book is that the secret to success in high productivity retailing is having the right people with the right attitude, which is dependent upon having the right culture. Exhibit number one is the *Bleeding Orange* culture at The Home Depot.

This people preference may surprise some. Retailing generally has been considered an industry with low pay and high employee turnover. Employees often tend to accept retail jobs as entry-level work until something better comes along. Management's emphasis is too often on quantity instead of quality.

This is unfortunate. There is a correlation between low pay and low productivity. It does not have to be that way, and it shouldn't. Investing in the right people provides the productivity that pays for itself.

Industry watchers were often amazed to find great sales associates with outgoing personalities and super product knowledge at The Home Depot. They wondered where we found such people. The truth is you don't always find those kinds of people. *You most often have to create those kinds of people.*

This means hiring career-minded people, paying them what they are worth, investing in their education and training, and then keeping them by rewarding success and celebrating their contribution to the company.

Frontline sales associates are the face of the company. What your public relations statements proclaim or what your advertising promotes doesn't matter nearly as much as what your own people believe, how they behave, and what they say.

For example, when a customer enters a store, the length of time it takes to be recognized and the quality of that greeting incredibly impact the customer's inclination to like (or not like) the store and trust the brand. This can create a lasting brand image in the customer's mind. Millions of dollars of advertising can quickly be negated with the wrong response by that first contact with a sales associate.

SELF-SERVICE—THE PEOPLE IMPERATIVE

In chapter 17 we said, *Self-service is the best service.* Now let's go into more detail on how that premise impacts store staffing.

Great service requires self-service store layouts and customer-friendly displays—*plus great sales associates.* These are not conflicting ideas. The customer is in search of a solution. Making it easy for the customer to obtain the right solution quickly will create sales now and engender loyalty in the future. You must think through the customer's questions and provide ready answers in your displays and signing. You need the right technology in the store and online to make all relevant data readily available to the customer.

What does this have to do with having good salespeople?

SPENDING LABOR DOLLARS WHERE THEY COUNT

A self-service store that is customer friendly will allow you to move labor hours into key areas where more intimate and personal customer service is required. This is critical at customer-service counters at the store's front end and in departments where product knowledge and selling skills are needed to help design customer projects. Payroll dollars need to be focused where they will be most productive: providing the talent to transport the customer through the project continuum from idea to completion and satisfaction. Investing in good people means focusing on quality, not quantity.

If you simply hire more people because they are cheap, you may have quantity and still be within budget. But you will not provide the best service and implement the best practice. When your focus is on quantity instead of quality, you will, of necessity, pay low wages. This may be the path chosen if you accept the premise that more people automatically means more service. However, it more often means the opposite.

Minimum wage people do not generally have product knowledge or selling skills. Also, the turnover of people at this level of income tends to be high as well. The company may hesitate to invest in the training necessary to impart those skills. Furthermore, some people simply don't have the education and background to benefit from such training. You must have people with product knowledge and digital competence or the ability to become competent with proper training.

ASSURING COMPETENCE

Paying people well will create a workforce of perhaps fewer people but one that can be more productive and committed to a long-term career. This can then provide management with the confidence to invest in the proper training and tools to create a highly competent team. Such motivated people will be able to multitask and outperform numerous lower paid and less productive people. Good people pay for themselves.

When customers interact with knowledgeable salespeople, they will quickly recognize that this is a superior retail shopping experience they are not likely to experience elsewhere. This is an excellent way to ensure that your customer bonds with your brand. Bonding is the result of customer service that is superior to all the alternatives.

Today's customers are more educated and knowledgeable than ever before, thanks to the internet. They can quickly discern whether salespeople are truly able to help them with their project. They have already done the basic research and are looking for sales assistance to take their project to the next level. When you value people and invest in them, you get serious about providing the kind of superior service that becomes a *unique, sustainable, compelling, competitive advantage.*

STAFFING CRITERIA VARIES WIDELY BY RETAILER

In advising retailers across Europe, Asia, and the Americas, I have found an interesting correlation between employee pay and the quantity of people it takes to accomplish the same tasks. A typical big-box, 100,000-square-foot home center that does about $30 million annually in sales varies widely in its full-time-equivalent (FTE) sales staff, depending upon its geographical country location. FTE is computed by dividing the store's total payroll hours by forty.

If the store is in Western Europe, it will have approximately 110 FTE employees. The same store in North America will have 120 FTE. A parallel store in Eastern Europe will have 160 FTE. Jump to South America and the store will have 300 FTE. Then consider China. I experienced stores there with over *500 FTE!*

Should the operations manager in one of these overstaffed stores be asked to reduce the headcount, he would most likely claim the store could not operate with one less person. He would, furthermore, tell you his main job is to hire people, which takes virtually all of his time. The obvious problem with this is that the management should be addressing other priorities, in addition to hiring.

This creates a continuing cycle of low productivity for both the manager and the employees. The manager may point out how busy both he and his staff are, but busyness does not indicate productivity.

WEAKER SYSTEMS, MORE WORKERS

The number of people hired tends to be a function of the cost of labor. When people are cheap, the store design, processes, and systems tend to be more labor intensive. There is a hesitance to make laborsaving investments and an assumption that it's easier to throw people at the problem or opportunity.

This means the stores lack technology that would improve the customer experience. Further, logistics that would make the supply line more efficient or the store more productive are missing. Also in short supply are good signing, customer-friendly packaging, and self-service displays, on the assumption that one of the many salespeople will provide the missing information.

The problem, however, is that low-paid sales staff tend to be ill informed and cannot provide the missing information. When a store is not focused on self-service, there tends to be a tremendous amount of product movement from sales floor to storage areas and vice versa. The movement of all this merchandise must be accomplished by the pure muscle power of manual labor, so people are hired for their strong backs instead of their strong minds.

DEFAULTING EMPLOYEE COMPETENCE TO A VENDOR

This reliance in emerging markets on low-paid, entry-level, uneducated salespeople, often prompts vendors to put their own salespeople on the store's floor to protect their brand and boost sales of their own products. I often found, for example, these vendor *promoter*s were the primary sellers of products on the sales floor of many South American and Chinese home-center stores. Of course, the manufacturer has to add the cost of these people into the price of goods.

Shortsighted retailers think this labor is free and continue to abdicate their responsibility to *hire the right people, train the right people, and keep the right people.* These vendor *promoters* are not free, and they are a crutch that ultimately prevents customers from receiving the great service they deserve.

When the vendor's promoters are selling product in your store as well as in your competitor's store, you have lost the competitive advantage of superior service. Another problem of putting vendor salespeople on your sales floor is that they will promote their own brand and denigrate any other product. The importance of private-label merchandising to both sales and profits has been already explained. You don't need a Trojan horse on the sales floor bad-mouthing your own products.

Regardless of how many employees or vendor promoters are on the sales floor, a deficiency of great salespeople displays a poor commitment at the top of the company to a quality shopping experience. If knowledgeable sales associates can become a core competency, you will have an incredible competitive advantage in the underserved world of retailing. This will put in place an important element toward developing a unique and valuable culture.

PRODUCTIVITY REQUIRES PEOPLE INVESTMENTS

Poorly paid and untrained associates also create a morale problem. Ambitious employees inevitably begin to discern the lack of motivation in the troops and management's lack of respect for good people. They conclude there is no assurance of a process that can lead to a meaningful career path. People who perform above the norm are scorned by other employees and told to slow down. The good people leave, and the remaining people reinforce bad habits that impact customer service.

Customers quickly discern when employees are bored and uninterested. They can sense a salesperson who is motivated to help versus one who is simply putting in time. It only takes moments for the customer to tell if the salesperson is knowledgeable, competent, caring, and involved. Customers know if they have entered the right portal to fulfill their project needs.

The truth is, there is generally an inverse relationship between the number of people on the sales floor and the quality of the customer service. Higher paid people are simply more knowledgeable and productive. They are able to offer more assistance to more customers. Lower paid people find themselves doing the manual labor of moving products or simply *making work* to look busy. The overstaffed store is not truly customer-service oriented; it tends to be task oriented.

SMART INVESTMENTS INCREASE PRODUCTIVITY

When labor is costly, there is an openness to invest in equipment, systems, and technology to accomplish tasks at more competent levels with fewer people. The self-service store will be designed so that many customers are able to get in, select their items, and get out without hand holding by the sales staff. This frees the higher-qualified sales associates to give focused personal service to clients who need hands-on assistance with their projects. This dual focus on both self-service and personal service makes the shopping experience easier and more enjoyable for all the customers.

Simply having a warm body on your sales floor is worse than having no body.

The definition of great service is not more people, it is better people in a customer-friendly store.

Many companies brag that they are the *best place to work*. This is based upon *best-place-to-work campaigns* promoted by consulting companies. They coordinate testing regimens and create reports over time, showing how well their program is improving the morale of the workers. There is an assumption that better morale will create improved customer service and satisfaction. This seems reasonable, so the best test of such a program would be to measure the change in the customer's perception of these people. However, this test is often missing.

Unfortunately, the unstated fact of many retail *best-place-to-work* programs is that they want to be the best place for *minimum wage* people to work. This qualification changes everything. It would be far better for the company, the employees, and the customer to commit to being *the best place to self-actualize and build a career*. This would put the emphasis on developing better people, which in turn would create an environment more focused on delighting customers.

GOOD LEADERSHIP IS FOCUSED ON PEOPLE DEVELOPMENT

It bears repeating that providing superior customer service requires you to *1) hire the right people, 2) train the right people, and 3) keep the right people.* Here is a look at each of these elements.

THE PEOPLE CRITERIA: HIRE THE RIGHT PEOPLE

An important hiring criterion should be to search for mature people who have years of experience selling or using the products being sold. A mature person is likely to have product knowledge, but he or she also has had life experiences that often create a more extroverted and friendly personality. It is easy to trust the person with white hair when he or she gives you guidance regarding your project. How often have you been given advice in a store but discounted its value because the *kid* didn't seem to know much about the project you had in mind?

Why are mature people often missing from the sales floor? One reason is that store management tends to clone itself and believes that younger people have more energy and, therefore, are more versatile. They can work the sales floor this morning, chase shopping carts at noon, and unload trucks in the afternoon.

This kind of logic fails to appreciate the value of a person who can interact with the customer to create sales. Sales associates are needed who can and should multitask, but there is also a critical need for sales experts who can design projects and close sales. Creating sales must always be the top priority.

A second erroneous reason for not hiring experienced people is that the more mature person may wish to have special hours or only work part time. This may not fit into the manager's schedule. There is a false assumption that part timers should be paid less and are expendable.

In reality a part time person often has wide knowledge that makes him or her incredibly valuable. This type of sales associate can give helpful assistance to the customers but also be a great mentor to other employees. Offering some scheduling flexibility can make it possible to obtain some excellent talent.

Rate of pay can be the main problem in proper staffing. The managers may not be willing to move off a preset minimum wage scale. This can be a blind spot that requires retraining to understand the true value of people. The management team must appreciate the value of people before they will pay them what they are worth. When this realization sinks in, they will see it is not only a cost issue but also an investment in customer service that pays off in sales and customer loyalty.

Think about it—why would anyone want to hire minimum wage people for any reason other than charity? It is always smart to hire people who bring skills and talents to the company or who have the ability to learn these skills and abilities. In both cases, the odds of obtaining a winning employee start with being selective and looking for quality, not quantity.

Too often the case arises where a young person who has proven to be a sales expert gets married and the couple is expecting their first child. He goes to the store manager and asks how to make more money. The answer is to enter the management-training program, which means he will be directed into new activities and will no longer be on the sales floor, providing assistance to the customer and selling projects. This is a tragedy.

The real need is to hire and keep people who would be very pleased to make a career of being great salespeople. Just as there is a career path for management positions, there must be a clear and rewarding career path for professional sales experts.

Unfortunately, the structure and culture of many retailers does not accommodate positions for sales experts who can design projects and close the sale. This is why the best and most knowledgeable salespeople are most often found in specialty retail stores but seem sadly lacking in big-box mass merchants.

Another criterion for a good employee is to be drug free. A person who abuses substances will not be helpful to your customers. Even worse, he or she will make other good employees uncomfortable. They won't want to work with that person, and they might even leave the company. This is a real morale problem. Add to this the danger of accidents or theft. Mandatory drug testing is smart and appreciated by your clean employees. Are drug-free people available? The answer is yes if you reward them with pay and recognition.

THE PEOPLE CRITERIA: TRAIN THE RIGHT PEOPLE

When you have hired the right people, you must train the right people. This requires a calendar of scheduled training sessions that focus on: 1) company history and culture, 2) systems and procedures, 3) technical skills, including digital competence, 4) selling skills, and 5) product knowledge. This is level-one basic training, but it does not stop here. Advanced training must continue as you educate your people in leadership and management skills so they can continue to grow and accept new responsibilities. Education and training must be standard operating procedure, not a one-time event. Every manager in a growing company must consider it his or her first job to be a trainer. This means formal training sessions should be planned into the work schedule every week and every month. In addition, during the normal course of work, a good manager will look for opportunities to turn problem situations into teaching opportunities.

The human resources department should provide good curriculum and training tools. A tracking system should ensure good training discipline throughout the company. Ongoing follow-up should show what training has been achieved for each employee. The process must *train, measure, and retrain* to constantly improve competence. Fortunately, there are good electronic systems that provide self-learning tools capable of providing much of the training and monitoring the progress of each employee. Knowledge benchmarks must be established to measure learning, recognize accomplishments, and reward achievement. On-the-job and classroom learning are also important. The operating management team must buy into the value of well-qualified and well-trained people. They must be the role models and the hands-on trainers to create the right attitudes that lead to a winning culture.

THE PEOPLE CRITERIA: KEEP THE RIGHT PEOPLE

The bottom line is that it is important to make it *cool* to help customers. Being a sales expert must be seen as a prestige position that is recognized and rewarded. It needs to be honorable to go above and beyond the call of duty to delight the customers. People who excel do so more for ego satisfaction than for money. Good people want to feel good about themselves. They want to be recognized by their peers as successful. They want to contribute. They want to be part of something worthwhile. Accomplishments must, of course, be rewarded with monetary incentives. However, it cannot stop at money. Salespersons must truly be and feel appreciated.

The result must be an organization that has a structured program to recognize and reward competence in customer service and selling skills. Great salespeople need to know they can support themselves and their families as a kitchen salesperson or millwork expert. It is in the company's best interest to make sure that such career paths are available and that the culture of the company is to applaud and celebrate successful sales and great *voice-of-customer* scores.

The customers can quickly sense employee attitudes when it comes to taking pride in customer service. They know if they have come to the right place and can put their project in the hands of competent people who will take pride in a job well done.

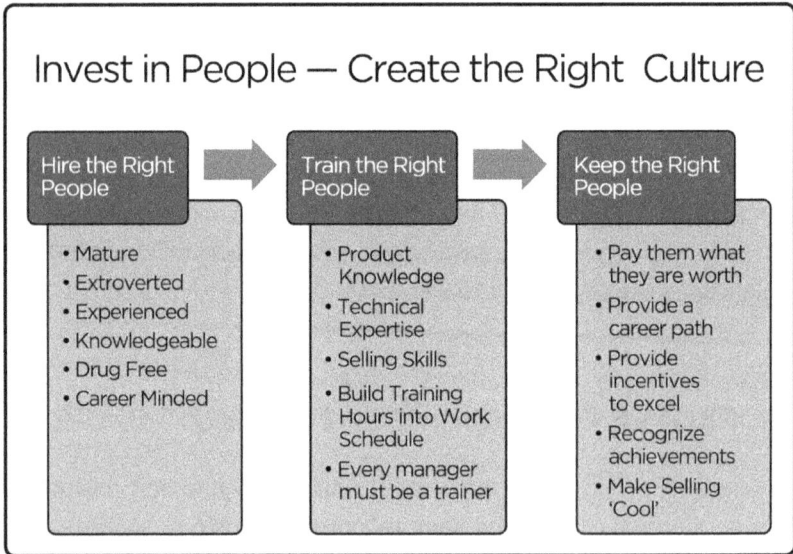

Invest in People — Create the Right Culture

Hire the Right People	Train the Right People	Keep the Right People
• Mature • Extroverted • Experienced • Knowledgeable • Drug Free • Career Minded	• Product Knowledge • Technical Expertise • Selling Skills • Build Training Hours into Work Schedule • Every manager must be a trainer	• Pay them what they are worth • Provide a career path • Provide incentives to excel • Recognize achievements • Make Selling 'Cool'

The Home Depot's secret weapon was always the *Bleeding Orange* culture, which created a positive ambience the customers could feel. Great salespeople are the most effective means of promotion. *Hiring the right people, training the right people, and keeping the right people* is the cornerstone of building a company with a strong culture. At the end of the day, the culture makes a company great. The key to strong morale is providing both monetary and emotional rewards for a job well done.

COMPANY CULTURE
PRINCIPLE 10:
CULTURE DRIVES PERFORMANCE.

One of our hardware vendors at The Home Depot was a company named Hager Hinge. Their tagline was *Everything hinges on Hager.* I would like to modify that tagline for our purposes to say, *Everything hinges on people.*

What turns ordinary people into extraordinary dynamos? What makes them willing to walk through walls if necessary? What turns a job into a cause? What is the lighting in a bottle? That is what this book has been all about.

All the principles and guidelines boil down to the search for that ingredient that separates mediocrity from superiority. That one thing for The Home Depot was its *Bleeding Orange* culture. The culture of a company is set by the values, beliefs, ethics, ideals, integrity, and code of conduct exemplified by the CEO and the rest of the C-suite.

CULTURE IN THE DECENTRALIZED RETAILER

The retail business, by its nature, requires a decentralized organization. It is important to push decisions down and out into the stores, which are close to their customers. A thousand variables are at play at any given time in the retail world, and it is important to have empowered people who are engaged with their customers and who can respond appropriately to those challenges and opportunities. Employees at every level need to be self-starters who understand they are empowered to do the right thing and will never be punished for giving their customers the benefit of the doubt and going the extra mile for them.

The retail business requires constant innovation. A certain amount of experimentation—and even a little chaos—facilitates this. When the management goal becomes centralized control and total standardization, creativity dies. A comfortable balance between centralized control and decentralized empowerment encourages innovation and allows experimentation at the local level. A strong self-starting culture springs from an attitude of ownership.

"Culture makes the difference, and great people are actually everywhere. What separates them is the culture in which those people are operating."

— Kevin Hancock

Of course, there is a difference between decentralization and anarchy. A decentralized corporate structure that can be defined as a matrix organization is critical. Such an organization involves a great deal of local autonomy and authority. However, at the same time, key principles that define the brand must be taught, internalized, honored, and maintained. So while you must encourage local initiatives, there must ultimately be an understanding that core principles cannot be violated. Your most important asset is your brand. The brand represents the values of the company, and veto power must reside in the protectors of a consistent brand image.

CONFIDENCE TO DECENTRALIZE

True decentralization can only move forward with the understanding and support of the CEO. A smart CEO understands he or she must delegate to grow. There can be no quantum growth and increased scalability without delegation and no delegation without confidence in the team. In a multi-store retail business, decentralization is critical to assure responsiveness to the local market.

The CEO must be surrounded by people who are experts in their field and are empowered to create magic for their customers. For most positions the definition of best people is not necessarily based upon academic achievement as much as a history of being a mover and shaker. Too often companies base their hiring criteria primarily upon education for a certain job and end up with employees with a sense of entitlement and the wrong attitude toward hard work. There is a world of well-educated dunderheads. My experience with such people is that they love bureaucracy and, strangely, seem to have trouble hearing, since they think they already know all the answers.

Strive to attract people with a strong work ethic and a hunger for success. Do not underestimate the ability of ordinary people to accomplish extraordinary results, when given the right direction and motivation. People with the right attitude will eagerly follow the model established by senior management—who must, in turn, walk the talk.

Once people buy into a strong culture, they will move mountains to achieve the common goal. They will always exceed expectations. It is a matter of attitude.

The smart people making management decisions need to understand that before they issue brilliant edicts *from above*, they need to empathetically listen to the people in the stores. The store staff is on the frontline and has the best understanding of the customers' needs and attitudes. Listen to them carefully and then respond with urgency. This is how the management team shows servant leadership responsiveness.

GETTING THE RIGHT MESSAGE TO THE TROOPS

Decentralization requires education and training to assure smart decisions. Education helps the employee understand why a policy is needed and the goal it is intended to achieve. Training explains how to perform the processes to achieve the objectives to reach that goal. Education and training together are the prerequisites for decentralization and empowerment.

Part of the education process is explaining the company's history and the vision that created it. It is important to tell and retell the stories of success in serving the customers and growing the business. There must be a celebration of what the company has achieved and a shared vision of where it is going. People want to be part of positive movement. They want to feel good about their job and what they do.

The importance of the *Bleeding Orange* culture at The Home Depot cannot be overstated. Every orange-blooded employee embraced the following beliefs:

1. Our number one job is to delight the customers. We must give the customers no reason to ever shop elsewhere for their home-improvement needs. We can't tolerate our customers' standing in our competitor's stores.

2. We must be the complete, one-stop project source for both products and services for repair, maintenance, and remodeling.

3. We are committed to driving down the cost of home improvement and improving the standard of living for our customers.

4. We price at everyday low prices (EDLP), so there will be no limited-time sales. It will always be the right time to buy.

5. Our price guarantee assures the customer of always buying at the lowest price.

6. Each employee is empowered and expected to provide complete satisfaction to every customer.

7. Our goal is to consolidate the market. We will not conspire to share the market with our competitors.

8. We are measured and rewarded based upon ROI (return on investment) metrics.

9. Our company is an asset to the community, and we want to give back our time and money to help those in need.

10. We are part owners of the company, and as it grows, so will we.

CONSISTENT MESSAGING

The company culture must be embraced at every level of the company structure and constantly reinforced and rewarded by management. It is important to have tangible victories in the marketplace and to celebrate those accomplishments. Employees want to be part of a winning team. They work for money but are more likely to stay for acceptance and appreciation. They need to see that they are not only benefitting the company but also helping customers and improving the community in which they live. The company can be the vehicle for self-actualization. This creates a zeal that is much like a religious movement.

Indeed, a strong company culture is not unlike a religious or political organization. There must be a clear set of beliefs, a corporate goal, a stated enemy, and a future reward. The Home Depot *Bleeding Orange* culture was incredibly strong in each of these elements, and every employee was proud that they bled orange.

However, as seen in chapter 9, a vibrant culture is fragile. It can be destroyed inadvertently by inconsistent management or by design, as illustrated by the story of the change in management when the original founders left The Home Depot.

ROLE MODELS

It is said that a company is the shadow of the person at the top. This is true. Employees are very observant of what the senior management says—and of what they do.

They look to the senior management to define the vision and mission of the company. They watch and listen for this stated direction. Then they watch and observe. What is the management team's attitude at the end of the month when the financial results are reviewed? What are they looking at and what is emphasized? Are they more interested in gross margin percentage than sales? Is the focus on long-run growth or quarterly results? Does delighting the customer take precedence in decision making?

Are people really rewarded for doing the right thing? Is management involved at store level? Does senior management have true empathy when it comes to the stores? Do they demand a servant attitude of the corporate staff? What happens in store walks? Does the senior management make eye contact with every customer and start a conversation? Does the management team stop to determine the core reason there are out-of-stocks on the sales floor? Do store visits include the bathrooms, lunch rooms, vault, and receiving areas? Does the management team know who has made new sales records at this store, and do they take time to acknowledge and recognize great service? Is the corporate management team willing to put on the company apron or uniform and walk in the sales associates' shoes? Does the management team even come to the store at all? There can be no hypocrisy—consistency to the stated culture is critical.

WALKING IN THE CUSTOMER'S SHOES

When we really listen to our customers, we essentially change our whole point of view. I loved to do store walks with my associates at The Home Depot, and I still like to walk the stores with my clients.

It always surprises the group I am with when we walk up to any random counter in a store, and I can point out so many things we can improve for customers. Often we see blatant problems that can be embarrassing.

RETAIL DETAIL #49

The right questions are never asked when you know too much.

The question often arises: "How does Jim always happen to walk directly to the one bay in the store that has a problem?"

The answer is that *every* bay has a problem, if you stop, put yourself in a customer's shoes, and simply ask, "What do I need to know and what do I need to do to make the right purchase?" The problem is that most of the time we think we know the answer, so we never ask the right question.

The Obvious Solution

Many things become clear when you are actually standing in the store. This applies to both internal and external stakeholders.

During my time with The Home Depot, I was contacted by the national account representative for Newell, which supplied us with Levolor mini blinds. He said The Home Depot purchases resulted in a 35 percent return rate. Given this situation, Levolor was afraid they could not continue to sell their blinds to our stores. They were about to fire their best customer!

Neither of us knew why this was happening. I suggested that if the representative wanted to solve the problem, he needed to spend time in our stores to observe customers purchasing the blinds.

He agreed, went to one of our stores, put on an orange apron, and spent an entire weekend on our sales floor, helping customers who were shopping for window treatments.

Each window blind came in a cardboard carton sealed inside a thin cellophane wrapping. He observed that every customer tore off the cellophane film on the box of the size of blind they were interested in buying and opened it to see if all the mounting parts were included. When they were sure all the parts were there, they would select an unopened carton to take to the register.

Our stores would then send the opened carton back to Levolor for credit.

The solution was easy—do not wrap the carton in cellophane. Make it easy for the customer to open a flap on the carton to see the contents before purchasing.

The cellophane wrapping had no real function, but this was the way it had always been done. Nobody questioned why—until real-world store observation made the solution obvious.

Problem solved, with cost savings for both the vendor and the store.

CULTURE REALITY

Arthur Blank used to say, "If you do not know the answer, you need to love the question." The right questions always need be asked.

Is customer service really job number one, or is that just a cliché?

Does customer service apply to the whole enterprise, or is it just another department?

Are customer returns handled in a friendly manner?

Is there a clear focus on the company's mission to delight the customer?

Do the key performance indicators (KPIs) reflect this common goal?

Do the corporate departments have a servant attitude toward the stores?

Are the stores free from needless paperwork, reports, and meetings?

Are employees educated about the history of the company and the founders' values?

Do the employees understand and believe the company's promotional claims?

Are customers problems or complaints treated with respect?

Is there a comprehensive program to both educate and train employees?

Is there a career path for people who love to sell and help customers?

Is great customer service celebrated and rewarded both financially and emotionally?

Do all employees feel empowered to do whatever it takes to help the customer?

Are employees encouraged to provide input to improve the company?

Do employees have immunity to speak of problems without retribution?

Do the employees feel appreciated? Is their personal success celebrated?

Is customer satisfaction the stated and actual policy?

Are employees given opportunities to help their communities?

Are both base pay and fringe benefits above the industry norm?

Does the company provide emergency funds to assist employees with unexpected or catastrophic emergencies?

Is there an opportunity to participate in ownership of the company?

All questions are really asking, "What is the culture of the company?"

The culture must instill a deep conviction in every associate that "We will give the customer no reason to ever shop elsewhere." You cannot make any money from the customer who is standing in a competitor's store. The customer must feel and experience the difference that can only come from interacting with associates that believe. This is the most important prerequisite for customer loyalty.

THE MAGIC OF CULTURE

The message of this book is that the right culture can be magic. It can overcome many obstacles and other shortcomings. It can create a force that is unstoppable. It is the most important ingredient in developing a successful business. What are the elements that define a culture? It is not just a feel-good statement. You must identify each element that creates your unique culture. Then, for each element you must develop an action statement that assures fulfillment. It is critical to define the culture at the beginning, and it's important to reinforce that culture every day. Celebration of success is the best ingredient for future success.

It is always important to step back and ask, "What is this company all about?" It can't just be about the numbers in a particular quarter. The numbers will come as a result of doing the right thing. The optimum numbers result from the dollar votes of the customers, which in turn derive from their favorable experience both online and in the store. Customer loyalty is driven by experience, which is impacted by the company culture they encounter at every touch point when they shop the store and website. Following a transaction with their favorite home center, the customer's attitude should be, "I am glad I have a friend in the home-improvement business." This chart expresses how the customer should see this "friend" and the feelings that should result.

The Customer's Viewpoint

- Competent — • They Know Their Stuff
- Dependable — • They Always Deliver
- Trustworthy — • They Have My Back

So what drives the culture? Like so many things that are hard to define, you know it when you see it—or, more accurately, when you feel it. Culture is driven by a consistent attitude that becomes powerful when it is shared. Leadership is shown in attitude and action that don't just salute the flag but also carry it into battle.

The culture will define so many aspects of the business, from innovation to implementation and on to market dominance. There must be a big idea that establishes the path forward and a team of zealots committed to follow with a passion. These leaders must exhibit a set of beliefs and values that can rally the larger team around this vision. Such a team can accomplish the seemingly impossible. They will resolve to win. A person who knows he or she is part of something special exhibits a certain swagger. At The Home Depot we were proud of our orange blood, and it showed.

The rallying cry will not be *Bleeding Orange* in every company, but a clarion vision must exist. Whatever color that vision is, it must be clear, shiny, and bright. It must be painted in bold primary colors, not pastel. It must be the magnet that pulls everyone to the company's "true north" goals and objectives.

I have relayed some success stories from The Home Depot experience and some cases where we failed. Making errors meant we were pushing the envelope, evolving new processes, finding new products, and creating new services. The important thing is to move forward and learn from the experience. It is not wrong to fail; it is very wrong not to learn in the process. The Home Depot was a learning machine. This was an important part of our Bleeding Orange culture.

> *"Every morning in Africa, a gazelle wakes up and knows it must outrun the fastest lion or it will be killed. Every morning in Africa, a lion wakes up and knows it must run faster than the slowest gazelle or it will starve. Whether you're a lion or a gazelle—when the sun comes up, you'd better be running."*
>
> — Christopher McDougall

Culture is about being passionate. At The Home Depot orange was our passionate color. We were proud to wear the orange apron. That apron symbolized our common bond to grow The Home Depot by giving the customers no reason to ever shop at a different store for their home-improvement needs.

What are you passionate about?

What is your color?

I hope you wear it proudly!

EPILOGUE

What is the store of tomorrow? This is the topic in every retailer's board-room today. Change is a constant in the retail world, especially in historic moments such as the one in which this book was written: the pandemic of 2020.

There is not one store of tomorrow; there are many stores of tomorrow. Precise data tools that measure customers' demographic and psycho-graphic needs will continue to define market segments. Our societies will be subdivided into more and more separate, specifically defined homogeneous groups.

It is already possible to see this fragmentation in the market for groceries. In today's grocery business a wide range of formats compete for specific niches in the marketplace. These range from giant hypermarkets to warehouse clubs, neighborhood grocery stores, fresh food specialists, private-label discounters, and local dollar stores. Then you can include the numerous home-delivery prepared food options to this list. These formats differ widely in product assortments, online and off-line services, and prices. It takes different strokes for different folks.

The marketplace will continue to fragment by customer segment—but it will be dominated by the most efficient retailer within each segment. There will be fewer but stronger retailers. These winning retailers will focus on the customer's motivation and will engineer the right solutions for their market segments, which will gravitate to one of these three main customer groupings:

• The value-conscious customer driven by price

• The discriminating customer driven by unique products

• The full-service customer driven by solutions to needs and desires

Technology will drive and empower the retailers who focus on each of these customer groups. The systems and disciplines developed will zero in on different digital tools to define each retailer's *unique, sustainable, compelling, competitive advantage.*

The value/price-oriented retailer will rely on technology to provide systems that will drive down logistic costs in order to offer the very lowest prices in the marketplace. The retailer focused on the discriminating/product-oriented customer will use technology to design and introduce a flow of unique proprietary products. The retailers driven by service/solutions will be focused on speed and accuracy to provide services and will use technology to uncover needs and then supply intimate customer-oriented solutions.

A large segment of our society desires high degrees of service and convenience. The dominant retailers for this customer will be the omnichannel formats that integrate their online and off-line business. The integrated format gives the customer the best of both worlds: virtual and physical. The customer does not have to make a limited choice; he or she can have it all—for a price.

Niche players—some off-line but primarily online—will develop specialized offerings for incredibly unique products that do not make economic sense to the mass marketer. These will be retailers that can afford the significant cost of marketing and distribution to low-volume markets by operating with the high margins that exclusivity allows.

Another segment of our society is very much driven by price and is willing to travel a little farther and make extra effort to save. This group will drive a new wave of no-frills, price-oriented outlet retailers. These physical stores will give their customers an economic reason to make the trip to their brick-and-mortar locations. History shows the evolution of stores eschewing high overhead expenses and calling themselves "*cash and carry* stores" or "*discount outlets.*" We will see retailers avoiding e-commerce and delivery services to continue serving the price-motivated consumer.

While there have been repeated predictions that e-commerce would bring about a *retail apocalypse,* the truth is that physical stores that define their target market segments, embrace change, and invest in the appropriate technology to put them on the cutting edge will continue to grow and prosper.

And what about our home-center businesses? The big-box home center is alive and well, and it will continue to evolve. The store must be seen as simply one step in the supply chain from producer to consumer. The store will continue to add value in multiple ways:

Time value will be added by facilitating and expediting the flow of merchandise from the store to the customer's home or jobsite. The store can also be a pickup terminal for products ordered in advance. Getting this right will require reconfiguring the flow of product for fast, convenient, contact-free transactions.

Price value on the most needed and purchased items will continue to be a big-box store advantage. The ability to source directly and move product in full truck quantities from producers to the stores is critical to maintaining this customer benefit.

Information value will be increasingly important to the customer. This may come in the form of providing inspiration, supplying specifications for a project, explaining how a project can be done, or giving the customer the confidence to move forward on a project. This information may be offered electronically and/or by knowledgeable salespeople. The store must become a showroom that displays the product ideas available both off-line and online in an inspirational environment that makes project planning easy.

Choice value will be achieved by having product authority in regard to store inventories as well as more choices via online options. Many of these new choice values will be unique private-label products that are proprietary to the home-improvement retailer.

Service value will be achieved by becoming the online portal for all home-improvement desires and needs for products and services. This will be a wide range of services performed by the store as well as in conjunction with third-party providers. The transition from product orientation to service orientation will be striking.

The winning home center of the future will not be smaller; it may be larger, but it must be reconfigured to better serve customers' changing needs. The store's digital presence must grow to encompass all the goods and services required to repair, maintain, or remodel a home.

The home center's brand must represent "total home solutions" and be at the front of the target customers' minds. The infrastructure to support such a wide-ranging solution portal will require combining the resources of the home center retailer with those of product vendors and service suppliers in efficient, transparent partnerships focused on delighting the customer.

In today's digital world, the customer is in control and will force both manufacturers and retailers to provide the right products and services and will have full knowledge of the right prices to pay. Whether the issue is lowest prices, unique products, or intimate service solutions, customer demand will be fulfilled by responsive retailers.

The winners will be the retailers who embrace change and invest in the technology required to perform with excellence. This will enable them to be clearly seen as the best, trusted choice for their targeted customers. Which retailers will achieve this preferred status? This will ultimately depend upon the culture of the company. Everything hinges on people!

JIM'S RETAIL DETAILS

RETAIL DETAIL #1

Innovation hardly ever comes from the industry leaders. In fact, they will fight with all their power to maintain the status quo.

RETAIL DETAIL #2

To be the Everyday Low Price Leader, you must also have the Everyday Low Cost Supply Chain!

RETAIL DETAIL #3

Most retailers price defensively and consider pricing a threat. Winning retailers price offensively and consider pricing a tool.

RETAIL DETAIL #4

Increasing GMROI is always a winning strategy, while increasing gross margin percentage can be a dangerous losing strategy.

RETAIL DETAIL #5

The best loyalty program is simply to be the best store! Give the customer no reason to shop elsewhere.

RETAIL DETAIL #6

When you focus on the customer first, the right numbers are likely to follow. The opposite is not true when you start with the numbers.

RETAIL DETAIL #7

"You either make dust or eat dust." — H. Jackson Brown, Jr.

RETAIL DETAIL #8

"I began a revolution with eighty-two men. If I had it to do over again, I would do it with fifteen and absolute faith. It does not matter how small you are if you have faith and a plan of action." — Fidel Castro

RETAIL DETAIL #9

Whenever possible use the KISS method: "Keep It Simple, Stupid." - Kelly Johnson

RETAIL DETAIL #10

"Culture eats strategy for breakfast." — Peter Drucker

RETAIL DETAIL #11

The Art of the Ambush is to do what your competitors least expect.

RETAIL DETAIL #12

Increasing sales covers a multitude of sins.

RETAIL DETAIL #13

There are two types of people: those who see an opportunity and say, Why?, and those who see the same opportunity and say, Why not? The latter group are the merchants.

RETAIL DETAIL #14

The day you start to believe your own glowing news reports is when innovation and progress stop.

RETAIL DETAIL #15

"Success or failure in business is caused more by the mental attitude even than by mental capacities." — Walter Scott

RETAIL DETAIL #16

Heard on a visit to Havana, Cuba: "They pretend to pay us, and we pretend to work."

RETAIL DETAIL #17

If you think good employees are expensive, try bad employees.

RETAIL DETAIL #18

"The key to failure is to try to please everyone." — Seth Godin

RETAIL DETAIL #19

Most customers do not trust most retailers—and they shouldn't.

RETAIL DETAIL #20

It's hard to win a war when everyone has the same weapons. Dare to be different.

RETAIL DETAIL #21

The deal you turn down today is the deal you will have to compete with tomorrow.

RETAIL DETAIL #22

When all vendors get their fair share of your product assortment and shelf space, you cannot possibly be buying at the lowest cost.

RETAIL DETAIL #23

"One area where I think we are especially distinctive is failure. (We have had plenty of practice.) Failure and invention are inseparable twins."— Jeff Bezos

RETAIL DETAIL #24

"Innovation can't be forced, but it can be quashed." — Mat Ridley

RETAIL DETAIL #25

"To ask is to grow."— Rabbi Lord Jonathan Sacks

RETAIL DETAIL #26

"All of my best decisions in business and in life have been made with heart, intuition ... not analysis. If you can make a decision with analysis, you should do so. But it turns out in life that your most important decisions are always made with instinct and intuition, taste, heart." — Jeff Bezos

RETAIL DETAIL #27

"The essential ingredient for success is a steady stream of innovation." — Peter Drucker

RETAIL DETAIL #28

"Rules and models destroy genius and art. — William Hazlitt

RETAIL DETAIL #29

The "Godfather Rule" of merchandising: Make them an offer they can't refuse.

RETAIL DETAIL #30

"Whenever I talk about balancing the art and science of retail, I'm careful to emphasize that we will always start with the art." — Ted Decker, The Home Depot

RETAIL DETAIL #31

"You have to give people a license to say what is going wrong. Otherwise, everyone is smart enough to realize that their career isn't made by identifying problems." — Frank Blake, former CEO of The Home Depot

RETAIL DETAIL #32

"There are three kinds of people: Those who make things happen, those who watch things happen, and those who wonder, What happened?" — Nicolas Murray Butler

RETAIL DETAIL # 33

"Hierarchies were built for a slower, older time when we could all wait in line for an audience before the throne." — *Kevin Hancock*

RETAIL DETAIL #34

"Behold the turtle. He makes progress only when he sticks his neck out." — James Bryant Conant

RETAIL DETAIL #35

Management gets what management inspects.

RETAIL DETAIL #36

Customer accommodation is always better than customer manipulation.

RETAIL DETAIL #37

Retailing is a race with no finish line.

RETAIL DETAIL #38

If we want the customer to believe we have the best prices, the solution is very simple: Have the best prices!

RETAIL DETAIL #39

Remember that zero gross profit dollars are generated when the customer is standing in a competitor's store.

RETAIL DETAIL #40

The customers' perception of their shopping experience today potentially impacts a lifetime of purchases—not just their own but often those of their social group.

RETAIL DETAIL #41

Any time products stop moving, costs escalate.

RETAIL DETAIL #42

"People do not buy goods and services; they buy relations, stories, and magic." — Seth Godin

RETAIL DETAIL #43

"Without promotion, something terrible happens: Nothing!" — P.T. Barnum

RETAIL DETAIL #44

You can't make sales out of an empty wagon.

RETAIL DETAIL #45

The customer sees only one brand for any retailer. The experience online defines the band image off-line and vice versa.

RETAIL DETAIL #46

The Amazon is an impressive river, but then, so are the Nile, Mississippi, Yangtze, Ganges, Danube, Volga, Mekong, and Congo. There is not one right way to the customer's wallet.

RETAIL DETAIL #47

Simply having a warm body on your sales floor is worse than having no body.

RETAIL DETAIL #48

'I believe that culture makes the difference, and great people are actually everywhere. What separates them is the culture in which those people are operating" — Kevin Hancock

RETAIL DETAIL #49

The right questions are never asked when you know too much.

RETAIL DETAIL #50

"Every morning in Africa, a gazelle wakes up and knows it must outrun the fastest lion or it will be killed. Every morning in Africa, a lion wakes up and knows it must run faster than the slowest gazelle or it will starve. Whether you're a lion or a gazelle—when the sun comes up, you'd better be running." — Christopher McDougall

JIM'S 10 CORE PRINCIPLES OF RETAIL

Principle 1:
Merchandising is an art embracing change.

Principle 2:
*Your brand is your most valuable asset—
and it resides in the mind of the customer.*

Principle 3:
The right price is solely determined by customer perception.

Principle 4:
*Success is measured by GMROI
(gross margin return on inventory investment).*

Principle 5:
Everyday Low Price demands Everyday Low Costs

Principle 6:
Advertising is an investment, not an expense.

Principle 7:
Self-service is the best service.

Principle 8:
Retailing must transition from product orientation to a service agenda.

Principle 9:
Hire the right people, train the right people, keep the right people.

Principle 10:
Culture drives performance.

FURTHER RESOURCES

REFERENCE BOOKS

You may find these books on retail and the home center industry interesting:

Arthur Blank, *Good Company* (New York: Harper Collins, 2020).

Donald Katz, *The Big Store: Inside the Crisis and Revolution at Sears* (New York: Viking Penguin, 1987).

Rajiv Lal, Jose Alvarez, and Dan Greenberg, *Retail Revolution: Will Your Brick-and-Mortar Store Survive?* (Boston: Harvard Business School, 2014).

Bernie Marcus and Arthur Blank, with Bob Alderman, *Built from Scratch: How a Couple of Regular Guys Grew The Home Depot from Nothing to $30 Billion* (New York: Crown Business, 1999).

Chris Roush, *Inside Home Depot: How One Company Revolutionized an Industry Through the Relentless Pursuit of Growth* (New York: McGraw-Hill, 1999).

Michael Treacy and Fred Wiersema, *The Discipline of Market Leaders: Choose Your Customers, Narrow Your Focus, Dominate Your Market* (Boston: Addison-Wesley, 1997).

Kevin Hancock, *The Seventh Power: One CEO's Journey Into the Business of Shared Leadership* (Post Hill Press, 2020).

REASEARCH REPORTS

These research companies have excellent retail data.

Cleveland Research Company, www.clevelandresearch.com

Wolfe Research, LLC, www.wolferesearch.com

ABOUT THE AUTHOR

James W. Inglis is a world-renowned expert with fifty years of experience in the retail home-improvement industry. He served in executive positions with The Home Depot for thirteen years, where he held the titles of Vice President of Merchandising, West Coast; Executive Vice President of Merchandising; and Executive Vice president, Strategic Development. He also served as a member of the corporate board of directors.

Jim has helped shape the industry worldwide as a special adviser to the boards of leading home-improvement retailers around the world: Sodimac, Santiago, Chile, the largest building material and home-center company in South America, operating in seven Latin American countries; Hornbach, Bornheim, Germany, one of the largest home-center chains in Germany, operating in nine western and eastern European countries; Bunnings Warehouse, Melbourne, Australia, the dominant home-center operator in Australia and New Zealand; and Komeri, Niigata, Japan, which operates more than 1,200 stores selling hardware, home, and agricultural supplies in Japan.

He also is a past member of numerous boards of directors: Home World, Tianjin, China, a pioneer in developing home centers and hypermarkets in the Chinese market; Chamberlain Manufacturing, a producer of garage door openers and other security entry hardware; K&G, a chain of U.S. discount clothing stores; and the National Kitchen and Bath Association.

In 2015 Jim was honored with the Lifetime Achievement Award from the Global Home Improvement Network and the European DIY Retail Association.

He is a member of the executive committee of the Storehouse of World Vision, a board member of Help the Persecuted, and past board member and board chairman of the Atlanta Mission. In addition, he is a member of The Church of the Apostles in Atlanta. He and his wife, Susan, have two daughters and eight grandchildren and maintain residences in Atlanta, Georgia, and Palm Coast, Florida.

www.ingramcontent.com/pod-product-compliance
Lightning Source LLC
Chambersburg PA
CBHW030450210326
41597CB00013B/603